HOW TO PLEASE THE COURT

A MOOT COURT HANDBOOK

PAUL I. WEIZER
PROFESSOR, FITCHBURG STATE UNIVERSITY IN MASSACHUSETTS

KIMI LYNN KING
DISTINGUISHED TEACHING PROFESSOR, UNIVERSITY OF NORTH TEXAS

LEWIS RINGEL
MOOT COURT DIRECTOR, CALIFORNIA STATE UNIVERSITY AT LONG BEACH

NICHOLAS D. CONWAY
ASSISTANT PROFESSOR, SAN FRANCISCO STATE UNIVERSITY

ANDREW B. SOMMERMAN
SOMMERMAN, MCCAFFITY, QUESADA AND GEISLER, LLP

McKINZIE CRAIG HALL
ASSISTANT PROFESSOR, UNIVERSITY OF LOUISIANA AT LAFAYETTE

WEST
ACADEMIC
PUBLISHING

The publisher is not engaged in rendering legal or other professional advice, and this publication is not a substitute for the advice of an attorney. If you require legal or other expert advice, you should seek the services of a competent attorney or other professional.

© 2019 LEG, Inc. d/b/a West Academic
    444 Cedar Street, Suite 700
    St. Paul, MN 55101
    1-877-888-1330

West, West Academic Publishing, and West Academic are trademarks of West Publishing Corporation, used under license.

Printed in the United States of America

ISBN: 978-1-64242-667-0

In memory of Frank Guliuzza

Table of Contents

HOW TO PLEASE THE COURT

A MOOT COURT HANDBOOK

Introduction

How to Please the Court: A Moot Court Handbook is designed to familiarize you with and to succeed at moot court. This overview will serve as an introduction to both the chapters to follow and to moot court in general. It will proceed by addressing several subjects and questions that students engaged in moot court, both new and experienced, should find useful.

WHAT IS MOOT COURT?

Moot court is the simulation of appellate advocacy. A trial or some other lower court proceeding has occurred and one side (the losing side) has appealed some aspect of the lower court's decision to an appellate court. Appellate courts decide if lower courts made any correctable errors insofar as their rulings on matters of law not facts. Appellate advocates do not argue innocence or guilt—rather they argue if a trial decision correctly interpreted/applied the law. It is a very cerebral exercise with far less emotion and none of the drama associated with trials. Moot court can take more than one form and can involve both oral and written advocacy. This book is designed to teach you how to engage in both of these forms of appellate advocacy.

ORAL ADVOCACY

Oral advocacy simulates oral argument. Student-advocates, also known as mooters or appellate advocates, stand at a lectern in front of a panel of judges (usually two or three and seldom, if ever, more than nine) and argue an appellate case against a competing team of student-advocates. In the process of doing so, student-advocates answer questions and concerns raised by the judges. Oral advocacy, at its finest, is a conversation between the advocates and the judges. Judges can interrupt to ask questions at any time and typically they can ask about any subject related to the case before them (some will even ask questions not germane to the immediate case). Rounds at the undergraduate level typically last forty minutes (twenty minutes per side) with the side that is arguing that the lower court erred (known as the Petitioner) getting a short (2 or 3 minute) rebuttal. The side that defends the lower court's ruling goes second and does not get a rebuttal. This book will identify a number of strategies to assist you in developing and presenting oral arguments.

WRITTEN ADVOCACY

In a real appellate proceeding, attorneys submit a series of written briefs to courts. These briefs follow specific rules and processes and they precede oral advocacy. The judges in real appellate cases and in some law school competitions will have already read the briefs and will have specific questions about their arguments.

When it comes to undergraduate moot court competitions, written briefs are not typically required and if they are they required they are graded separately, meaning that there are distinct competitions for written and appellate advocacy.

Developing into a good and effective legal writer is an important skill and there is no better way to do it than by mastering the written brief. In real life, not all attorneys appear in trial court and few engage in oral advocacy. But they all have to write. The authors of this chapter and of this textbook have all coached teams in appellate advocacy and we have all spoken with attorneys about our students' successes. If there is one accomplishment that impresses these attorneys the most, it is when we tell them that one of our teams won a written brief award. As with oral advocacy, this book will identify a number of strategies to assist you in developing and presenting written arguments.

WHY MOOT COURT?

There are several reasons to participate in moot court. The first is that it is fun. Secondly, it will teach you valuable life and legal skills. Finally, it is a rare opportunity to put into practice what you are learning.

Moot Court Is Fun

Moot court is not for the squeamish. To do it correctly involves a significant amount of work and a lot of dedication. That said, moot court can be the best academic experience of your academic career. Whether you are mooting (yes it is a verb) as part of a class or in a club, it offers a chance to bring you together with singularly-minded, hard-working people in a common quest. If you compete in tournaments, such as those affiliated with the American Moot Court Association (AMCA), you will likely travel the country from competition to competition appearing in front of panels of judges that can include law students, attorneys, law professors, and even real judges and justices. This can be a lot of fun and in our experience many of our students repeat moot court, which means that unless they are gluttons for punishment, they must enjoy it. Moreover, many of our students have become friends for life—there are even some mooters who marry and become partners for life—there is something special about the bonding that occurs when you work as a team (whether with one classmate or with your larger group of classmates) toward a common goal and succeeding. When it works, and for most of our students it does, it can be truly magical.

Preparation for Your Future

Every law school requires that their students participate in moot court or in trial advocacy, and many law schools require both. Mooting in college, especially in both written and oral advocacy, will help prepare you for what will come in law school. Put simply, you will need to develop these skills if you go to law school, and even if you do not go to law school, there are few professions that will not value the ability to read and present complex materials in a manner that is clear and concise to audiences. In more practical terms, the authors of this book have all sent former mooters on to law school competitions and we are pleased and proud to report that they typically kill these competitions. They are far ahead of their fellow law students in their written and oral advocacy skills and they are quite comfortable and even confident when appearing in courtrooms in front of real judges and justices. We know how to get you to that step—the choice to do it and to do it right is your choice to make.

Moot Court Teaches Valuable Life Skills

Moot court will assist with the development of your critical thinking and analytical skills. Whether or not you want to be an attorney, these are skills that will be invaluable for your future. Mooting can help you gain self-confidence and self-awareness. You will encounter stressful situations and come into contact with difficult people you will have to deal with. It will cause you to face many of your fears, and it will reinforce the value of winning and losing with dignity, as well as the value of good sportsmanship and of being an ethical competitor. In this way, moot court is a reflection of life and in many ways (hopefully good ways such as being a graceful winner) it will help prepare you for your professional life.

DO SOMETHING

We all have taught and taken classes that require you to learn about strategies associated with different fields typically for purposes of taking exams. There is nothing wrong with these classes. We raise this point not to complain about these courses (as we say we all teach them) but rather to extenuate what we think is one of the best qualities of moot court. Moot court is a special sort of academic experience because you actually do what you are taught. That is, you argue cases in front of judges—often real jurists. There are real attorneys who, depending on what type of law they practice and how well they did in moot court or trial advocacy in law school, who cannot make that claim. Imagine how that will look on your law school applications. Mooting will offer you the rare opportunity to do what you are taught now and not have to wait until after graduation when you can have your dream job. To our way of thinking, it does not get any better than that and it is one of the best reasons to moot.

CHAPTER 1

Moot Court: Commitment and Rewards

DO YOU WANT TO BE A "MOOTER"?

Here is the thing: there is a decision to be made and it is yours to make. You are a student justice considering the facts of a court case in an appellate simulation known as moot court. A moot court is an academic exercise in which students "try" a legal case before an appellate court. This is not to be confused with a mock trial. In a mock trial, students try facts before a trial court. To try facts is to judge innocence or guilt or, in a civil matter, to decide if a party, such as a corporation, is liable for an action or if a party, such as a government, exceeded its powers or violated some civil law. There is a prosecution and a defense team, comprised of students, who deliver opening statements, examine and cross-examine witnesses, and deliver closing statements. In a moot court, there is no trial. The trial has already occurred; someone or something has already been found innocent or guilty, someone or something has already had a civil issue settled, or someone or something has already been told that their or its actions violate some section of a constitution. In a moot court, someone or something is protesting the validity of a trial court decision. The issue is not did the trial court misconstrue the facts? Appellate courts do not try facts. The question is did a trial court make any errors in how it interpreted or applied the law? Lawyers argue for some set time period before a panel of judges, which may ask questions before retiring to talk among themselves and render a verdict. This decision may be accompanied by a written opinion that explains the rationale or justification for the decision and provides some direction for future courts deliberating similar issues.

You have participated in a question-and-answer session with other students known as oral argument. In this session, two legal teams, comprised of students, presented their argument and answered whatever questions you and your peers asked. Now, you are in a secret conference with your fellow students and your instructor for the purpose of deciding the case and arriving at some common rationale for your decision. The court is deadlocked. You hold the decisive vote. If this were a real decision it would affect the nation; perhaps the world. The issue might be whether to free a man from jail or whether the death penalty is constitutional. The case might require you to judge whether certain words or ideas can be censored. The decision might compel you to define the president's war powers in the case of a terrorist attack or whether some act of Congress intended to promote racial or gender equality compromises states' rights or individual property rights. Want to experience what making such a decision might be like? This is your chance.

Fancy yourself a player? Does being a judge sound too much like being a referee? Perhaps you would prefer to be a moot court litigator, developing an argument and supporting it, answering questions, and rebutting your opponents. Sound good? This is your chance.

Perhaps you like writing and research and thinking up arguments but you do not want to appear before the court to make an argument or answer questions. Do not worry. Few real lawyers are litigators. Moot court needs lawyers to perform research that assists their team to develop their case and anticipate the other side's arguments. Writing an appellate brief can also be a rewarding experience. Depending on your instructor, you may be able to participate in your group without speaking in oral argument. Sound good? This is your chance.

SO YOU THINK YOU WANT TO BE A "MOOTER"?

If you answered "yes" to any of the questions in Section I of this chapter then chances are you want to be a "mooter." What is a "mooter"? "Mooter" is the non-technical term for devotees of moot court. There is no single form of moot court. Some are in-class simulations that find student lawyers arguing before a student-run court. Some moot courts involve a tournament. Courts in such tournaments often consist of non-student justices such as lawyers, professors, or members of the state or federal bench. In a tournament, courts will select the *best* team rather than deciding the merits of the case itself. The most persuasive argument will prevail. The cases used in moot courts can be fictional or real. The court is usually one of last resort like a state supreme court or the United States Supreme Court. They are called courts of last resort because they are the final arbiter when it comes to issues within their jurisdiction such as questions of state or federal law.[1] Because they have the final word over matters exclusive to their domain, the justices in your moot court cannot pass the buck to a higher court to resolve the issue at a later date.[2] This fact should add a degree of gravity for the lawyers and judges. Sounds good does it not?

---

[1]   State courts sometimes decide federal issues. State courts share this jurisdiction with federal courts. If a state court's resolution of a federal question is at odds with federal court's, it is the federal judiciary's interpretation that is to be supreme. Federal courts lack any proper jurisdiction to decide questions of state law insofar as interpreting state constitutions or other laws. If a conflict raises both state and federal questions, federal courts can, if they choose, resolve the case on federal grounds. Such a resolution tends to be rare. Under a pair of long-standing doctrines, the doctrine of equitable abstention and the doctrine of independent and adequate state grounds, federal courts, in cases that raise both state and federal questions, will generally allow state courts an opportunity to remedy the situation under state law. In certain exceptional cases, such as *Bush v. Gore*, 531 U.S. 98 (2000), federal courts will resolve federal questions despite the fact that state questions still exist.

[2]   If your instructor has chosen to have your class simulate the United States Supreme Court, the only way your court could be reversed would be if it changed its mind, or through a constitutional amendment. See, for example, the history of the Eleventh Amendment to the United States Constitution.

WHAT IS MOOT COURT?

Simulations of appellate court proceedings, also known as "moot court" or "mock Supreme Court," have been a feature of the legal education landscape for hundreds of years, with origins in pre-medieval England. Moot court is well established around the world as an educational tool. Intercollegiate moot court tournaments are currently conducted in a number of European countries including Austria, France, and Germany. Undergraduate tournaments are also regularly organized in Australia, Canada, and New Zealand, and in other areas of the world. Moot court is a common requirement in the curriculum of all American law schools. Inter-collegiate tournaments are regularly organized concerning a variety of legal issues: communication law, environmental law, the First Amendment, mass media law, and so forth.

Two fundamental forms of American undergraduate moot court coexist: in scholastic moot court students of a single undergraduate class, such as constitutional, international, or business law, or a communications/speech class (among other academic subjects), are required to participate as a condition of successfully completing that class. This may take various forms ranging from simulating the arguments in an actual case to dealing with a hypothetical set of circumstances. Some classroom models will be more sophisticated than others and more true to form of a legal dispute.

The second form of undergraduate moot court is the tournament, involving undergraduate students voluntarily competing for trophies or other personal rewards. In these tournaments, students play the role of attorneys and argue before actual attorneys and judges as if they were in a court of law. All of the rules and protocols of a regular appellate courtroom are followed in tournament competition. Students must respond to questioning from judges and forcefully advocate for their client. Additionally, in tournament competition, students will argue both sides of a case in order to test their skills and ensure fairness in the process.

In the United States, undergraduate moot court competitions are overseen by the American Moot Court Association (AMCA). The AMCA annually hosts a series of regional qualifying tournaments leading to a national championship event. Several hundred teams representing more than a hundred colleges and universities compete in these events, looking for championship glory.

WHAT DOES A "MOOTER" DO?

Because there is no one type or form of moot court, there is no single or simple answer to the question "what does a 'mooter' do?". The answer will likely depend on your instructor or facilitator, the type of moot court in which you are engaged (e.g., tournament versus classroom), and/or your assigned role (lawyer or jurist). Having issued that disclaimer, there are certain aspects or attributes that most moot courts will have in common. Much of the work that "mooters" will do will involve legal research. This work may involve reading judicial opinions, legal periodicals, newspapers, statutes, legislative histories, or state constitutions. A good amount of this research can be done online, using a variety of legal search engines or other resources, or in a library where students will find an assortment of books and articles as well as court cases.

The remainder of this section attempts, in general terms, to give students a greater understanding of what will be expected of them. Again, please note that these expectations will depend in great part on decisions or assignments that your instructor or facilitator makes. For purposes of organization, we have provided separate discussions with respect to expectations for lawyers and judges. Please note that there are certain basic tasks or expectations that lawyers and judges will share.

Lawyers

One thing that moot courts will have in common is that there will be student lawyers divided into legal teams. The size, organizational makeup, and hierarchy (if any) of these teams will vary. Some legal teams may number as few as two or in excess of ten. In some simulations, there will be lead attorneys charged with the task of allocating team resources, deciding on roles, and ensuring that the team does its work. In other instances, there are no official leaders, and matters are decided more informally (perhaps even democratically). In some simulations, the legal teams will be assigned specific sides to represent far in advance of moot court. Under a different scenario, the legal teams are not told who they will represent until a short time before oral argument.[3] Whatever the size or nature, "mooters" who are lawyers can expect to work with others to research, develop, present, and defend a legal argument for the purpose of representing their side as best they can. This teamwork may include producing a legal brief on behalf of the team that lays out and provides for your side's argument.[4] The purpose of this team brief is ultimately to get your point of view expressed to the court in a forum in which you cannot be interrupted or thrown off track by questions from the justices (those will come in oral argument). A related purpose is to get your team familiar with the legal issues and to spot any potential problems in your argument prior to court. This teamwork may also include working as a group to put on a practice moot court. Using such an exercise, your team can address certain issues or provide tips for the speaker(s) such as eye contact or delivery style or how to answer expected questions. Your team might use this as an occasion to practice rebutting the other side.[5]

Lawyers would do well to expect to be responsible for producing some written work for moot court. The exact work will depend on your instructor or facilitator. Common assignments include writing your own legal brief, producing a majority opinion that you would suggest the court adopt, or researching a specific issue or precedent relevant to

---

[3]   Such a scenario is most common in tournaments in which the teams are assigned to the appellee or appellant by some random drawing. In such instances, the legal teams will need to be prepared to represent either side at a moment's notice.

[4]   A legal brief is a document that communicates a legal party's argument to the court. Legal briefs can vary in length and format.

[5]   This can be done by having some team members pretend to represent your opponents.

the moot court case. These assignments are excellent opportunities for you to hone your writing, legal research, and critical thinking skills.

Judges

In some ways being a moot court justice is similar to being a moot court lawyer. For one, you will be expected to engage in legal research and will likely submit a writing assignment. For another, you will work with a group to prepare for moot court. Lawyers, of course, strive to win on the behalf of their clients. Your client is the nation and its constitution. If your court votes on the cases and produces a written court opinion, your goal might be to compete with opposing blocs within the court (if one exists) in the scramble to form a majority that supports your view and is willing to make it the law of the land. Another similarity is that the court, like the legal teams, may—or may not—have some hierarchy. You may have a chief justice and in some simulations the justices may be ordered by seniority. While a degree of independence will no doubt hold sway, justices may be assigned by the court certain tasks to perform on the group's behalf. This might include providing a balanced brief for the court that summarizes certain key cases, or it may include outlining for your fellow judges the key arguments made by the legal teams.

Justices should expect to be responsible for producing some written work. The exact work will depend on your instructor or facilitator. Popular assignments include writing a majority opinion based on your views, researching a specific issue or case relevant to the moot court case, or learning about a specific Supreme Court justice and emulating his or her views, manners, or tendencies in oral argument and in an opinion that he or she might be expected to produce. These assignments are excellent opportunities for you to hone your writing, legal research, and critical thinking skills.

MOOT COURT: KNOWING WHAT IS IN IT FOR YOU AND WHAT IT TAKES

Like most academic assignments you will get out of moot court what you put into it. Put another way, those who work hard and take it seriously, tend to enjoy the experience (and earn a better grade) than those who do not. A chief reason for the correlation between high levels of involvement in moot court and student satisfaction is that moot court will require considerable time working with fellow students outside of class. Moot court is a hands-on experience and gives you more room for you to be involved than other classroom assignments or projects. Students may organize their teams (e.g., divide labor, assign roles, review, and evaluate each other's work); students develop their arguments or their questions; students defend their views or ask questions of one another, and students may determine how the case is ultimately adjudicated. Even those simulations, such as tournaments, which may involve non-students in significant roles rely heavily on student contributions. This level of student involvement means that you may glimpse the fruits of your labor in an uncommon fashion not readily available or possible in other academic assignments.

Based on our own observations of "mooters" and the feedback forms that we have our students complete, we know that for most students moot court is a great experience that many will rank as the best of their academic careers.

Moot court can be a good deal of work and at times even a little frustrating. How much work and how frustrating this experience is may be dependent on other variables. For instance, the case your instructor chooses and the work that he or she assigns will affect your experience. So might your role in the simulation (lawyer or justice), or the court's willingness to consider the arguments your team wishes to make. Your experience may depend upon the dynamics and makeup of your group. Some groups work quite well; others do not. It is not always apparent why some groups function better or smoother than others. This text, and your instructor, can offer advice for how to have a good group dynamic, but there is no magic solution to the issues groups face. As we said, you will likely get out of moot court what you put into it. So, even if your group does not always function to your liking, do your best to benefit from this unique experience.

At this stage you might ask, what are the benefits to which you have alluded? There are several. Of course, no one can guarantee exactly what course your moot court experience will take. That said, there are considerable benefits associated with moot court that we believe far exceed any costs or frustrations that some might experience.

Based on moot court feedback forms, discussions with past students, and our own experiences either as student "mooters" or as coordinators of numerous moot courts, we would summarize the main benefits students experience into the following categories:

- Obtain good preparation for graduate study
- Learn about yourself and your interests or your abilities
- Experience leadership
- Learn about the law and the judicial process
- Experience being a judge or a lawyer
- Experience the thrill or rush of competition
- Improve your self-confidence or self-esteem
- Improve your critical or analytical thinking
- Overcome shyness/improve your public speaking
- Work with a team for a common goal
- Get to know your fellow students

CHAPTER 2

Getting Started with Moot Court

Now that you have seen the benefits of being a mooter, we need to address the steps necessary to become a successful moot court advocate and develop a successful program. There are two facets to developing a successful moot court program that need to be considered: (1) development of skills and (2) development of resources. In the chapters that come, we discuss moot court skill development. In the present chapter, we introduce you to the necessary ingredients for getting started with moot court and development of resources.

This chapter will introduce the basic framework for generating a program at your home institution. While each educational institution is structured differently from another, a canvass of the most successful programs in moot court indicates there are several factors that contribute to their organizational success. Most important of these factors are the following components: (1) formal organization, (2) funding, and (3) recruitment. Successful development of these features of a moot court program will enable the greatest level of success for your home institution. While there are several moving parts to this aspect of moot court, taking advantage of the insights provided here will put your program in the best position to be successful at your home institution.

FORMAL ORGANIZATION

Formal organization is a necessary component to getting started with moot court. Without a formal organization in place it is easy for new mooters to get lost in the development process. If rudderless, your members can individually spin away from the center of gravity that is the team and/or the program. It is important, then, to maintain a sense of organization in developing moot court.

While educational institutions have various types of structures, as mentioned in previous chapters, it is relatively common for moot court programs to be structured by two forms: (a) moot court as a co-curricular activity or the "moot court club" and (b) moot court as a scholastic activity or the "moot court class."

Typically these two types of organizational structures occur simultaneously with the existence of a "moot court club" that is open to all students of a campus, and, a "moot court class" that is a part of a school's curriculum. While it is fairly common for students to be engaged in moot court in both the "club" and the "class," it is not necessary that a student participate in both.[1] Because both forms of organization ("club" and "class") are often utilized by the top moot court programs, we will discuss how to employ both organizational forms. Understand, however, that the distinct components of your home institution may require some melding of these two organizational forms.

Moot Court as a "Club"

When we speak of moot court as a "club" we mean moot court as a recognized student organization (RSO). Each school has a distinctive process for creating recognized student groups on campus. There might be the "Chess Club," or the "Mathematics Club," or even a "Pre-Law Club" on a college campus. Establishing moot court as a club

---

[1] Unless, of course, simultaneous participation is required by university/college requirements.

provides institutional and financial benefits that can have a tremendous impact on the growth of moot court within a campus.

The first step in creating a club requires interested mooters to understand how their respective educational institution establishes recognized clubs. At many institutions, the process typically requires students to start this process with a student organization division. This division could be a Dean's office, or, the student assembly or council. The point is, whatever division of your respective educational institutional that handles these matters should be consulted.

After ascertaining which entity on campus establishes and oversees student groups, you will want to begin the administrative process of establishing a student organization. Sometimes a university will require a minimum number of students. Typically this number is fairly low to accommodate new and developing student groups. However, you will want to be mindful as to whether there are any such minimum member requirements at your home institution. If you find yourself below this number, consider our recruitment discussion *infra*.

Another important feature of establishing a recognized moot court organization is development of the organization structure. Often recognized student groups will be required to have officers. These officers serve as the student leaders for their respective organization. Typical officers will include a President, a Treasurer, and other leadership roles, such as a Vice President or Secretary. Whatever officers your home institution requires, understand that you will want to strategically choose who should fill these positions. For instance, individuals who are good at overseeing others and who are dedicated to moot court as a student activity should be considered for the President position. This individual is typically the point person for the organization and will represent the organization within the campus community. Having someone who is responsible and focused in this position, and who works well with the organization's "advisor" (discussed below) should be considered. Relatedly, those who have experience managing the financial resources of a student organization or who are detailed oriented should be considered for the Treasurer role. Regardless of what officers your home institution requires for student organizations, the point is to consider who will fill these spots and what strengths they have which will make them effective in those roles.

Intelligently filling these officer roles has important implications for developing a moot court program. Having distinct officers with clearly defined distinct tasks allows for efficiency in organizational operation. Individual officers within the student organization are not engaged in redundant action. Moreover, distinct lines of authority for operations permit individuals to become expert at their respective tasks. Let us evaluate a concrete example to expand on this point. Assume your organization is created and is allotted a certain amount of money to be expensed for moot court activities, such as traveling to tournaments. Often, these funds are paid back to students (or advisors) on a reimbursement basis. As a result, after returning (from your hopefully victorious) trip, you are required to submit reimbursement paperwork and related materials (such as receipts for travel, lodging, etc.). If after every tournament a different person takes the lead on the reimbursement process, it will require several different individuals to become familiar with such bureaucratic procedures. This process results in redundant efforts and does not maximize group efficiencies. Additionally, the group loses efficiency through repeated, non-redundant startup costs (i.e., the cost and time associated with each person becoming skilled in a certain task). College students often feel they have severe constraints on their time. Inducing inefficient behavior in these organizational actions can impinge upon one's already busy schedule. Thus, having separate officers who can become expert in their specific "task domains" can increase the efficiency of the program as a whole.

Another important feature to consider when establishing a moot court club is the role of a constitution (sometimes called organization by-laws). Often a university will require students to prepare a guiding document for the internal workings of student organizations. Some features of this document, or constitution, will be set by the university (i.e., every organization has to follow some specific processes no matter the organization). However, other parts of this document might be amenable to change or editing. If so, there are a few considerations students might wish to consider when preparing the moot court constitution.

First, it often makes sense to ensure that each officer delineated in the constitution have clear roles (as discussed above). Second, it is worth considering planning for growth (and relatedly, competition). If your moot court program succeeds and begins to grow in size, it is quite possible demand for financial resources might outpace actual financial resources. What would this scenario look like? Here is an example: suppose you have eight people join the newly created moot court club. This would mean you have four teams who can compete. You follow the steps in this book and become excellent mooters ready for your first tournament. However, you find that your organization can only afford to send three teams. Assuming you cannot obtain the requisite funds to send everyone in the club to this competition, how should you go about deciding who should go? A founding constitution could provide an avenue for solving this problem. For instance, some programs of which we are aware require students to compete in an in-house competition to decide who goes. In the example, the top-three teams (using whatever competitive mechanism is put in place, such as a mini-tournament, or round-robin competition) are determined to be the best teams to send to the competition. Having a student organizational document or club constitution, which states in advance how it will be determined who can attend a tournament, can prevent internal dissension within the organization. Third, a constitution can be adopted which details the minimum membership requirements for participation in the club. Many schools have a requirement that officers of a student organization maintain a specified grade point average (as an example). Perhaps the moot court club wishes its members to exceed this level. Or, perhaps this student organization wishes members of the club perform certain tasks for the greater good of the organization (requiring members to engage in a certain amount of recruitment hours). Whatever the preferred aims of the organization, the point is to codify such requirements within the foundational document to ensure there is compliance with specified activities.

A final requirement often made of student organizations is to have an official advisor. Typically, the entity that manages student organizations will require that the advisor be a current university or college employee. Often times this individual will be a faculty member. It is possible your home institution will allow a member of the local community to be an advisor (perhaps a local attorney even). You want to check with the entity that governs student organization at your university or college to determine who can serve in this advising role.

In going about choosing an advisor for your new moot court organization, we can offer several insights. First, it is always great if someone already has an interest in establishing a moot court club. For instance, perhaps you have been encouraged to start moot court by a faculty member. In this case, the faculty member who has already expressed an interest in forming a new group would be a terrific person to serve in this advising role. If this situation is yours, consider yourself lucky and begin the above processes in forming your recognized student group.

It is possible, though, you have a desire to start a moot court program which stems from your own initiative. If this situation is the case, you might not have a potential advisor in mind. Where should you look and whom should you consider? If you are in this specific circumstance, it would behoove you to begin looking for faculty members who can serve as an advisor. Many times, faculty members who serve as moot court advisors are employed by the university in departments where there is an interest in the law. For example, a quick look at the Board of Directors of the American Moot Court Association (AMCA)[2] reveals almost all of these board members (and moot court coaches) are faculty at a university. University departments

---

[2] *See* https://www.acmamootcourt.org/board-of-directors.

such Political Science, Government, Legal Studies, Communication/ Speech, or Philosophy often have faculty members who are versed in the law and can serve as an advisor to a moot court student organization. From the students' perspective, it is important to understand that many faculty members are busy. However, most faculty desire to see their students succeed, so it can never hurt to ask a faculty member about potential student organization advising. Indeed, such advising will often count towards that faculty member's tenure requirements (i.e., "university service") and thus some faculty have their own self-interest in serving in such a role.

Having an advisor who has experience in the practical applications of the law or moot court can also be beneficial. If you are aware of a potential advisor who formerly practiced law, for example, or who previously participated in moot court while a student, they could be a great person to ask to serve as an advisor. There is also another reason why such an individual might be best poised to be an advisor: they can serve as a coach. Having an advisor that not only can shepherd the student organization as a whole, but who can also provide insights into how students can improve their specific moot court skills, is a bonus. Asking around your university, or viewing the *curriculum vitae* of faculty, can help you ascertain if such a person exists at your home institution. The point here is, be strategic in finding an advisor. They will likely have a large role in the development of your program, and in establishing your recognized student organization.

Once you have engaged in these multiple endeavors to establish your club, what are the benefits? The benefits for being a recognized student organization can be quite substantial, depending on your home institution. Often universities and colleges will provide tangible benefits to recognized student groups, including moot court. For instance, being a recognized club on campus could provide you with access to use of school facilities (such as classrooms or other areas that can be used as locations for club meetings or practices). Additionally, educational institutions, either through themselves or a governing student body, will often give student organizations some amount in funding. The importance of funding will be detailed later in this chapter, however, it is worth emphasizing here that having funds for moot court activities (including, for instance, travel to competitions) is critical for continued prosperity and growth of this activity. Getting those funds, then, helps serve this purpose. Finally, there can be advantages in logistics for the club if one obtains recognized status. For example, some schools will allow clubs to have an official "University" mailing address and official "University" email account. Having these channels for official communication adds an element of prestige to your group, but also allows for streamlined communication, both within the group and to outside persons and entities.

As we have detailed, there are many reasons why when starting a moot court program, you would want to found a student club. The benefits we have discussed will be quite helpful in establishing solid moot court opportunities at one's home educational institution. In the next section, we detail another manner for getting started with moot court: as a class.

Moot Court as a "Class"

A second method for creating formal organization for your program can be through moot court as a classroom activity. Building moot court into the fabric of a school's curriculum can ensure focus remains on the activity in an institutionalized manner, and, allows for the reinforcement of moot court skills (which are discussed later in this book).

In Chapter 6 we provide detail on how to operate moot court as a classroom activity. The information there goes into the specifics of how to incorporate moot court into the parameters of a course. This information is useful in establishing and cultivating moot court skills in the confines of the course experience. For those specific tactics, please refer to the later chapter. While the classroom dynamics are explained in great detail in Chapter 6, we do want to emphasize a few points here about teaching moot court as a class from a more general, and larger perspective.

As with developing moot court as a club activity, operating moot court as a class comes with its own strategic considerations. The first, and perhaps most obvious, is to create the moot court class. Some schools presently have moot court built into its curriculum. However, perhaps you are reading this book at a school where moot court is not presently enshrined in the university's course bulletin. If the class is not, you will want to perform such tasks as required to get the class "off the ground," so to speak.

At most colleges and universities, adding a course to the curriculum can include several steps, including justification of the course to university administration. If so, you will want to begin that formal process in order to utilize moot court as a classroom activity. Demonstration of student interest will certainly not hinder this process. As noted, moot court advisors come from a variety of departments. However, often moot court classes are offered within the social sciences or government departments. Ensuring that the class is housed within one of these departments can assist in serving as a nexus between an advisor and the actual classroom activity. Indeed, it is often the case that moot court club advisors are also the coaches/instructors for related moot court classes. Departments (or colleges) also typically have a faculty curriculum committee. These committees work to ensure student curriculum is maximized within the respective home institution. Be sure to indicate to such a committee the desire to create a moot court class. It is important to help the curriculum committee understand the value of moot court as an academic endeavor. Universities and colleges across the country are stressing the importance of experiential learning activities where students gain hands-on experience and build their skills that can help them succeed in other classes, post baccalaureate education, and in the workforce. As you can see throughout this book, moot court provides just this kind of experience and helps you improve writing, research, and speaking skills. Administratively, such a committee can serve as the gatekeeper for development of the classroom activity and can assist you in the process of getting the course off the ground and running.

Even if a class is not "presently on the books" of your university, and there is a need to move quickly in establishing such a course, note that sometimes a university or college will permit the use of a previously-established course number that rotates in topics (e.g., "Legal Issues"). If that situation is the case, you might inquire as to whether, in the interim and short run, a moot court course could be taught utilizing one of these pre-established course numbers. Again, much of these specifics will depend on your home institution. However, the ability to fast-track the creation of a course in this manner should not be overlooked.

Finally, recall our suggestion earlier that it may take a blend of moot court as a classroom activity and as a club in order to be successful at your home educational institution. Be sure to know whether there might be any university regulations that permit or disallow the linking of these two activities. Again, the extent to which such overlap exists varies widely depending on the curricular and extracurricular regulations at distinct schools. That said, be advised that when developing the course as a classroom activity, you will wish to consider this connection between the two types of formal moot court organization.

We will leave here the topic of moot court as a classroom activity and reconvene on the topic in Chapter 6. You will find specific pedagogical and curricular advice there. For now, consider the aforementioned larger concepts when thinking about how to create the moot court class itself.

FUNDING

The second factor in developing a successful moot court operation is funding. While scarcity of financial resources is often an unfortunate problem in higher education, the reality is funding for moot court can be very important to development of the formal organization. We will detail for you a few considerations to make when thinking about obtaining resources for your growing moot court organization.

The first and primary consideration is to understand why funding is so important in getting started with moot court. If you operate moot court as a classroom activity, it is likely the case there is no additional requirement for funding per se. Students pay tuition, that tuition goes to the university, the university pays the moot court instructor, the school pays to keep the lights on in the classroom, etc. In this regard, participating in the classroom requires no more funding in general than the funding necessary for any other course. If, however, the class (or indeed, a club) wishes to engage in the competitive circuit of tournaments for moot court, then funding is important as it typically costs money to register for, travel to, and compete in scholastic moot court tournaments.

Second, funding for tournament participation is important because moot court skills are sharpened in the competitive environment. Chapter 7 details the ins-and-outs of running a moot court tournament. Here, we wish to make clear that those who do go to tournaments are required to exercise the skills they learn in moot court. Traveling to and participating in several moot court tournaments only serves to strengthen students' overall moot court skills. Again, as noted above, this travel may be pursuant to class requirements, or, under the auspices of the moot court club. Regardless of what vehicle serves to pursue tournament experience, such tournaments serve to develop students' skillsets. And, going to such tournaments will typically cost. Thus, one should keep funding in mind as they get started with moot court as it relates to skill development.

Finally, it is important to keep in mind university constraints on how money can be spent. Bureaucratic regulations on expenditure of funds are quite common in higher education. Whether a private school, or public, whether a big school, or little, educational institutions often have limitations on how certain types of funds can be expensed. Understanding how these different "pots" of funds operate together can strategically leverage maximum dollar value. To give an example, the author of this chapter once coached a moot court team at a university where they had three separate accounts to manage expenditure of funds. Lodging could be expensed from any of the funds, but food on tournament trips had to come from a specific pot; checks written to pay for tournament registration could be issued from another set of funds, but not from the others; and etc. If you have created a moot court organization and have full control over a single account, rejoice. If, however, you are a student (or even a faculty member) at an institution with more regulation in place, knowing how to balance the differing "pots of funds" in order to maximize the resource allocation will be critical to getting the most out of the allotted dollars.

Where then should folks look for funding? The first comment in answering this question is to consider the requirements and regulations of your respective school. Whatever regulations are in place regarding funding and financing, be sure to follow them. Second, in getting started with moot court, many emerging programs find they have to resort to a combination of fundraising endeavors. We provide some examples of these funding efforts. Keep in mind, however, that this list is non-exhaustive and might need to be adjusted depending on your home institutions' rules and regulations.

Potential Funding Sources

1. Student Organizations Group

2. Department/College Support

3. Donations

4. Grants

As noted before, one obvious place to look for funds (if you have a moot court club) is with the student organizations group. Some schools provide each organization with a minimum number of funds each academic year. If so, take advantage of such opportunity. Additionally, student organization groups (such as a Student Senate) will sometimes have supplemental funds for which groups can apply. Determine if your home educational institution has such funding opportunities, as they could be obtained and added to your growing group's total pot of funds.

Consider broaching the department or college where moot court is "housed" (e.g., "Department of Political Science") for funds. This request could be made to a department chair/head or to a college's dean's office. Funding for academic programs like moot court can often find funding friends in these places. When making your pitch, be sure to have a budgetary breakdown on how many funds you will need for each moot court activity. School administrators are often budget-oriented; clearly presenting a budget for your needs will assist these individuals in procuring funds.

Donations can also constitute a source for moot court funding. Perhaps there are alumni from your home institution with an interest in donating funds for moot court. To this end, it can be useful to coordinate such fundraising efforts with the college or university's development/endowment group. These offices typically have expertise in fundraising and can provide you with an avenue for tapping into outside donors. Students can also engage other donation avenues such as "profit shares," where a student organization coordinates with local businesses to receive a percentage of profits for some specified period of time. These are but a couple considerations for securing donations; many others might be appropriate for your specific situation. No matter the course, be sure to follow your home institutions rules and regulations when attempting to secure outside donations.

The final category for funding consideration is grants. Some schools, especially those within a larger university system, might be eligible for system-wide grants. For example, perhaps the university system has a program for sponsorship of activities related to classroom experiential learning. Instructional related activities of this sort fall squarely within the ambit of moot court, namely, travel to competitive tournaments. Application for such funds is often done well in advance of a given academic year, so be sure to prioritize these submissions to timely file such requests. These funds, however, can often be used to significantly supplement funds derived from local home institution support, and, can provide a sturdy foundation upon which to build a moot court program.

Individuals getting started in moot court, especially those developing a class, should also ascertain if their home educational institution provides grants for curricular development. It is common for universities to provide some support for development of new classes. If you wish to create a moot court class (either as a student, or, a faculty member), it would be wise to determine if your home school provides funding for curricular development. It is possible such curricular development would encompass funding for experiential learning activities, such as tournament travel. When combined with other forms of funding, these funds can add to the growing body of resources required to effectively build a moot court program.

Having made suggestions of funding avenues for starting moot court, we want to turn to the final component of getting started in moot court, namely, recruitment.

RECRUITMENT

If you thinking of starting a moot court program, the absolute base minimum required—even before organization and funding—is people. You must actually have people interested in learning moot court. If you are reading this book, you are clearly someone interested in learning moot court. But, what about finding others to assist in the development of this activity? In a word, the answer is simple: recruitment.

Recruitment for your new program can take many forms. And, as noted before, some of those endeavors will be structured by the constraints of your home institution. However, there is one key ingredient necessary for effective recruiting: finding like-minded individuals, i.e., other students who are similarly interested in the development of moot court skills.

Students with an interest in the underlying skills of moot court can often be found in pre-law organizations on campus. If your school has a pre-law organization, consider approaching that group about beginning a moot court program. Relatedly, if your college or university has a pre-law advisor, reach out to that person, as they might be able to pitch the idea of moot court to the students they advise. This person could be a great resource for linking into the stream of pre-law students on campus.

It is also worth approaching the chair of the respective department where moot court will be housed (e.g., Chair of the Political Science Department) to see if you can visit professors' classrooms to make a short pitch to their students about the new program. You could also contact professors in departments where you are likely to find pre-law students (e.g., Political Science, Government, Legal Studies, Communication/Speech, or Philosophy) and see if you could do the same short sales pitch to those students. Reaching out to these students is likely to cast a net wide enough at least to stir the interest of some potential recruits.

If your emerging program is in the process of establishing a student club as a recognized campus activity, it is advisable to use the student organization governing structure to your advantage. In many instances, the governing body for student organizations will provide specified days where student groups are permitted to advertise their groups in public forums (e.g., Student Center). These events, sometimes called "tabling," are an opportunity for the organization to present themselves to the general campus public and reach potential recruits. Having a dedicated student or students in a growing program working these events can be a successful avenue for obtaining new members.

Whatever approach you take to recruiting, be mindful of the law of numbers. The reality is, not everyone who starts moot court will finish moot court. People leave endeavors and organizations for myriad reasons; moot court is no different. If you need a minimum number of students to be interested to start a class, for example, be sure you extend your recruiting beyond what you feel is the minimum in order to account for attrition.

Additionally, be sure that your recruitment activities happen at optimal times and occur repeatedly. As an example, student "tabling" events often happen near the start of semesters; be sure your plan for using this process is in place in time to make it effective. Relatedly, ends of semesters are typically very busy times, for students, faculty, and administrators. Attempting to recruit during these periods, when people are not only occupied, but also, distracted by other concerns (like final exams), would not be an effective recruitment approach.

Finally, it behooves emerging moot court organizations to repeatedly recruit. What we mean by repeated recruitment is recruitment in order to fulfill not only growth of the program, but also to ensure attrition does not negatively impact the group. Year after year, students graduate and move on to other endeavors. In that process, moot court, like any student activity, can lose students as they move on. As a result, there is a need to replenish the human resources necessary to maintain an effective program. For example, having a moot court program entirely comprised of seniors, while perhaps advantageous from a competitive experience standpoint, can be disastrous to a program. If all these students graduate, and no recruitment is done, then the following year will be difficult to have a functional moot court campus activity. Thus, in our example, recruiting for future members while the seniors are all on the team would be a best response to this potential human resource pitfall. Engaging in repeated recruitment over time is the best way to ensure sufficient generation of interest by, and contact with, likeminded students.

CONCLUSION

In this chapter we have discussed the development of resources necessary to get started with moot court. Successfully establishing formal organization, securing funding, and effectively recruiting will set your moot court organization on the best resource path for success. We will now leave the organizational and resources concerns and turn to discussions centered on moot court skill development.

CHAPTER 3

Understanding Legal Research

Legal research seems overwhelming, but jurists and lawyers have devised systems to help find materials quickly. Once you see the pattern for how legal materials are accessed, finding the law becomes almost routine. Learning the different sources available and how to use each one most effectively is the most difficult part. After that, it is a process of going on treasure hunts to find the clues you need to solve your own particular legal puzzle.

This chapter[1] helps you conduct legal research for your moot court argument. It contains two components to help you hone your research skills. The first section presents an introduction to law and the structure of the legal process. It includes the principal sources of law widely used by those in the legal profession, as well as information about how sources of law relate to the legal process. The second section introduces you to finding and searching legal sources and also provides you with information to access both text-based and electronic materials. Here we include suggestions about how to conduct research through online databases that require paid subscriptions such as LexisNexis Academic Universe and Westlaw (these may be free through your library). We also provide information on free websites such as http://www.findlaw. com, the Cornell Law School Legal Information Institute, and government websites. The goal of this chapter is to provide you with materials to consult when you are doing research.

---

[1]   The authors recognize Adam Whitten who was a co-contributor to this chapter.

FINDING "THE LAW"

There are multiple sources of "the law"—it is not monolithic—and legal professionals use different sources to make their arguments depending on the context in which the "law" is used. Whenever you are making a legal argument, always remember to come back to the underlying source of law that you use for forming the basis of your premise or supposition.

What Is the Law?

It is important to distinguish between the law and the interpretation of the law. Generally, the "law" refers to sets of rules put in place by public officials that have the sovereign government's authority and backing. Rules are dynamic, and as they are amended, implemented, and interpreted, laws may be in conflict with one another or may be interpreted differently by various parties. This leads to many of the disputes that you encounter.

Anglo-American jurisprudence during the Nineteenth Century was based primarily on *common law*—interpreting the law on a case-by-case basis. Lawyers and judges use prior court decisions to determine the legal precedent of previous cases to determine how a dispute would be resolved. Judges were the primary source of interpretation—so they not only modified the law, they were also instrumental in creating it. By the turn into the Twentieth Century, reliance on common law changed dramatically as democratically elected legislatures codified rules and case decisions into statutes.

During the New Deal in the U.S., the government played a more prominent role in society and codifying the laws. *Codification* is the formal statement of the law transcribed into the legal structure. Rather than relying on a case-by-case interpretation of the law, codification standardizes the law into written form. Along with increased emphasis on formal legislation, the growth of the bureaucracy at all government levels (federal, state, and local) expanded the sources of law available. While writing laws down helps decrease uncertainties about its proper meaning, it is still judges who interpret those rules and who change the meaning of the law.

Sources & Types of Law	
Source	**Law**
Primary	Constitutions
Primary	Statutes, codes, and session laws
Primary	Court decisions and cases
Primary	Regulations, administrative codes, and administrative agency hearing decisions
Secondary	Encyclopedias, treatises, and hornbooks
Secondary	Law reviews, American law reports, and journal articles

Sources of Law

The principal sources of law are constitutions, statutes, case law, administrative regulations, and procedural rules.

1. *Constitutional Law*

Relying on a state or federal Constitution can be the ultimate endgame for litigants because these sources of law have the greatest legal weight and potential impact. Constitutions have authoritative legal force for prescribing principles of government. The root in Roman of *constitutio* or *constitutiones* means "enactments, decrees or regulations by the sovereign", and in Latin it is derived from *constituere*—meaning "to cause to stand" or "to fix, set, or make" a thing.

Constitutions tend to be broad, designed as frameworks for interpretation. The U.S. Constitution is rather concise with more than 4,400 words, seven articles, and 27 amendments. Yet this document has survived 230 years of political turmoil and is the oldest democratic constitution in the world. Keep in mind that some constitutions are very specific. For example, the Texas state constitution (as of 2017) has over 196 pages and 98,000 words, with 498 amendments covering freedom of speech to requiring Constitutional amendments every time the state seeks to abolish a county office.[2] While many refer to England as a "constitutional government", it's constitutional framework is function Parliamentary laws and court decisions handed down over time.

Both federal and state constitutions operate side by side, and if a state or federal law is in conflict with the U.S. Constitution the courts determine whether the law is *unconstitutional*. Do not just assert that some law or action is unconstitutional because such statements are general—always specify what constitutional provisions are in conflict within the case you are arguing. Generally, laws are declared unconstitutional only as a last resort when it interferes with a fundamental principle within one of the articles or amendments of a constitution. Moreover, a law may be constitutional *on its face*, but the implementation of that law *as applied* (e.g. actions taken by public officials) may violate the Constitution. Ask yourself, what part of the law being questioned interferes with a specific part of the Constitution? How do prior judicial opinions support or oppose the law under inquiry?

Most founders (the persons responsible for authoring the federal and state constitutions) debated the purposes of individual provisions. As such, there are historical records relating to the *framers' intent*. Judges look through founding documents to be sure that they are interpreting the law as intended by those writing the law. These explanations can differ from one judge to the next, so you may want to find the original materials yourself to help understand what was meant.

The primary source for constitutional law comes from the written constitutions themselves, but most interpretations of constitutions

---

[2] SCOCAblog. 2017. California Constitution Center and the Hastings Law Journal. "California's Constitution is not the longest." Available at http://scocablog.com/californias-constitution-is-not-the-longest/ and last accessed July 10, 2019.

come from case decisions that increase our understanding about constitutional inquiry. Through these interpretations, judges are able to articulate whether some specific action or law violates a constitutional provision.

2. Statutory Law

Statutes, passed by federal or state legislatures, are codified laws for judges to apply. After a law passes the legislature, it receives a Public Law number citing the year of the legislative term and chronological approval of the bill within the legislative session. Federal statutes can be found within the *United States Code (U.S.C.),* the *United States Code Annotated (U.S.C.A.* beginning 1926), and in the *Statutes at Large (Stat.).* Most helpful are the *U.S.C.A.* citations because this source includes the statute, and all key federal and state cases where the federal law is cited. State courts can interpret some federal laws, so there may also be state opinions associated with the federal statute. Thus, when you use the U.S.C.A. you get the text of the statute, along with a list of cases useful for understanding the law's application over time.

Every state legislature passing a law also gives it a numerical designation, but every state is different in terms of how it assigns names and numbers of the statute itself. All of the 50 states have online access to their state legislative histories and codes, discussed in the section for finding the law.

Frequently judges want to examine the *legislative history* and debates surrounding the enactment of a statute to understand what the legislature intended when it passed the law. Judges and their law clerks examine this *legislative intent* to argue why a law should be construed a certain way. Needless to say, these interpretations are subject to controversy about what the legislature truly intended when it passed the law. Occasionally you will see references to these hearings—either to the Senate or House—and pay close attention to the name of the committee or subcommittee that held the hearings. You may need this information to track down the hearings and the debates. Remember that while legislative history is a useful tool, it is a secondary source and is not controlling law.

Sometimes legislatures issue new statutes to overturn court decisions via *statutory reversal.* You want to be sure you know the history surrounding the passage of such statutes. These *new* laws, however, may also be overturned as *Texas v. Johnson*, 491 U.S. 397 (1989) illustrates. After the High Court voided a Texas statute which made it illegal to burn the flag, Congress passed a federal statute prohibiting flag burning. When that new federal law was challenged a year later, the Supreme Court once again said federal law violated the First Amendment's protections of free speech and indicated that the only way to prohibit flag burning was to pass a Constitutional amendment (*U.S. v. Eichman*, 496 U.S. 310 (1990)).

3.   *Case Law*

Case law—also known as common law or judge-made law—is the result of judicial interpretation about all relevant laws at issue in a case, including constitutions, statutes, prior cases, procedural rules, or administrative regulations. Courts use past case law (called *precedent*) as part of the doctrine of *stare decisis* ("the decision stands"). Judges establish rules consistent with precedent to help resolve current disputes on a case-by-case basis. The courts themselves may reverse prior precedent, and although infrequent, it happens. Between 1790 and 2017, the U.S. Supreme Court reversed itself in whole or in part at least 236 times (approximately 1.04 times per term).[3]

In the vast majority of trial cases, only one judge typically sits to hear arguments, and depending on the substance of the litigation, there may also be a jury involved.[4] Judges make decisions daily, but the only

---

[3]   Government Printing Office. 2017. *Constitution of the United States of America: Analysis, and Interpretation-Centennial Edition-Interim.* "Supreme Court Decisions Overruled by Subsequent Decision (1790–2016). Available at https://www.govinfo.gov/app/details/GPO-CONAN-2017/GPO-CONAN-2017-13 last accessed May 4, 2017.

[4]   Three judge panels at the federal district court level are mandated either by law (Congressional statute) or when there are constitutional challenges to federal and state reapportionment activities. Available at https://www.law.cornell.edu/uscode/text/28/2284

record of the decisions made throughout the case is within the trial transcript. When a trial judge does hand down an opinion, she or he may not necessarily issue a written opinion but may make a *bench ruling*. Therefore, there may be no record of the decision.

When it comes to appeals of trial court cases, the federal system and 40 state court systems have an *intermediate appellate court* (IAC) that hears cases before they proceed to the highest court levels. These IACs typically have judges that sit in three-judge panels to review lower court appeals, and some states, such as Alabama, New York, Pennsylvania, and Tennessee, have multiple IACs depending on the jurisdiction granted by state law. All states have a "court of last resort"—usually referred to as the "supreme court" at the federal level and in most state court systems. In general, supreme courts are courts of *general jurisdiction* meaning that the judges hear cases concerning a wide variety of legal issues, and they are not restricted to certain substantive areas, such as family law, torts, etc. While 48 states have only one highest court with general jurisdiction, Texas and Oklahoma have divided their supreme courts into two institutions—the supreme court hears civil cases and the court of criminal appeals hears criminal cases.

4. *Administrative Regulations*

Administrative regulations have emerged as dominant since the New Deal, and after the passage of the Administrative Procedures Act (1946), this body of law covers almost 60 different federal agencies. Administrative rules and regulations as those enacted by public agencies to clarify, further define, and implement statutory laws or executive actions. These agencies, as part of an office within an executive branch (at the federal, state, county, and local levels), have *quasi-legislative* and/or *quasi-judicial* functions over different substantive areas of law.

---

and last accessed May 3, 2019. A majority of trial cases involve verdicts by a judge (called a bench trial) rather than a jury. Federal and state governments both have rules regarding eligibility for jury versus bench trials.

Quasi-legislative powers refer to the prospective authority administrative agencies have to make rules and regulations to carry out the laws passed by the legislature. Legislation, when it is passed, may not provide comprehensive guidance on how the law should be implemented, and so legislators delegate *rule-making authority* to administrative agencies and their personnel who handle the daily operation and application of the law. The administrative agency adopts rules to clarify the laws which has force of law even though the legislature has not voted on it. Agencies announce these proposed rules in the *Federal Register* and hold a "notice and comment" period where individuals and groups give feedback. The agency may or may not hold public hearings, and once the rule is "final", it is published in the *Federal Register* and the *Code of Federal Regulations* with most agencies publishing material on their websites. This process is comparable for state administrative agencies.

Quasi-judicial powers refer to the retrospective ability of agencies to hold hearings, conduct fact finding, and issue decisions regarding the implementation and violation of the statutory laws for substantive areas over which the agency has jurisdiction. The U.S. Congress may delegate this *dispute resolution authority* to administrative agencies because legislators believe the agency needs direct control over a substantive area, because of the complexity or volume of cases associated with the regulation, or because of a desire to keep certain conflicts out of the courts. In the typical case, an administrative agency with subject matter jurisdiction issues a sanction against a party for violating a law. It may then hold hearings where the accused party challenges the charges. After this, the administrative official (whether agency personnel or an administrative law judge) reach a final decision. Quasi-judicial powers have the force of law, but the case is not heard before a trial judge, but the decisions are usually published online and can be appealed (to one of the circuit courts of appeal in federal cases). The only way to overturn an agency decision is if the agency's actions were "arbitrary and capricious." Needless to say, courts tend to defer to the findings of the administrative agency.

5.   *Procedural Rules*

Every state and federal has court has rules for filing motions, briefs, responses, and other legal documents. Most rules are similar across jurisdictions, and they govern everything from the procedures for judges to follow while on the bench to ethical standards for attorneys to follow, and these are codified giving them the force of law. Different rules apply depending on the court procedure. For example, the U.S. Supreme Court has procedural rules which it applies in cases proceeding before it. Rule 38 of the High Court requires a $300 filing fee for hearing a case via the writ of certiorari. Congress codified the authority of the Court to set these fees under 28 U.S.C. § 1911.

In addition to these rules, there are a variety of rules that are organized according to the issue area governing the court's jurisdiction (*e.g.* criminal, civil, or evidentiary matters for both federal and state court systems). The common cites in federal cases are to the Federal Rules of Civil Procedure, the Federal Rules of Criminal Procedure, or the Federal Rules of Evidence. These rules are not used frequently for most substantive research, but if you are focusing on procedural aspects of a case, you may need to refer to them. State courts also have similar procedures that you may need to know.

RESEARCH

Now that you know the sources of law, it is time to go about finding it. In today's legal world there are multiple ways that you may access legal sources, and you want to be sure that you have the most current and up-to-date materials.

Text-Based (Print Copy) or Electronic-Based Searches?

The logic for finding statutes, cases, and law review articles is similar, and almost all of the information is in a comparable format. You simply need to find the right sources and know the following critical information. In addition to the *primary sources* of law that were discussed earlier, there are also *secondary sources* that can assist you with your research journey. Primary sources are the actual laws themselves, but secondary sources summarize, synthesize, and clarify those laws. Secondary sources can be rather helpful for assisting you in better understanding the impact or interpretation of some laws. As such, you will almost always use secondary research in conjunction with your primary sources. Make no mistake: secondary sources *never* have the same weight of authority as the actual laws themselves. No matter what type of source you use, you need to allocate your time accordingly so that you still have time to carry out the research for both types of sources. Plan a research schedule so you can be efficient in your research.

Conducting legal research today is far different than it was even two decades ago. The advent of the Internet and the wide dissemination of electronic legal resources and databases such as LexisNexis Academic Universe, Westlaw, and FindLaw (http://www. findlaw.com) have radically changed how you access information. Law students these days are almost overwhelmed with the number of sources available, and you should begin to find what methods work best for you given what materials are accessible to you. While electronic searches have become the most popular way for doing research, all law schools still teach the old-fashioned way to find text-based materials. Therefore, as we go through each resource, we provide you with both manual and electronic searching skills.

1.   *Text-Based Searches*

The classic image of an attorney at work in the office is looking through piles of law books and stacks of papers to find what she needs for her client. The truth is, text-based materials tend to be much less expensive than subscription-based electronic databases, but the days where lawyers rely on written texts seem to have passed. Replacing them are fast, efficient, and frequently free electronic research platforms available online.

Text-based sources tend to be viewed as more reliable (over free electronic sources) but are less efficient to access. Most text materials tend to be archived so you can go back to earlier periods in time. Because of the exponential increase of information, many electronic materials are not archived as well as text-based sources, and some students may be frustrated to find a resource one day only to check back later and find it has "disappeared." You may also find that legal reference sources such as dictionaries or words and phrases indicia are easier to use in text format because you can visually scan the table of contents or indicia to help you find key words and phrases that you may need to begin doing research on your topic. And of course, there is really no substitute for having a book in your hand to read and learn the law.

2.   *Electronic-Based Searches*

Electronic-based resources have become the standard in law offices and judges' chambers nationwide. There are a number of useful free resources available online that provide both updated primary sources and some secondary sources of law. Access to *subscription-based* materials (sources where a monthly fee is paid to search a legal database) is costly, and many law firms cannot afford such sources. Most university and college libraries have at least one subscription service that they provide to their students. We focus in this chapter on two of the most commonly used subscription service sources, LexisNexis (for business and Academic Universe available for colleges and universities) and Westlaw, although there are other options.[5] Both have been available since the 1970s, and a majority of schools have access to one or both. We have also included a summary of other electronic resources (see Major Electronic Publishers appendix) to help you find some of the more useful electronic sources. Some are paid services, but we have

---

[5]   Ravel a legal data visualization research platform was publicly available until it was acquired by LexisNexis in 2017. It covers over 14 million documents from both state and federal courts over an extended time period, and it has comprehensive coverage of unpublished cases after May 15, 2015. Prior to LexisNexis acquiring Ravel, it had a cooperative agreement with Harvard Law School to digitize U.S. case law.

concentrated on free services. The only danger in learning to use electronic data sources is that you can become overwhelmed because of *too much* information. Learning when to stop doing research is just as important as learning to do the research in the first place.

3.   Search Possibilities

Regardless of what type of sources you search, you need to know the different techniques and possibilities that exist for conducting searches, and these methods vary depending on whether you are using text- or electronic-based materials. The techniques can apply for searching on the wide range of primary and secondary materials discussed next. Essentially when searching for materials where you do not have a specific citation, you have the following options: key words or controlled language; Boolean search logic; and natural language.

a.   Key Words or Controlled Language

Using key words or controlled language means that you are dependent on the linguistic structure that the publisher uses for cataloging the material. It is what is used exclusively in text-based where you have words or phrases indicia. These phrases are designed to be critical expressions that are commonly used. The advantages to using key words or controlled language are that you can browse the topics to peruse different search words that may be useful and find relevant terms for your research. Moreover, all libraries rely on some form of this type of search in one or more of their materials, and the materials cover broad concepts so that if you are just beginning your search, you can gather ideas about how your information may be organized. The disadvantage is that you are dependent on the publisher's topics and these may not be consistent across sources. It can also be time-consuming, especially if you already have an idea about the information you are trying to find.

Westlaw has a unique feature known as KeySearch which is a comprehensive catalogue of topic areas divided into categories of substantive legal issues. Each topic and category has a unique key number associated with it so you can identify the terms and key numbers most relevant to your research. Once you have identified those, Westlaw creates a query for you to find the areas that you are the most interested in searching. You can also scan the list of topics and subtopics and then specify whether you want to search cases, law reviews, etc. for those key numbers.

b.   Boolean Search Logic

LexisNexis Academic Universe, Westlaw, and almost all electronic research online operate on the Boolean search string system named after George Boole, who developed a process used in algebraic calculations. You should think of it as a way to solve a puzzle by searching through materials and specifying the criteria you need for your subject. It operates on the same principle as when you use a word processor to find a phrase you used somewhere in your paper but just cannot seem to remember where it is. Essentially you are stringing together words with terms and connectors much like an algebraic equation only you are building a word formula to be solved. You are telling the computer to find only those documents that fit the equation you have given.

Use Boolean searches when you need to get comprehensive results, to be sure that each of your key phrases appears in the documents you are seeking or to establish specific relationships between topics. The advantages to such searches are that you can control the results to get only the most complete, relevant, and precise documents you need. The disadvantages are that it takes time to learn to use it effectively, and you need to have knowledge of your subject and to formulate that knowledge into a specific query. It will take time to do precise searches that are neither too broad nor too narrow, so be sure to plan to practice before you begin doing your research. Do not search on common words—try to use distinctive words so as to be more precise—and be sure to spell the words correctly. Moreover, depending on the database you are using, you will need to learn its specific terms and connectors because it varies across publishing source. All search databases provide a legend of their specific Boolean operators as well as an "advanced search" feature that provides specific fields and limiters to use in your searches. Use Boolean search logic when you are getting specific about the type of information you need. It is the most advanced and sophisticated of all the search possibilities because it allows you to use key terms to specify your search (see the Common Boolean Terms and Connectors appendix).

Example: LexisNexis Academic Universe

Searching for materials on affirmative action in higher education that relate to the Supreme Court's decision involving the University of Texas law school. (Note: the italicized words are the words you are searching on and the bold capitalized terms indicate the Boolean terms and connectors that you use (not words you are searching).

search string: *Affirmative* **W/2** *action* **WP** *higher education* **OR** *university* **OR** *college* **W/200** *Supreme Court* **AND** *Texas* **AND NOT** *Bakke*

Translation: This tells Lexis to go find all documents that contain the words *affirmative* within two words of the word *action* and within the same paragraph as *higher education* or *university* or *college*, and to be sure that within 200 words the phrase *Supreme Court* appears along with the word *Texas*, but that we do not want documents that contain a reference to the *Bakke* decision. Lexis will find only those documents that meet these criteria. Note we include college or university because those words might be used instead of "higher education."

Some data sets (like LexisNexis Academic Universe and Westlaw) allow you to limit the date and to search through the titles of specific documents. You can also expand your search by using an 'expander' such as an exclamation mark (!) so that you can search variations on words. Both techniques can help make the search more accurate, but you have to learn the language and format used by the source.

Example: Westlaw

Searching for documents that deal with perjury in trial courts by state government officials or public employees.

search string: *testi*! **/S** *perjury* **/P** *proceeding* **OR** *hearing* **OR** *court* **AND** *government* **AND** *public* **/10** *employ!* **OR** *offic*! **AND DATE (AFT 12/31/2002)**

Translation: This tells Westlaw to find documents that contain some variation on the word *testi!* (this can include "testify", "testimony", etc. because the "!" point leaves it open ended) within the same sentence as *perjury* and within the same paragraph either the word *proceeding* or *hearing* or *court*. Further, we need only documents that have a reference to government and public within ten words of some variation on the word *employ!* (including "employer", "employee", "employment", etc.) or the word *offic!* (including "officer", "official", "office", "officially", etc.). Note that we have also used a date limiter so that we get only documents that are published after December 31, 2002.

---

c.   Natural Language Search

Many databases now follow the example of Westlaw and LexisNexis Academic Universe that developed the natural language searches in the 1990s. Both Lexis (Freestyle) and Westlaw (WIN) allow you to avoid precise terms that you need for Boolean search logic. This is identical in practice as your standard Google search.

Example: Is gay marriage or same-sex marriage legal?

After you submit your query, the computer translates the sentence into a search string by relying on common terms in much the same way you use a thesaurus. Based on what documents it finds, the individual program uses an algorithm to choose the documents that are most relevant to your question. The advantage is it makes it much easier for newcomers to start doing research because the computer formulates the query for you (unlike the Boolean search string where you have to do it). Moreover, you do not need in-depth knowledge of subjects and terms, and you can refine your research based on the results you receive. The disadvantages are that you are dependent on the way in which the computer interprets your request, and you will probably receive some weird or unrelated results depending on how you formulated your question.

You should use natural language when you have broad topics but are unfamiliar with the specific language that might be used regarding the legal treatment of the topic. It is also helpful when you are starting your research and you are looking for broad categories of materials.

Each of the search possibilities depends on your level of expertise and the material you are searching. As you become more adept at using primary and secondary sources you will find there are certain techniques you prefer in the process. Remember the most important thing about conducting legal research is that you learn to find what works best and most effectively for you.

Primary Sources

Searching online is similar to doing research with traditional written texts. You need to have narrowed your topic with key phrases that relate to the cases you are researching or have specific citations to the sections or case that you are trying to find. In advance of your search, sit down and write out a list of phrases and cases so that when you begin your search, you have some idea of the broader topic areas you are trying to find. This is especially important to help you accomplish work more efficiently and effectively. It may be helpful for you to look through *Words & Phrases Digest* (a reference source your library may have) or one of the encyclopedias (listed in the section on secondary sources) to ascertain what key legal phrases are used in reference to certain topic areas.

1. Constitutions

Finding federal and state constitutions has become a much easier task with the advent of online communication. Depending on what aspect of the U.S. Constitution you are researching, you may want to do a Google search of key words that you may need to use. The federal constitution is online at the U.S. House of Representatives site (http://www.house.gov) and is also available at the FindLaw site. There is an excellent analysis and history of the United States Constitution from the Government Printing Office (https://www.govinfo.gov/content/pkg/GPO-CONAN-1992/pdf/GPO-CONAN-1992.pdf). While virtually all libraries have compiled copies of state constitutions, we suggest that you go online. First, find the official state web site for the state you plan to research through the United States government's own site (http://firstgov.gov/Agencies/State_and_Territories.shtml). Follow the links and search within each state. Remember that every state web site is different, and typically you may need to search under subdirectories containing information about the "judiciary," "judicial branch," "courts," or "law and law enforcement." Second, you can take a shortcut and go to FindLaw.com and search under "States." That takes you to all the legal resources available for the 50 states. You can also find state constitutions on LexisNexis Academic Universe and Westlaw under the "state" data bases.

2. Statutes

There is no end to the number of sources you can use for finding both federal and state laws, but there is a consistent pattern in how the laws or codes are cited by various governments. Once you learn the tricks, you should be able to find the laws easily. If you have a specific cite to the law in question, your search is always easier. If not, be sure that you have a series of key words or phrases that help identify the substantive area of the code you want to find. Be sure to use unique words where possible.

a.   Federal Law

There are three different citations and four different ways to find federal laws. When laws are passed, they are assigned a Public Law number according to the Congressional term and chronological passage of the bill during that legislative session.

At that point, it is still considered to be a "slip law." At the end of the legislation session, the slip law is then assigned a number in the U.S. Statutes at Large (abbreviated as Stat.) which contains published records from 1845 forward (the Government Printing Office took over official responsibility in 1874). The first number listed is the volume where the statute appears, and the second number following the Stat. abbreviation indicates the page number where the law begins. Also note that if you do not have the specific citation, a list of laws in particular volumes is provided in the back of each volume where it appears.

> **Example:** *Lilly Ledbetter Fair Pay Act*, Pub. L. No. 111–2, 123 Stat. 5 (2009)

For the Public Law citation, the law was passed during the 111th Congress and it was the 2nd law to pass that session. For the Stat. citation, the law appears in volume number 123 and begins on page 5.

You can also find laws that have been codified by Congress after it has been assigned to a United States Code (U.S.C.). Finding a law here is slightly different because the first number to appear before the U.S.C. refers to the titles where the actual statute has been indexed. The U.S.C. is broken up into 50 different titles, and within each title there are separate parts: chapter, subchapter, and sections. Inside each of the volumes you can find an index for all of the titles, chapters, and subchapters. You can also find the statute and the case law associated with it listed under the United States Codes Annotated (U.S.C.A.). The numbers to both the U.S.C. and the U.S.C.A. are identical, the only difference is that the U.S.C.A. contains citations to cases, law reviews, and law reports that address the substance of the statute. The citation for the U.S.C (and U.S.C.A.) refers only to the title and the statutory section. You do not need to refer to the chapter and the subchapter. We discuss them here only so that you understand that each of the titles is broken down into chapters and subchapters.

> **Example:** 42 U.S.C.A. § 1982 relating to actions for civil rights violations. The statute is in Title 42 of the U.S.C.A., and the section of the statute is 1982. For example, if you went to find the cite, you would find Title 42 (titled Public Health and Welfare), Chapter 21 (Civil Rights). The section does not appear on *page* 1982 but appears in the part of the title where *section* 1982 begins.

> **Example: New York State**
>
> 1)   *McKinney's Sessions Laws of New York*—unofficial full text of all public and private laws passed since 1951. Published by West.
>
> 2)   *Laws of New York*—official full text of all public and private laws passed annually by the New York Legislature.
>
> 3)   *Local Laws of the Cities, Counties, Towns and Villages in the State of New York*—official full text of laws passed by local governments pursuant to the New York Constitution, the Municipal Home Rule Law, Statute of Local Governments, or other statutes delegating particular powers to local governments.
>
> 4)   *Consolidated Laws Service Session Laws*—unofficial full text of all laws passed annually by the New York State Legislature with supplemental material limited to governor's annual message since 1976. Published by Lexis.

Inside each of the U.S.C. and U.S.C.A. volumes there is a complete table of contents, as well as a summary of all the titles. By looking through the table of contents, you can find the page where the section first begins. You need to have that to find the appropriate section. Note that most of the sections go on for multiple pages, even volumes! Some of these lengthier laws are broken into "parts." Try to always have the "part" number available to find the material.

From time to time Congress amends the laws and different dates may follow the code's cite. As a general rule, the volume and the section follow the same number when the law is amended, but on occasion, Congress gives an overhaul to certain sections, and thus new numbers may be assigned—it is important to pay attention to the date following the U.S.C. (U.S.C.A.) cite. That date tells you that *as of that date*, you can find the code listed at the volume and section number that follows. Do not be concerned if you do not have the exact date that corresponds to your statute. Most sections do not change frequently, so if you have a cite that contains an earlier date, chances are good that the same section still applies for the volume you are searching. If you are searching online, the sections are always updated, so you do need to worry about having the correct date.

Searching on LexisNexis Academic Universe or Westlaw you should find that having the exact citation makes life easier. Otherwise you need to be sure you have a fairly specific search string that examines the particular section of the code you are interested in finding. Perhaps the best strategy is to have used secondary sources to come up with a list of key words or phrases that you can search, and then rely on electronic sources to find the actual law. When you search http://www.findlaw.com you can browse through the titles and sections and that may make it easier to get key words that you use for more specific sections.

b. State Law

Finding state law is a similar process, but state laws vary in terms of how the information is presented. Like federal laws, each bill passed has a public law number attached to it, along with a numerical number indicating the legislative session in which it was introduced and passed. Unlike federal law, however, when the law is placed on the books, there are myriad possibilities for how it is numbered. Moreover, the codes of the different states are called different things depending on the system's governmental structure. In many states there are both official and unofficial publishers of statutes that cover different periods and materials.

States also vary by subdividing their codes into various substantive sections such as civil or criminal, although all the states follow the practice of establishing titles or chapters with various subdivisions. These variations in citations mean that you may have to dig deeper to find your law, and each state has different methods for cataloging material or uses different types of search engines and techniques for tracking materials. Be sure you know multiple search techniques when you go to find the law. Generally speaking, searching by text requires the use of key words and controlled language. State materials should contain an index either as a separate volume or a summary of key titles and chapters in the back of individual volumes. Be sure to check with your library to find out what state statutes they maintain as most libraries keep the statutes of their own state and perhaps those from neighboring states. Rarely do most libraries contain all the state statutes, although larger law libraries may.

When you search electronically, however, you will probably utilize key words, Boolean searches, or natural language techniques. As with other state materials, much of this information is online. One of the best sources is http://www.findlaw.com using the "State Resources" link that allows you to access all 50 states.

Before beginning your search online, be sure to check the "searching tips" section that the states provide because this saves you time and energy and allows you to be sure that you have conducted a comprehensive search. Where you can use exact phrases, you increase your ability to narrow your topic.

Example: Massachusetts Law

Conducting a search in the General Laws of Massachusetts for "driving under the influence" returns nine different possibilities including: Title XIV. Public Ways and Works. Chapter 90. Motor Vehicles and Aircraft. Section 24. Driving while under influence of intoxicating liquor, etc.; second and subsequent offenses; punishment; treatment programs; reckless and unauthorized driving; failure to stop after collision.

---

3.   *Case Law*

Case law constitutes written opinions issued by judges. When a judge hands down a decision, the judge may direct the clerk of the court to send a copy of it to the different publishers and electronic distribution outlets that make cases available. These *reporters*, or sources of case law, are the primary way in which legal professionals access materials. The reporters are available in both text-based and electronic format. Numerous reporters catalogue cases according to: 1) when the decision was rendered; 2) the company that printed the opinion; 3) what level of court heard the case (trial or appellate); and 4) what state or federal court decided the case. In the late 1990s, many of the federal and state courts began publishing their opinions online as well. Many of the cases in the text-based reporters are also available electronically, but this is not always the case. It is helpful if you know what level of court and geographic area you are searching on, but if not, you can still find your cases.

Both federal and state reporters compile cases according to the date the judge or justices issued the case. Reporters contain only information regarding the case opinion and include all relevant facts, the judges or justices who decided the opinion, the attorneys who participated in the case, and the body of the opinion including the legal reasoning and the judgment (who wins, who loses). One final note about finding cases—after you have done so, you need to be sure that your case is still "good law." As such, you need to use either Shepard's or Westlaw's KeyCite citator service to be sure that you have only the most up-to-date materials (see the LexisNexis Shepard's Citations & Westlaw's KeyCite inset). Both Shepard's and KeyCite are pay services offered through LexisNexis and Westlaw, respectively. It is possible to determine the current status of a case by using free case search databases, including FindLaw, Google Scholar, Casemaker, and Fastcase. These methods are, however, more time-consuming and less reliable unless you are practiced in legal research and case law. It is recommended that you use Shepard's or KeyCite (or both!) if you have access to them.

a. Federal

At the federal level, judges routinely issue written opinions to provide the lower courts with precedent that can be followed in future cases. At the trial level, however, the decision to write an opinion is at the judge's discretion, and judges may rule from the bench without issuing a written opinion. As such, you may find appellate opinions but then be unable to find the trial court opinion that goes with it. The U.S. Circuit Courts of Appeals hear cases from the trial court level, and the federal circuits are organized geographically according to the circuit court that has jurisdiction for that region. These eleven circuits plus the D.C. circuit are courts of general jurisdiction reviewing cases that originally started in one of the 94 federal district courts. Do not confuse the U.S. Court of Appeal for the D.C. Circuit with the U.S. Court of Appeal for the Federal Circuit which only hears tax, patent, and international trade cases.

In contrast, the U.S. Supreme Court always issues an opinion, but while there is only one "official" cite, there are four text-based places where it is reported, in addition to multiple electronic sources. First, the official reporter of the U. S. Supreme Court is the United States

(U.S.) reporter with cases reported in sequential volumes. Second, the Supreme Court Reporter (S.Ct.) is published by West Publishing Company. Third, the Lawyer's Cooperative Publishing Company publishes yet another version of the opinion in the Lawyer's Edition (L.Ed.) through multiple series. Fourth, the Bureau of National Affairs (BNA) issues the United States Law Weekly (U.S.L.W.)—a publication addressing legal issues presented by recent Supreme Court decisions. Be careful using U.S.L.W. because it is not as comprehensive as the other three sources. Both LexisNexis Academic Universe and Westlaw assign their own numbers to cases, plus www.findlaw.com and Cornell's Legal Information Institute also publish High Court decisions. Thus, potentially eight different sources with four different citations appear for one case! When U.S. Supreme Court cases are cited, typically all three of the traditional reporters are listed (U.S., S.Ct., and L.Ed). Lawyers refer to this as *parallel citation*, and three forms are given so that if attorneys are unable to access one set of reporters, they may be able to find the case in another set.

All cases—whether federal or state—are easy to find, and the cites to a particular case are listed according to the following formula, with the same logic applying to all cases. The name of the primary two parties comes first with the reporter where the case is found coming second, and the page number where the case begins to appear. *Party A v. Party B, volume number* name of reporter *page number* (year).

> **Example:** *Obergefell v. Hodges*, 576 U.S. ___, 135 S. Ct. 2584, 192 L. Ed. 2d 609, 83 U.S.L.W. 4592, 2015 U.S. LEXIS 2333 (2015)
>
> The volume in the U.S. Reporter (U.S.) is 576, but there is no page number assigned (it is a slip opinion). You can also find the case in the Supreme Court Reporter (S.Ct.) volume 135 beginning on page 2584; in volume 192 of the Lawyer's Edition, second series (L. ED. 2d.) beginning on page 609; and in volume 83 of the U.S. Law Weekly.
>
> If you use the "Get a Case" function on LEXIS, enter cite 2015 U.S. LEXIS 2333. The page number is where the first page of the opinion begins—the actual opinion may go on for quite a few (even hundreds of) pages.

Federal appellate and trial court opinion citations follow the same logic, but information in parentheses provides additional information to assist you in knowing what lower court decided the case. The same logic for party names, volume number, reporter name, page number, and date applies, but you also include the circuit or district court where the case was heard. In some instances, with the district courts, there is more than one district court in the state. Be sure you get the correct district court.

> **Example: Federal appeals courts**
>
> *U.S.A. v. Kimler*, 335 F.3d 1132; 2003 U.S. App. LEXIS 13586 (10th Cir. 2003). This means this case is in volume 335 of the Federal Reporter, third series, beginning on page 1132. The information in the parentheses tells you the Tenth Circuit decided this case in 2003. Note that you can find it on Lexis in the U.S. appeals database (volume 2003 and page 13586).

> **Example: Federal district courts**
>
> *U.S.A. v. Reynard*, 220 F. Supp. 2d 1142; 2002 U.S. Dist. LEXIS 21855 (S.D. Cal. 2002).
>
> Here the case is in volume 220 of the Federal Supplement series, beginning on page 1142. The case is out of the Southern District of California in 2002. The same logic applies to LEXIS in this example.

b.   States

State cases are compiled in both state and regional reporters published by West (Thomson Publishing), and these reporters provide the full text of state court opinions. Most libraries have at least their own state and regional reporters, but, depending on resources, may not have all the text volumes for every state. Increasingly, libraries are relying on electronic sources for more recent cases. In addition to the individual state reporters, there are also regional reporters where state cases are organized by date and according to the geographical location of the court. Remember, these are *state* court opinions, and the reporters are *not* grouped according to the federal circuits. The format is identical to federal cases (volume, reporter name, page number, and date), but commonly you see two parallel citations—both to the regional reporter and to the state court reporter. Not all states have official state reporters, and even the regional reporters are not considered the official reporters.

A note of caution about one of the most frequent mistakes made when researching both federal and state law. The "2d,", "3d", or even "4th" references you see in different citations refers to the volume series. Legal materials are compiled chronologically, and rather than let volumes continue endlessly, when a reporter volume reaches a given number, the publishers begin a new series and renumber the series accordingly. For the first series of the Federal Reporter (F.), the volumes went up to 300, but for the Federal Reporter, second series (F.2d), the volumes went up to 999, and they are now in their third series beginning in 1993. Be sure you have the correct series number (2d, 3d, 4th, etc.) because otherwise you may not find the material. Most series of reporters or other materials are well into the second series.

> **Example: Illinois appellate case**
>
> *People v. Daly*, 792 N.E.2d 446; 275 Ill. Dec. 215, 2003 Ill. App. LEXIS 865 (2003). The volume is 792 in the Northeastern reporter, second series, beginning on page 446. You can also find the same case in volume 275 of the Illinois decisions, beginning on page 215. Note that as with federal cases you can also find the citation on LexisNexis Academic Universe under the section titled state law.

4. *Regulations*

Regulations from a variety of agencies may also play an important part in determining the meaning of the law. Further, regulations may be from either federal or state agencies.

a.   **Federal Regulations**

There is an extensive process for the development of these rules and a formal set of laws that govern the implementation and interpretation of rule-making authority. The *Administrative Procedures Act* (1946) includes a notice and comment period so the public can respond or provide feedback to the agency. As such, you should access materials from the *Federal Register*, but also in the *Code of Federal Regulations* (C.F.R.). As with other reporting volumes, the volumes are divided into subject areas depending on the legal issue (and federal agency) implementing the regulation. Regulations exist for most everything that exists. Understanding how and where to find regulations (even if you don't understand the need for them) is a very useful skill. Like the U.S. Code, the first number listed refers to the title and the second number refers to the section where the regulation appears. Most regulations are subdivided into subparts which are the numbers that appear after the decimal. Pay close attention to each of the titles, sections, and sub-parts when trying to find a cite.

> **Example:** Catsup/Ketchup has been subject to regulation since 1953, and the U.S. Department of Agriculture devotes eight pages to what constitutes the different grades of catsup, including Grade A Fancy. The regulation that governs what can be called catsup requires that the "consistency of the finished food is such that its flow is not more than 14 centimeters in 30 seconds at 20 degrees Celsius when tested in a Bostwick Consistometer" (scientific ramp device with approximately a 30 degree angle). 21 CFR 155.194. The citation indicates that it is in Title 21 of the Code of Federal Regulations appearing in section 155 and subpart 194.

b. State Regulations

The citation format of state regulations varies according to the state but is set up similar to the federal system. Each state has a publication to disseminate information about regulations that are being considered. After comments from the general public and interested parties, the rule is published via an official publication and posted. The text-based form of these materials is made available to all the state's depository libraries. Typically, the code for each state is published on a state web site. You may find that the further back in time you go that you have to use text-based sources for these materials because states do not archive the materials for more than three to five years. In a number of states, a private publisher may have a service that compiles the state regulations as part of their materials on different substantive areas. LexisNexis Academic Universe and Westlaw also have materials regarding state regulations. Check with your reference librarian to find out what resources may be available to you through your university. The quickest source that we recommend is through http://www.findlaw.com.

5. *Procedural Rules*

Most undergraduate students do not do research on substantive issues surrounding procedural rules, but when you get to law school, you will have to access both federal and state rules. On occasion as an undergraduate you may need to look up a procedural rule to read it in its entirety because it is referred to in your materials. Every state publishes a text-based version of its rules that are available at most university book stores. The easiest thing for you is to rely on federal and state materials found at http://www.findlaw.com. This is particularly helpful because a number of ethics and courts rules are posted as well (by state). In addition, Cornell's Legal Information Institute has a full-text version of all federal rules of procedure (including criminal, civil, and evidentiary). You can also purchase a downloaded version. Be sure to have at least some idea of the substance surrounding the rule if you do not have a specific rule number.

Secondary Sources

Secondary sources are materials that are summaries of primary source conclusions and arguments about the correct interpretations regarding the rules of law enunciated by primary sources. Secondary materials are often more helpful and easier to understand than primary sources, but you must be careful to remember that only primary sources have binding authority. Many persons use secondary sources to help synthesize complex legal issues but rely on primary materials for making their legal arguments. Be sure that you do not solely rely on secondary sources because there is no substitute for reading the primary source material.

1. *Case Digests*

Case digests are helpful guides summarizing legal cases according to the legal issue that is presented in the judicial opinions. These volumes are a chronological quick reference to a comprehensive set of cases for court opinions so you can compare how federal or state courts have decided legal issues. Rather than reprint an entire case opinion, and because one case may encompass several legal issues, Thomson Publishing hires attorneys or legal scholars to comb through the cases and write concise summaries of the legal points. These points are then categorized according to legal area and topic, so you need to use a subject approach to find your topic and the cases that relate to it.

Each digest has a "Descriptive Word Index" volume of topics that you should skim to find the most appropriate topics that relate to your issues. Additionally, a "Table of Cases" volume can help you find the cite to cases and "key numbers" that are associated with the topic area. Finally, West also provides a "Defendant-Plaintiff Table of Cases," so that if you do not know the plaintiff's name, you can look up the Defendant instead. These volumes are located at the end of the stack of volumes covering the digest.

You do not cite to the digests, they are just helpful for summarizing information quickly and finding cases that you may want to use. These are only in text-based format, and increasingly some researchers find them to be limited compared to the vast majority of electronic searches you can do. Digests can be helpful if you know the subject area that you want to examine, and they are particularly helpful because they summarize all federal *and* state cases according to the topic of the case. They can also be overwhelming if you have no idea about the topic area where you should begin to look.

2. *Legal Summary Materials*

Legal summary materials take a wide variety of forms. The most common—law review articles, annotated law reports, legal encyclopedias, and practice manuals—are discussed in the following sections.

a. Law Review Articles

Law review articles are great sources of secondary information because they provide you with analyses of issues that you are interested in researching. These lengthy articles are written by law professors, judges, practitioners, and, on occasion, law students. The information contained in these articles is superior because these scholars have spent a great deal of time studying the issues and providing frameworks about the issue being considered. Law review articles cover a broad range of subjects, and the inquiry ranges from case notes to broad surveys of legal topics including arguments about the legal interpretation or questions about whether certain rules of law should be changed. Case notes are articles that focus exclusively on one particular case, usually by the Supreme Court. These are in-depth analyses and are excellent for providing you with extensive detail about the case. Other law review articles provide you with legal evaluations or current controversies. Scholars propose their ideas about why a certain legal standard should be adopted or whether certain court decisions were decided correctly (or incorrectly!). Law reviews save you hours of doing research because they provide synopses of key cases and relevant points. In a sense, legal scholars have done a great deal of the busy work for you!

If you are using text-based materials, the easiest thing to do is to peruse the subject areas listed in the *Index to Legal Periodicals* with the lists of all articles that relate to that topic. Using the index is helpful in getting you started because it provides a quick source of topical issues. Unlike digests or encyclopedias, it is not organized according to legal topic area, but is instead organized according to common terms associated with cases (e.g., flag burning, abortion, freedom of religion, etc.). We recommend you look through it first if you are unsure about how to begin your legal research. Most students find that LexisNexis Academic and Westlaw are the easiest way to access law review articles because you can search by natural language and Boolean searches. Moreover, you can limit your search to looking within titles or by certain dates so that you obtain specific materials, as well as only the most recent works available (see the Common Boolean Terms and Connectors appendix). Be careful, because if you use an idea that comes from a law review, you must cite the author and source. Remember, given the easy access to electronic information, one of the downsides in the age of the superhighway is that it is much easier to check on plagiarism. If you are in doubt about whether you should cite some particular source, cite it. Lawyers are very conscientious about documenting where they obtained their information.

LexisNexis Academic uses a template for doing searches to guide you. When you access the database, go to "Legal Research," then "Law Review." While you have two options—either a "Basic" search or a "Guided" search—we suggest using the guided search because you can search on specific areas, such as title, author, citation, or full text. You need to specify on the pull-down menu which category you are seeking to search. Some of you may already know a specific author, citation, or title for which you are searching. Many of you, however, may want to do full text searches to find out what types of articles have been written—in that case, use the "full text" search. If you use the "full text" option, you should rely on your Boolean search strategies and choose words carefully to ensure an accurate search. Also be sure to specify a date delimiter. LexisNexis goes back to 1981, so if you are looking for articles before that time, you should use other text-based sources.

Example: LexisNexis Academic Universe search string:

separation **W/2** *power* **WP** *executive* **OR** *presiden*! **WS** *congress*! **OR** *legislat*! **AND NOT** international

This search string, done in full text mode, says find all articles where the word *separation* appears **within two words** of *power* and **within the same paragraph** the word *executive* or some variation of the word *president* appears **within the same sentence** as a variation of the words *congress* or *legislate*, but not the word international. When limited to the dates 08/01/02 to 08/01/03, we found 19 articles.

Westlaw operates in much the same way as LexisNexis Academic in that you have options for how you go about your search. It varies slightly when it comes to the language that you use for conducting the search. You may also want to rely on Westlaw's KeySearch system for getting comprehensive access to case digests, law review, and encyclopedia materials.

Example: Westlaw

TI(*free*! **or** *hate* **and** *speech*) **and** *KKK* **& DA(AFT** *09/01/1999* **& BEF** *09/01/2019*)

This search string says find all law review articles where some variation of the word *free* or *hate* appears along with the word *speech* in the **title, and** somewhere else in the article the phrase *KKK* must also appear. The **date** is restricted to only those articles written **after** *September 1, 1999*, and **before** *September 1, 2019*.

Law review citations resemble closely the pattern used for case law—volume number, law review title, and page number. When you cite a law review article you need to cite it in the following manner: author first and last name, title of article, volume number of the article, abbreviated name of law review, page on which the article begins, and the date or year of publication. The hardest part of getting law review citations is figuring out the abbreviated version of the law review titles that are used. You can find a summary of these inside the *Index to Legal Periodicals* and also online.

Example: Taylor Ledford, "Foundations of Sand: Justice Thomas's Critique of the Indian Plenary Power Doctrine", 43 *Am. Indian L. Rev.* 167 (2018). Note that the citation indicates that the article is found in volume 43 of the American Indian Law Review beginning on page 167.

Pay close attention to the footnotes in law review articles because authors rely heavily on footnotes to place information tangential to the direct issue being analyzed. Here you can find other references and citations. Occasionally, there are important facts that may bear on the legal analysis. This reliance on footnotes IS NOT something used frequently when you begin actually writing your legal brief. Unlike other college papers that you write, most legal briefs do not place great emphasis on footnotes or endnotes. Instead, the relevant material is placed in the full body of the brief itself following the idea that you are supporting. Check with your professor or teacher to find out what format he or she prefers for your assignment.

b.   Annotated Law Reports

Annotated Law Reports (ALRs) are similar to law review articles, except these reviews are much more comprehensive and exhaustive in their analysis. As such, the reviews can be helpful, but trying to comprehend all of the information provided can be overwhelming. You may want to identify only the key ALRs that are relevant to your research, and then use the topics to search for other materials. Published by Lawyer's Cooperative since 1888 (the same group that publishes the Lawyers' Edition of Supreme Court cases), each ALR has selected (but not all) state and federal court opinions followed by an analysis of all the legal issues presented by the case. It was originally called the *Lawyers Reports Annotated*, but in 1919 the title changed to the *American Law Reports*, and two series of the *Lawyers Reports Annotated*, as well as six series of the ALR exist, including one that comprises only federal cases, statutes, and regulations.

You may find using the manual volumes easier than researching the information online if you do not know where to begin because you can view the different topic areas. Each ALR volume encompasses between twenty to thirty cases, and a table of contents begins each of the annotations. The ALR has a "Quick Index" that is organized according to descriptive topics. You should look through the index to see which topics apply to you. This index does not cite the specific authorities but gives you cites to the annotated law reviews themselves. Remember: the ALRs are not jurisdiction specific, so check the "Table of Jurisdictions" when trying to find particular material. Depending on when the ALR was published some of the materials are superseded by recent decisions. Pay close attention to the publication date and check for pocket parts. Pocket parts are written supplements to the main text-based volumes. Pocket parts update the main volumes with recent developments in case law and the prevailing legal theories on any given topic. The publisher regularly produces and distributes pocket parts to ensure the main volumes contain and reference current and relevant law. Publishers use pocket parts as an economic means to supply their subscribers with relevant law; it is far cheaper to produce the pocket parts each year than it is to print new books! A search online or with electronic resources can sometimes be more efficient, however, when you are already familiar with the subject area's terms and annotations.

ALR citations are the same format as law reviews and case law, although sometimes no author is provided because an employee for the publisher wrote a specific article. Cite the ALR as: author first and last name (if appropriate), title of article, volume number of article, abbreviated name of law review, page on which the article begins, and publication date and year.

> **Example 1 (without author):** Annotation, *Use of Plea Bargain or Grant of Immunity as Improper Vouching for Credibility of Witness in Federal Cases*, 76 A.L.R. Fed. 409 (1986).
>
> **Example 2 (with author):** Theresa L. Kruk, Annotation, *Failure to Object to Improper Questions or Comments as to Defendant's Pretrial Silence or Failure to Testify as Constituting Waiver of Right to Complain of Error—Modern Cases*, 32 A.L.R. 4th 774 (1984 & Supp. 1992).

c. Legal Encyclopedias

Legal encyclopedias collect and compile the law and set it forth in an educational framework. They provide sometimes exhaustive summaries of each topic they cover. Publishers organize encyclopedias according to subject areas and then broken down into sections regarding the specific legal overviews. The two leading national encyclopedias are Corpus Juris Secundum (C.J.S.) published by West and American Jurisprudence (Am. Jur. 2d) published by Lawyers'

Cooperative. There are also encyclopedias covering some the law specific to certain states. The key difference between C.J.S. and Am. Jur. 2d is that C.J.S. is known for providing the general rule of law, an extensive list of cases, along with the exceptions and qualifications to that general rule, and Am. Jur.2d is known for providing broad principles and citations to the more important cases, along with statutes, rules, forms, and A.L.R. annotations.

It is important to have an idea of the key terms and signifiers of the subject matter within the encyclopedia collection you need to study because the encyclopedias are divided according to legal points. You should rely on the "General Index," which is divided alphabetically into separate volumes that accompany the encyclopedias (they are located at the end of all the subject area volumes). Reading through the index will guide you about what subject areas you can examine. If you are using the printed version, remember to check the pocket part in the back of each volume according to your subject section because there are almost always updates to the materials in the full volume. In the electronic or online volumes you can search on key words and use Boolean searches to make the task much easier.

Encyclopedias are useful, but the topics tend to be exhaustive; you are usually wise to narrow down your search once you are more familiar with your research topic. The outlines and tables of contents at the beginning of the chapters and sections are excellent "road maps" that you can use to refine your search for relevant law. After you find an entry of interest to you, go to the section of the encyclopedia where your topic of interest begins and scan through the outline at the beginning of the chapter of section. The outline itself may extend for several pages and include topic areas that may not necessarily be relevant to your research. The outline provides information about what section contains the discussion relevant to your needs. Each section contains information about applicable cases, statutes, and, most usefully, relevant sections in the encyclopedia so that you can continue researching issues related to the subject matter of your original search.

Additionally, the section may also contain references to relevant rules, regulations, or articles.

Citing the encyclopedias is straightforward because you are citing only the volume, abbreviated name of the encyclopedia, section number of the topic, and the date of the publication. In most instances when you are using electronic materials, you will also need to cite the current date on which you conducted your research or on which the article itself indicates it was last updated. While some searches yield hundreds of results, you should work on getting your searches to be as specific as possible. Practice using different Boolean and database-specific strings until you find one that yields the information you need.

d.   Practice Manuals

Although many attorneys and judges enjoy researching and answering legal questions for their own sake, or in preparation for an academic paper or presentation, the vast majority of legal research is conducted during the daily practice of law to further clients' interests. Accordingly, there are a plethora of manuals and treatises devoted to a specific practice area of law. Criminal prosecution and defense, real estate transactions, family law, environmental regulations—if a lawyer practices it there is probably a practice manual (and many times multiples!). These are usually written by experienced attorneys and law professors with deep knowledge about the area of law and are meant to provide specific guidance for daily practitioners. The cited law in practice manuals usually highlights the most relevant and recent case law and statutes affecting the area. Additionally, many include annotated forms that you can review to see the law as applied to a given area of law.

One of the most well-known practice manuals is Wright & Miller's Federal Practice and Procedure. This multi-volume manual includes extensive annotations for all federal rules of procedure and evidence, as well as key statutes. Another excellent resource for practitioners is pattern jury charges. The "charge" to the jury is form of the verdict a jury is tasked with answering when a case goes to trial (e.g., "Do you find that the Defendant committed murder beyond a reasonable doubt?"). Most of the federal circuit courts of appeals and state supreme courts publish pattern (or suggested) jury charges with reference to key cases explaining why the proposed form is correct given the current state of the law.

The benefit of practice manuals for your moot court legal research is that they can provide a start-to-finish outline of the type of case you are researching. This will be especially helpful if you are unfamiliar with the area of law. Moreover, many times the judges for your moot court competitions are practicing attorneys. You will gain significant advantage over your competition if you are able to explain the practical effects of your argument on hypothetical future cases.

CONCLUSION

Think of doing legal research as a treasure hunt that you are on for finding the materials you need. In the beginning, you start out with clues or ideas about general legal principles. After that, you begin systematically finding information that will help you in presenting your arguments or writing your papers and briefs. One of the most interesting things about studying the law is that in many ways it resembles a puzzle that you must piece together to form the arguments that you need for representing your clients. Preparation for doing legal research should not be an ominous task. Judges and lawyers need to be able to access information quickly whether it is in a text-based or an electronic format. Most of the difficulty associated with legal research and argumentation is understanding the sources of law, analyzing primary and secondary sources, and knowing where to find the different places where you may find legal information.

This chapter has provided you with an introduction to doing legal research, but the only way to become an expert is to go out there and start trying to find your pieces of the puzzle. As you go through sources, learn what works and what does not work for you. If you find that you seem to be running into dead ends for your research topic, consult with a reference librarian or your professor to find out how you can make your search process more efficient. Above all, remember that it takes time and patience to learn to access the different materials, and that as you grow more proficient, it will become easier for you. Happy hunting!

CHAPTER 4

The Basics of Oral Argument

Speaking in front of other people can be overwhelming, but once you understand basic principles, it can be rewarding. The ability to communicate effectively and persuasively is a skill virtually everyone needs throughout their lives. After mastering the ability to participate in moot court, most people find that they are less intimidated by public speaking in general. When judges, professors, attorneys, and law students have grilled you, everything else is easy by comparison!

This chapter[1] helps you prepare for your oral argument, and it contains two components to develop your speaking skills. The first component introduces principles of legal argumentation and underscores the importance of developing a "theory" about your case. It includes the fundamentals about structuring your argument so that it is coherent. The second component introduces you to principles of persuasive and effective speaking in the context of moot court. Here we include suggestions about how to improve your verbal skills and tips for successful moot court arguments.

PRINCIPLES OF CONSTRUCTING ARGUMENTS

Arguments arc statements that assert a situation, condition, or state of affairs to be true by providing *premises* (underlying statements) to support the *conclusion* (end result you are seeking). Most important,

---

[1]   The authors recognize Adam Whitten who was a co-contributor to this chapter.

structure your argument in a logical manner that follows your key points. On its face, your reasoning should be apparent, and you should weave a story that combines both law and facts into a persuasive case for your client on issues you are addressing. A successful oral argument presents the claims, uses logical reasoning and evidence to support the claims, acknowledges and refutes counter-positions, and summarizes why your arguments should be the preferred position.

A common mistake in argumentation is spending too much time refuting the counter-positions without fully developing *your* position and establishing its superiority. Another frequent mistake is to imply the conclusion by setting out only the premises. Finally, be aware of the logical reasoning that underlies the structure of your argument so you can be prepared to counteract potential criticism that may be leveled against you. You may use both deductive and inductive reasoning to present arguments, but the arguments must be internally consistent, and the premises should be valid.

An *inductive argument* is where you proceed from a specific observation to a generalization based on the premise of the specific observation. Inductive arguments are based on experience or evidence that may or may not be consistent with factual premises. It is concerned with empirical investigation upon which conclusions are reached or hypotheses tested (on the basis of experience, a generalization is made in terms of the probability). As such, inductive arguments depend more on the probability that the conclusion is true rather than pure logic that it can be proven to be true. As such, inductive reasoning can be easier to attack.

> **Example:** All students sitting at the table in a local bar are students on the moot court team. Those students at the table in the bar all party too much. Therefore, all students on the moot court team party too much.

A *deductive argument* is one in which you examine an issue by proceeding from general observations based on premises that are true to the specific statement about an individual observation that can be concluded based on the premises. Deductive arguments are based on knowledge that is already known and rely on declarative statements and establishing logical connections between known facts to generate conclusions.

> **Example:** Students who are on moot court teams study too much. A woman in my class is on the moot court team. Therefore, the woman in my class studies too much.

The biggest mistakes people make in structuring arguments are using logical fallacies and faulty premises to support their position. A fallacy is a defective argument that is based on a false premise (all arguments are based on some underlying premise that applies in the context of the issue with which you are dealing). Both formal and informal fallacies weaken your argument and cause you to lose credibility—your arguments are easily attacked. For both previous examples, discuss what problems you may or may not see with the statements as presented.

> **Example:** Wine is a beverage.
> Milk is a beverage.
> Wine is milk.

A *formal fallacy* is a flaw that can be identified by examining the structure of the statement presented. Such statements look like valid arguments because the premises seem true enough, but the conclusions are invalid.

Here the fallacy is in the structure of the syllogistic reasoning. One classification is not necessarily related to the other simply because they both belong to a similar category. In contrast, an *informal fallacy* is an identifiable flaw that can be seen by analyzing the content and structure of the argument. Such statements are invalid because they fail to demonstrate the truth of the conclusion that is reached and because they derive plausibility from improper usage of language and the structure of arguments.

> **Example:**   That man drank milk for twenty years.
>
> That man became addicted to cocaine.
>
> Milk causes cocaine addiction.

Here the fallacy is one of false causation—erroneously attributing two events to be related to one another when in fact they are not.

Before going on, be sure that you understand the different types of fallacies that can be made, the problems they can cause, and potential solutions by referring to "Common Criticisms of Arguments". We now turn to developing a moot court argument.

DEVELOP A THEORY OF THE CASE

To develop a coherent argument, you must develop your "theory" of the case. After examining the questions presented, begin asking yourself about the propositions that you want to communicate. *What* do you think is going on here? *What* are the underlying suppositions at the core of the arguments do you want to make? *Why* should the court decide in your client's favor? Why is your position the preferred outcome among a range of alternatives? A theory of the case requires a particular perspective on the legal and policy issues. By having a theory, you can easily revert to the major premises that underlie that theory and avoid making inconsistent arguments. The theory should be focused and framed in a definitive manner so that it is presented in a few short phrases that are easily understood. Each section of your argument should address the legal issues for that section and conform to the theory. Watch assumptions you make about your argument to be sure you remain consistent with the philosophy of the case. Your theory begins with the general position you want the court to adopt and then proceeds to the legal and policy reasons why it is preferred. You may acknowledge countervailing values in your theoretical statement, or you may reserve that for points in your main argument.

From your theory develop the major points, sub-points, and minor points. The entire structure of your argument follows from your theory, so invest some time in carefully articulating it.

> **Example:** The right to bear arms should not be infringed upon by the state because it is a core principle upon which this country was founded. The right to life, liberty, and the pursuit of happiness as embodied by the Second Amendment of the U.S. Constitution should be incorporated through the Fourteenth Amendment to apply to the states. The right to protect your personal integrity from the encroachment of others must be protected even if others misuse the right and carelessly disregard the responsibility of gun ownership.

RESEARCHING AND DEVELOPING AN OUTLINE OF THE LEGAL POINTS

Your outline is critical for setting out the structure of your argument, and it presents the broad strokes of your legal points based on your theory of the case. As such, it is more of a reference guide that you refer to throughout your argument. It should be no longer than 1–2 pages. ***NEVER use a speech that is written out on multiple pages.*** It makes you look unprepared, nervous, and judges are more likely to question you *more* vigorously as a result to try to get you "off notes". The goal of moot court is to have a robust, respectful debate and conversation with the judges in order to persuade them of your position; it is not the forum to read a paper to them.

To prepare your outline, begin by going through the lower court cases and records that are available. Next you need to begin doing legal research. (See Chapter 2 on understanding of legal research). The best place to begin is by finding the cases that are cited in the problem or case that you have been given for the moot court problem. In some instances, you have access to textbooks that can help you find key words to search on, so be sure to use those to help brainstorm key words and phrases. In other instances, you have what is considered a "closed case," meaning that you are confined to a limited number of materials and cases that you may use. (See the Important Legal Terms appendix). Read the resources that you are to use to help find the relevant issues. You need to be sure that you use the most up-to-date version of all your materials. The general rule is that material that is more than five years out of date should be double checked. Shepardize or KeyCite all cases that you intend to use. Shepard's Citations is a service by LexisNexis that allows you to see all the cases, statutes, regulations, and rules that cite back to or affect a particular case after it was published. Thompson West's KeyCite service performs the same function. Use of one or both of these services is critical because it is fundamentally dangerous to cite a case that has negative comments by other courts, or worse, has been overturned.

After collecting the cases that you might use, begin to read through and brief each of the most relevant ones to give you a better picture of the sources you have for developing your client's case. You cannot possibly use every single case you find if you are operating under an "open case" system. Roughly one to three key cases for each minute of arguing is about all you have time for, so be sure to select your cases carefully. Do not discard cases that have one or two key points because later on these may serve as additional or subsidiary sources of authority. As you did with your original case, divide your arguments according to those favorable to and those against your case. After you have done this, look back at your original case and begin the process of synthesizing and arranging by topic all of the legal points that seem most relevant to your theory of the case.

Outlining and Structuring Your Oral Argument

Your oral argument should be in outline form. Writing the presentation out longhand wastes space, forces you to depend on your notes, and increases the likelihood you "read" rather than argue. The argument should be typed on a computer because you should change it around as you practice and learn what works best. The argument should be structured by presenting your strongest points first and proceeding to weaker ones—keeping in mind the time frame. Generally speaking, you cannot get through more than four to five major points, and most people tend to rely on just two to three major points to clarify the crux of their case.

> **Example:** The First Amendment Establishment Clause prohibits the national government from funding school voucher programs to religious educational organizations because it creates an impermissible endorsement of religion.

Rely on Laws, Policy, and Precedent

You should use authoritative sources for your outline and for the points you are making. Primary sources of law are preferred because they control over any other authority. Primary sources are direct sources of law, such as court opinions, statutes, rules, and regulations. Secondary sources of law are not the law themselves but are instead sources that explain, summarize, or contextualize the primary sources of law. Examples of secondary sources of law are law review articles, legislative histories, and legal encyclopedias.

Supreme Court and appellate court opinions are more influential than trial court cases, do not discount a "killer" case from a trial court. If it supports your argument, use it. Pay attention to what cases come from which circuit and state. Opinions from the same circuit or state as yours are important, but they are not the final word. Find cases that are directly on point (similar fact patterns or arguments). If you have a case where a court ruled in a way that supports your opponent, think about ways to distinguish it from your case. Point to key facts that are different or find statements that show a judge was influenced by certain factors that are irrelevant to your client's case. How you use the case law is critical to whether you have a strong argument. Even if you have a case that seems negative because of the party that ultimately won the case, argue that it is the legal reasoning, standard, or principle established by the court that is important and that it militates in favor of your client.

Keep an eye open for "tests", standards, and key phrases that are used in legal sources because these help keep you focused on the issues. These phrases not only assist you in doing legal research, but they also help you structure your arguments and provide you with "punch lines" that can be used for answering questions. Your legal arguments should revolve around an analysis of these key phrases and whether the tests that the courts have used apply to your client's case. An example of a well-known test is "strict scrutiny", which is the highest level of judicial review to determine whether a governmental action (e.g., a statute) is constitutional. To pass strict scrutiny, a governmental action must promote a compelling governmental interest and must be narrowly tailored to achieve that interest. Thus, when performing legal research and formulating your arguments you can use the phrases "compelling governmental interest" and "narrowly tailored" to find cases relating to that test or emphasize points in your argument.

Do not use countless paragraphs and quotes of material from earlier cases. This is ineffective and increases the likelihood that you will read from your notes. While two or three key quotes may be effective and the quoting of precise terms or tests is preferable, using numerous quotes makes it looks like you are not able to analyze the issues yourself. It is your synthesis that the court is interested in hearing.

Secondary sources can also provide you with authority even though these are not from statutes or judges. These can be particularly useful for finding p arguments. Use the logical reasoning from these sources to support your argument and know the credentials of the authority that you are using. What is their background? Why are they experts? Why should the court listen to what they have to say about some issue? Remember—people who write law reviews are often experts in their field and may have prior legal experience.

Legislative histories are particularly helpful when formulating policy arguments because they reveal the intentions behind a statute's enactment, and they can reveal flaws and criticisms about the law that you may use to attack your opponent's argument. Use policy arguments from the debates on the legislative floor to point out the ramifications of a law. Examine whether the purpose of the policy has been met or whether it has been subverted as it has been applied in practice.

Preparing Your Materials for Presentation

After you have your basic outline and legal sources, you are ready to integrate the two into a comprehensive outline. Even though you have pages and pages of material, resist the urge to use everything. For each point you have on your outline you need to go through and establish one of the paradigms that follow for each of your points. Each stands for a formula you should use as you go through each of your points. Law schools, attorneys, and judges differ in terms of which ones they prefer, but the following summarizes your choices.

> **IRAC**—**I**ssue, **R**ules, **A**nalysis, (or Application), **C**onclusion
>
> **CRAC**—**C**onclusion, **R**ules, **A**nalysis, (or Application), **C**onclusion
>
> **CREAC**—**C**onclusion, **R**ules, **E**xplanation, **A**nalysis, (or **A**pplication), **C**onclusion

Issue—Refers to the legal subject under consideration by that point or section of your outline. What is it that has to be decided?

> **Example:** Peter (Texas resident) and Danielle (who runs off to Nevada) break off their engagement, and Peter sues for the return of a ring (total value $10,000). In federal district court he wins because the court finds that the ring was given with the understanding that Danielle would marry Peter—the items were *not* gifts. Danielle appeals to Fifth Circuit which overturns the decision on a technical error (Peter did not file his federal court case in a timely manner). Peter appeals to the U.S. Supreme Court which denies certiorari. Peter then files in the Texas state trial court. (continued)

Rule—Refers to the law or policy that is to be used for analyzing the issue. This can be either an established principle, or it can be a rule of law from a case that has been delivered. What is the law under consideration?

Explanation—Refers to the synthesis of the rule to the case facts where the rule comes from. How do rules from other cases assist in resolving the issues before the court in the case at bar?

Application/Analysis—Refers to the application of the rule to the facts for the case to clarify how the issue should be resolved. How does the law militate in favor of your client's case and position given the case at bar?

Issue: If Peter took the case to the highest federal court, is he prevented from suing in a state court?

Rule: The principle of *res judicata* requires that if a final judgment on the merits was delivered, the plaintiff cannot bring the same case against the same defendant in either the same or a different court. The case filed in federal court met all of the necessary elements outlined in federal and state law.

Analysis: When Peter appealed the case to the highest court, that judgment is the final statement on the issue. At that point he had exhausted all of his remedies because he had gone to the highest court of appeal. He cannot try to re-litigate the case in the state court.

Explanation: The federal elements of res judicata include: 1) identical parties in both suits; 2) prior judgments from court with proper jurisdiction; 3) a final judgment on the merits; and 4) the same cause of action involved in both cases. *United States v. Calton*, 900 F.3d 706, 713 (5th Cir. 2018).

Conclusion: Peter cannot bring his suit in state court after having lost in the federal court because the issue is barred by *res judicata*.

Conclusion—State what the outcome of the issue should be given the rules and how they are explained or applied in the analysis. Be sure to note if this is an extension of pre-existing law or if the position is creating any new precedent you are representing. What is the appropriate interpretation of the law?

You will need to go through your outline, and for each point you make do the same type of analysis. In this manner you are weaving law and facts together to build an argument that reaches a particular conclusion.

When you get to law school or begin practicing law, you will find that the most appropriate format can vary depending on whether you are writing a legal essay, memorandum, or brief, as well as whether you are presenting an oral argument to a trial or appellate court. Some court opinions even follow one of the styles depending on the preferences of the judge responsible for authoring the opinion. The common wisdom is that IRAC is best for written materials, but that oral arguments follow the CRAC or CREAC formula. The virtue of the latter two styles in oral argument is that you are stating up front what your conclusion is about the issue being addressed by your point. Advocating your case in a conclusive matter is more likely to persuade the judges that they should rule in your favor. You also tell the judge(s) where you are going with your argument and signpost what you expect them to support by the time you are finished evaluating and explaining the rule of law as it applies to your case. Use your own judgment to develop your own style and do what works best for you. In time, other authorities will dictate the structure, so enjoy the chance now to do what you like!

Develop a Style and Practice, Practice, Practice

As you begin to develop your style, use your native talents and natural qualities. Do not try to mimic someone else or be something that you are not—that usually translates into a phony performance. Most students find it helpful to think of their moot court personality as an extension of how they communicate in general. For some, this means keeping the tone, quality, and volume of their voice at the same level at which they usually speak. For others, this means they must be more conscientious about making eye contact and being assertive with the bench. The same also holds true for your physical mannerisms. More effective speakers have a straight posture that is firmly rooted showing command of the podium and the material presented at all times. This may not work for some who need to be more fluid and interactive. For them what works best is to lean forward to emphasize points and then resume a stance. One thing virtually everyone needs to watch is how they deal with their hands. Appellate style is much more formal than trial advocacy, so avoid flailing your hands about in the air. A few key hand gestures, mindfully and strategically deployed, can be effective to emphasize certain issues, but don't pound the podium or give it a death grip so your knuckles turn white! As you develop your style, get feedback from others who observe you. This helps you know what works and how others are perceiving you.

Always remember to whom you are speaking as your audience. In moot court, you will be in front of judges, attorneys, and law students (or even undergraduates), who will have different levels of knowledge about the case. Be careful not to insult the panel by assuming they do not understand the argument, but also be careful not to assume that they know everything about every authority you use. Try to find a middle ground where you are discussing your case in the context of other cases and authorities that are relevant for resolving the issue.

Extensive preparation and practice are the best thing you can do to develop your style and reduce nervousness while speaking. Try to work in as many practice rounds as you possibly can and get feedback from the people who are watching your presentation. Watch yourself in front of a mirror to help develop your style of argumentation and go over key phrases to hear what the most effective way is to highlight critical points.

Try to rely on the active voice rather than the passive voice when you are speaking. The active voice is direct and concise, avoids the use of flowery language, and clearly expresses the point. The passive voice tends to be more rhetorical and uses unnecessary words to express the point being made.

Example:

Active voice—The Supreme Court upheld a state legislature's practice of having a paid chaplain open sessions with a prayer.

Passive voice—The decision by the Supreme Court found that a state legislature could lawfully use funds in order to pay ministers for beginning legislative sessions with a prayer.

Listen to your voice as you are practicing and pay attention to your vocal mannerisms, including the speed and pace of your delivery. The most common mistakes that interfere with a person's style are unconscious statements and movements. Successful speakers use their diaphragm to control their voice and to give added authority to their speech pattern. Learn to pause effectively to emphasize key points and to raise the volume of your voice when there are particular arguments that merit distinction. If you are someone who says "ah, uhm, or er" regularly, practice just remaining silent when you come to pauses. Let your voice find a rhythm that is even without becoming "sing-song" or "rat-a-tat-tat." Also be conscious of how quickly you are speaking. When you rise to give your presentation you will probably be nervous and speed up your delivery. This is why you want to practice—you will already know how to keep the pace of your presentation at an even tempo.

Similarly, unconscious body movements are distracting no matter how persuasive you are with your voice. You should be careful not to wave your hands around, play with your hair, or toss your head back and forth. Plant your feet squarely in front of the podium so that you are rooted (like a tree) to withstand the onslaught of the questions. Watch your posture and avoid slouching over the podium.

The most useful tool you have is video recording your practice. You will see whether you are fidgeting, shifting your feet, or moving at the podium. You will also have audio to gauge your pace, tone, volume, and catch all the "ums" and "ahs" that inevitably occur. When you watch the videotape, also watch it in fast forward mode. That will highlight your overall style and what moves the most when you are arguing.

FROM START TO FINISH

Now that you know how to put your argument together, the following section is designed to help you present the argument in the most effective way possible.

Pleasing the Court and Easing Yourself

As difficult as it may seem, try not to be nervous when you are actually arguing and pay attention to your voice and your body while you are arguing. It helps to focus if you close your eyes and take several deep breaths (through your nose if possible) before getting ready to get up to speak. When you begin your presentation, relax your shoulders down to the floor and lift up the top of your head confidently to the ceiling so that your stance is forward looking and direct. Remind yourself that you have the inside scoop on how this is done. (See Appendix 8: "Things Someone Should Have Told You (but Probably Didn't)").

While the length of time may seem like forever at first when you are speaking, the time passes too quickly. Because you are going to be interrupted to answer questions, you need to allocate your time accordingly. There should be a timekeeper with cards so you can pace yourself, but if not, take a watch with a sweeping second hand so you can keep track of your time or have someone else keep track of time for you. While you have your written notes, do not be alarmed if you are unable to address all of your points. You *MUST at least try* to address each of the major points that you want to make. The judges want to throw you off course, so answer the question and get back to your argument. If a judge asks you a question that deals with a part of your argument that you were going to argue later, just argue that point when it is raised and move back to your argument. Do not be afraid of the judges (they rarely bite)! They want to illuminate issues and see how well you know your argument.

Your job is to crystallize issues before the court. You are helping your colleagues clarify issues and arguing on behalf of your client. Think of it as giving persuasive points about the most relevant issues that should be decided. Rather than see this as a hostile situation, think of it as a chance to engage in a dialogue with the judges about the critical issues. You are, in a sense, having a conversation with them about important points of law. Use phrases that will lead the judges down a particular road that you want to travel. You should not view the oral argument as an intimidating experience or else you may get defensive. No one has ever exploded while answering questions! Use the questions that the judges ask you to answer key points that relate to your argument. Part of the reason you should not read a set speech is that the questions will address the different legal points you have made, and many times will anticipate your future points of argument, undercutting your outline and plan for the argument. After you have responded to a question, move back to the organization of the argument and continue presenting your other points. Try to think of questions that you think the judges may ask you or arguments that your opposing counsel may make. What are the weak points about the argument that you are making? What points of the opponents do you need to address? What are the key points from the lower court opinion(s) that you feel need to be given consideration?

Winning at moot court is not just a function of performance— students who do the best are the ones who are well prepared and organized before they ever walk into a "courtroom." You should brief every case that you are relying on and take notes of ones that may be used by other student-attorneys. Make notes for yourself of the cases. It is helpful to use note cards that contain key cases and facts. For each case, do a "mini"-brief about the case, including the name, date, citation, holding, relevant tests or standards, and a brief fact summary. You may also want to write why the case is persuasive for your argument. Similarly, for cases that go against your argument, point out key facts that show why they should not apply to the case at bar. These note cards will help refresh your memory when you are actually presenting your argument. One helpful device is to use a manila folder and tape the outline on the left-hand side and the case "mini"-briefs on the right. Organize the cases according to the order in which you argue them so that you can flip a case up when you are finished using it. *YOU SHOULD NOT PLAN ON SIMPLY READING A SPEECH!* This is the most common mistake students make, and it is the one thing that is the easiest to change. If you read, it looks like you are unprepared.

Nuts and Bolts

The structure for your presentation is usually as follows, but ask your instructor or coach what the rules are for the simulation or competition. Time is divided between the two co-counsels, and the length of time can vary from 10–30 minutes. As for the rebuttal, only one speaker for the Petitioner/Appellant presents for a short period of time after the main arguments have been presented. It is up to the student-attorneys for the Petitioner/Appellant to determine who presents rebuttal. As a general rule, the stronger speaker does the rebuttal, but you should choose the person who thinks the best on his or her feet and who reacts well to arguments made by the opposing team. Some teams prefer to trade off. The Petitioner/Appellant gets a rebuttal because they have a tougher case to make (they lost at the lower level). Be sure that the counsel who is *NOT* giving rebuttal writes notes to co-counsel about which points should be addressed. You want to have coverage during the rebuttal—points should not be dropped or go unanswered. The following should help you with a mental picture of how a typical moot court proceeds.

Example for a 40 minute round:

1st Counsel for the Petitioner/Appellant—9 minutes

2nd Counsel for the Petitioner/Appellant—9 minutes + 2 minutes rebuttal

---

> 1st Counsel for the Respondent/Appellee—10 minutes
>
> 2nd Counsel for the Respondent/Appellee—10 minutes
>
> 1st or 2nd Counsel for the Petitioner/Appellant—2 minutes

With these time limits in mind, you should plan on spending about 30 seconds to 1 minute opening your argument and then transition to your main argument. The main argument should constitute about 90–95 percent of the time that you have allotted. Always keep in mind the central theory of your case to help guide you through the thicket of questions. The thrust of your main argument should be to take the known rules, laws, and policies and apply each to the facts of the case at bar. The most common mistake students make is that they emphasize one aspect disproportionately—either they focus on the case law and never apply it to the case under consideration, or they focus on the facts of the case and ignore the case law that supports their position. To be an effective advocate you need to entwine both law and facts for your client.

When judges begin to ask questions, stop speaking immediately, even if you are mid-sentence, and look directly at the judges to let them know that you are listening and responding to their concerns. This also helps you to analyze what type of question is being asked. (Is it a hardball or softball?) Engage with your eye contact and give facial reactions that indicate whether you are understanding the question. Pause briefly before giving the answer to the question to signal that you are reflecting on what was asked. Always be as direct as possible, and *frontload* by answering the question with a "Yes" or "No" answer before going on to explain why and the reasoning behind your answer. Answer each question directly and then segue way back into your argument with a transition. You may want to have some sample transition phrases ready to help you move more smoothly between questions and your prepared argument. Do not say "now returning to my argument" because that is a red flag for the judges to stop you right there for a question! If you do not know the answer, be honest and deal with it directly. You can tell the judges "I'm sorry your Honor, I don't have that answer. We would be happy to submit a supplementary brief on that issue." Always respect the judges, and do *not* be argumentative when you disagree with a judge's positions no matter what demeanor they are expressing toward you.

The goal of some judges is to keep you from being able to finish your argument and to identify weaknesses in the case that might militate in favor of your opposing counsel. Here the problem is trying to move through all of your points, and you may need to adjust accordingly by dropping some of the less important points. If you get a "hot bench," make sure that you focus on coverage and transition back to your argument as quickly as you can after questions. Still other judges are quiet or unprepared, and you may have just the opposite problem because the judges hardly ask you any questions. With a "cold bench" the problem is having enough material to fill in the time. Always adjust according to your bench and learn which sections you can drop if it heats up, and which points you can add if things cool down.

Within the last minute of your presentation finish the last argument you are making and go to your conclusion which is composed of a summary and prayer for relief. You want to be sure you leave enough time for a conclusion (summary) and prayer for relief. Your summary should hit those key points that you outlined in the roadmap, only this time, emphasize the key elements of those major points. Your prayer for relief is what you want the court to do. Be direct about how you want the court to rule and remind them of why they should reverse or affirm the lower court decision. State specifically how they should rule (either for or against what a prior court decision indicated) and reiterate why this is important for not only your client, but for principles of law that need to be protected.

You must adjust accordingly depending on the amount of time you have remaining. When there are about three to four minutes remaining, scan your outline and see which points you absolutely must hit and which points can be eliminated. In most cases, you will have had barely enough time to get through all of your argument when you receive the one-minute warning—watch time closely. You always want to use ALL of your time right up until the last second. Student-attorneys who do not prepare enough material may struggle to keep speaking. Some professors, judges, or law students take off points for not fully using your time, so keep going forward until time is up. It is better to err on the side of not having enough time than to err on the side of not having enough material.

In the event you run out of time, your sum and prayer should be very short, otherwise you may have judges take off points. In the event your time expires just as a judge is in the process of asking a question, ask the judge if you may finish answering the question and then *briefly* sum and pray. In most cases, judges will allow you to do this. There will be some judges who are terser with you and either ask you to be seated or else allow you to finish the question but will not give you permission to do a summary and prayer. Do not let it throw you off. Just answer the question and graciously thank the court for its time.

> **Example:** In conclusion, your honors, the execution of a person who is mentally challenged does not violate the prohibition on cruel and unusual punishment for three reasons. First, the death penalty is consistent with the Framer's view of the Eighth Amendment, and indeed was widely practiced at the time of the Founding. Second, views by religious institutions, public opinion surveys, or the practices of other states do not establish that there is a national consensus in the U.S. States should each determine whether such a policy is prudent for that state. Finally, regardless of the mental condition of the convicted murderer, that a jury of his peers has found that person to be a continuing danger to society. Moreover, the jury has determined that the only appropriate punishment is complete incapacitation of the defendant. We ask this court today not to take away one of the most powerful and effective tools in deterring and combating crime—the death penalty. Please affirm the Fourth Circuit Court of Appeal's decision

upholding the imposition of capital punishment. Thank you for your time.

Table 3.1—Common Criticisms of Oral Arguments

Mistake made	Problem	Argument Type	Solution
Attacking the individual, not the argument.	Makes it appear as though you can't attack the argument on its face.	**Ad hominem attacks**	Address arguments & not the person making it.
Appealing to bias, prejudice or fears of the population to support your position.	Makes it appear that you do not have facts & evidence to support your position & can backfire if your audience does not have the same bias.	**Ad populum attacks**	Address arguments with facts & evidence, not the audience's potential biases.
Assuming because one thing occurred before another, the former caused the latter.	Makes a mistake of construction—also called post hoc, ergo propter hoc ("after this, therefore because of this").	**Causal fallacy**	Establish the connection between events occurring by providing facts & evidence.
Re-asserting the claim's truth by repeating the claim in different words.	Wastes time & makes it look like you do not have evidence to support your conclusion.	**Circular reasoning (begging the question)**	Prove your major premise by discussing the fundamental question before arguing the conclusion.
Equates two meanings of the same word falsely	Forces you to lose credibility because of a faulty definition which is easily corrected.	**Equivocation**	Be sure to use words with their proper meaning & have definitions with authorities to support your position.
Assuming is similar to another, the conclusions drawn from one apply to the other.	Once the connection is attacked, undermines other analogies that may be valid.	**False analogy**	Choose analogies carefully to ensure that the similarities between the two are not superficial.
Presenting only two possibilities to a situation & forcing a choice of one.	Makes you appear unreasonable, dogmatic, & lackadaisical in your approach to analyzing a problem.	**False dichotomy**	Present sophisticated analyses that show why your position should be preferred among alternatives.

Providing only weak or limited evidence to support a conclusion.	Looks like you are relying on prejudice, superstition, "common knowledge" rather than known facts.	**Hasty generalization**	Avoid over-generalizations by providing facts & evidence to support your conclusion. Re-state your premise so as not to be so broad.
Presenting premises or reasons that are irrelevant to a conclusion.	Makes it appear as though you do not fully understand the logic of your argument.	**Non-sequitur**	Offer only evidence in support of your claim that is relevant to the issue you are discussing.
Assuming that something is true because an expert says so & ignoring evidence to the contrary.	Undermines your argument if other authorities with greater credibility are introduced.	**Overreliance on Authority**	Appeal to multiple sources for authority & have concrete evidence to refute attacks on your authority.
Appealing to emotions by giving easy answers to complicated questions.	Can be easily attacked with facts & evidence that will undermine your conclusions.	**Oversimplification**	Appeal to logical construction of premises rather than emotional statements.
Attempting to avoid the central issue by changing the subject or digressing into a tangential point.	Deflects the audience's attention from key points that need to be made.	**Red herring**	Emphasize your main points & only those arguments relevant to those points.
Selecting or emphasizing only the evidence and arguments that supports your claim while suppressing or minimizing other evidence.	Makes it look like you have not considered or evaluated all the facts & evidence.	**Slanting**	Recognize counter-arguments, propositions, facts, & evidence, but argue why your arguments & evidentiary proofs are preferable.
Asserting that if a course of action is taken, undesirable consequences will inevitably follow.	May not necessarily be wrong to make if you are trying to assert future harms. Be careful that you support the premise that the undesirable consequence will follow.	**Slippery slope**	Provide concrete evidence that the second event will follow based on other similar experiences or events.
Setting up a very weak version of an argument the	The opponent may never make (or may not actually be making) that argument	**Straw Man**	Be sure that the argument you are making is relevant to your own.

opponent might make, & then attack it.	so you waste time articulating it.		
Latin for "you too," it points to the opponent's hypocrisy in the argument.	Distracts from the argument because it is a diversionary tactic and serves only to deflect criticism of your own argument.	**Tu quoque**	Becomes fallacy only when it attempts to neutralize criticisms. Point out the contradictions in the argument and stay on the main points.

CONCLUSION

Beware! While the thought of oral argument scares most people when they first consider the challenge, after they have done so, they often find themselves addicted! There is a certain adrenaline rush that comes with being able to hold your ground under tough questioning and to present your client's position as an advocate. The ability to persuade others to your viewpoints is an influential skill that lasts with you no matter what profession you decide to pursue. With practice, most of you will find that improving your speaking expertise begins to permeate your verbal communication in general. It is not just when you are before judges, but even in your interpersonal discussions or in workplace meetings you will begin to notice that you are more effective and direct in addressing issues that arise.

This chapter has presented some of the basics of oral argument, but the real test is out there waiting for you. It is important to note that as you go forth to conquer that the circumstances of your presentation vary, and you need to be able to modify depending on your situation. To that end, we have compiled a list of tips that have come from over twenty years of comments that our students have received regarding what judges recommend or what they look for in an outstanding presentation. Note that not all judges agree on these. As we have noted elsewhere in the book, depending whether you are doing moot court for a class or for a competition, remember that styles and preferences vary. Undoubtedly anyone who engages in "mooting" finds that judges differ in terms of what they like to see. Modify your techniques and approaches accordingly depending on the type of feedback you receive from others. Do not be discouraged if you receive contradictory advice from different sets of people. That is part of the process of learning to create your own style and doing what works best for you. In the final analysis, doing moot court should be exhilarating, and yes, even fun!

CHAPTER 5

From Openings to Closings: A Step by Step Guide

INTRODUCTION

When you first listen to oral arguments, the idea of presenting your own research and withstanding questions from a panel of judges may seem daunting. What's more, thinking of the work that you need to put in to build an argument from the ground up could overwhelm you. But, as the old adage goes, to eat an elephant, you have to take one bite at a time. In this chapter, we break the elephant of oral arguments into a few bite-sized pieces. With each step, we give you tips and insight from our experiences. It is important to remember that you need to be familiar with what strategies work best for you. For example, we might suggest underlining key points, while you know that it works better for your learning style if you highlight and type out those points. It is appropriate and encouraged to adjust our strategies to your needs. Most importantly, as you complete each step, you will find yourself a little bit closer to winning your first oral argument and hopefully realize that it is not as intimidating as it seems.

1. HOW TO PREPARE FOR ORAL ARGUMENT

The best place to start is the problem. Read the problem and the cases cited in the problem. Familiarize yourself with the facts of the case and the major legal arguments at issue. Once you have an understanding of the key points, you are ready to start writing your argument.

As we note below, you should write an outline. Resist the temptation to write a script of everything that you want to say. A script has two disadvantages. First, if you become dependent on a script, it is more difficult to make yourself not look at your script to find out what you need to say next. Any moment you are looking down at your paper, you are not looking at the judges and you are not fully engaging them in the discussion at hand. Second, relying on a script makes it more difficult to answer the judges' questions and move back into your argument in chief. Judges will interrupt you mid-sentence and you will have to stop and answer their question immediately. If you have prepared using a script, you will be searching for the place you left off and it will be difficult to pick that sentence back up and continue your conversation.

Next, make sure you practice your argument with and without someone asking you questions. It can be off-putting for a speaker to have someone interrupt them. The speaker may lose their train of thought and have difficulty finding their place again. Practicing your argument with questions will help you develop the impromptu speaking skills that are necessary to listen to the questions, respond to them, and move on. Furthermore, sometimes, you will have a "hot bench" and judges will have a lot of questions for you. You need to understand which points are the best to stress when you have a shorter amount of time to get your argument out. Other times, you will have a "cold bench" and judges will not have many questions. In these instances, you will want to be able to communicate your message effectively and fill the entire time. Finally, practicing your argument with questions will help you think of your argument as part of a discussion with the judges. You are not debating against them. Instead, you are explaining your position and giving the judges an opportunity to help you explore your ideas in greater depth. As more people listen to you and ask you questions, you will learn that there are common questions that your argument brings up. You will be able to refine your answers to those questions.

2. HOW TO READ THE PROBLEM

First, start thinking of "the problem" as "the record." In your argument, when you discuss the facts of the case as spelled out in the problem, you will want to direct justices to "the record."

Before you start highlighting and taking notes, you should read the record once from start to finish. It is hard to know for certain what is important until you have an understanding of the big picture. Facts or arguments that seem irrelevant at the outset may become more important once they are put in context. Conversely, facts that initially seem dispositive, may have little impact in the final outcome.

After you have read the record once and have the general gist of the situation, you should reread the record from the position of the side you will be advocating on and keep track of key facts that help or hurt your position. Think of these facts as "good facts" and "bad facts." You will want to structure your argument to accentuate good facts and minimize bad facts. One helpful tip is to divide a sheet of paper in half—on the left side write all of the "good facts" for your side and on the right side write all of the "bad facts" for your side. Given you will need to argue both sides, you should read the record again from the position of the other side and keep track of the good facts and bad facts for this position. When you use these facts as part of your argument, make sure you keep track of the page number from the record that the fact can be found on. You want to be able to direct the judge to the particular place in the record that fact is discussed, especially if there is a dispute or discrepancy about that fact.

After you have a handle on the facts of the case, start using the legal research skills you learned in the previous chapter to build your argument. Just like you did with the facts, you should identify all of the strong arguments in favor of your side and put those on one side of the paper and identify all of the counter arguments that your opponents may use to challenge your position and put those on the other side of the paper. After you have summarized the key legal points, look over what you have written and give a rank ordering to what arguments you consider to be the strongest. Start your outline with the strongest argument. Any weak argument you need to use should be somewhere in the middle and then conclude with another strong point. Keep in mind that people will remember what they hear first and what they hear last most so you want to start and end with your strongest ideas. Below, we go into more detail about how to use the facts and the law to support your argument.

3. HOW TO WRITE AN OUTLINE

Rather than writing a script that you will read for your argument, you should construct an outline using key phrases to help remind yourself of each point. In the previous chapter you learned the importance of working from an outline written using key phrases to help remind yourself of each point. The outline should follow a structure similar to the IRAC structure introduced in the previous chapter.

You should focus on having each point being constructed with a thesis statement, a statement of the appropriate legal rule, an explanation of that legal rule, and an application of that legal rule to the facts in the record. You should expect to present two or three main arguments. In your outline, each of these main points should be supported using two or more sub arguments. Each of these sub-arguments should be constructed by stating your thesis, supporting that thesis with the law and applying the law to these facts.

Set out the strongest arguments for your side and issue first. If you are working with a partner, go over key points to ensure that you are not duplicating or contradicting one another. Stay focused only on the issue that you are presenting without addressing tangential points. This is one area where your theory of the case helps, as it will allow you to focus on the strongest arguments to illustrate that theory.

The outline should be a series of syllogisms presented in single sentences that persuade the court to rule for your client. Present each point as a one-sentence affirmative and argumentative statement that directly presents the legal issue you are arguing for your client. When the judges hear that statement, they should be able to quickly identify the issue, the law you rely on, and your position about which way they should rule. Stay focused on the legal issues and facts—avoid using rhetoric, clichés and colloquialisms. Your outline is a skeleton that you fill in with the substantive law and facts to support the central issue. Do not make peripheral arguments that do not directly address the theory of your case. In building your outline, break the major points down into sub-points that present each of the lesser points relevant to the main premise. The actual structure of your outline varies depending on the topical issue. While all major points do have sub-points, not all sub-points and minor points have lesser points (or divisions). Do not *hyper-structure* your argument. This occurs when you go into too much detail. The central points and conclusions are difficult to follow because they are lost in the structure. Avoid making your outline more cluttered with sub-points and minor points than it needs to be. What you want is a clear concise structure that you can present easily and that has sufficient detail to address your legal argument.

A helpful sketch of an outline might be:

I) Main point 1

    A) Sub-Argument 1:

        1. Case law (Rule)

        2. Facts from record (Application)

    B) Sub-Argument 2:

        1. Case law (Rule)

        2. Facts from record (Application)

II) Main point 2

    A) Sub-Argument 1:

        1. Case law (Rule)

        2. Facts from record (Application)

    B) Sub-Argument 2:

        1. Case law (Rule)

        2. Facts from record (Application)

4. FOCUS ON THE FACTS, THE LAW, AND POLICY

There is an old adage that lawyers should argue the facts. If that fails, they should argue the law. If arguing the facts and the law do not help, then they should argue policy. Consequently, when working on arguments it may help to put them into three groups or baskets:

(1) Factual Arguments: These come from the record.

(2) Legal Arguments: These come from the case law.

(3) Policy Arguments: These are big picture.

Facts

The facts are everything in your record that led up to the decision of the court(s) below. They do not include the legal analysis of the lower court(s). You should decide what are the key or dispositive facts for your side. There are different ways to perform this task. We recommend deciding what legal test you will argue or what case authority you will argue is controlling and then looking for facts that help advance those positions. Do not be afraid to tell the bench what facts are the most important. You may choose to do so are the outset or throughout your argument. You should also consider what facts hurt you. Rather than ignoring these facts or pretending that they do not exist, you should plan to explain why your side still prevails and/or explain why opposing counsel's reliance on these facts misses the mark.

Legal Arguments

These derive from the case law. It may be helpful to be prepared to discuss the rule and any key facts associated with the individual cases that are similar or different from the immediate case. Few moot court opinions lack case law that is beneficial to both sides. Use the facts of the record vis-à-vis the facts of the cited case law to get the judges to interpret the case law in a fashion that is advantageous to your side. Thus, ff a rule is contrary to your theory, show why the case does not apply by distinguishing facts or relying on later opinions. If a rule supports your theory, show how the case is analogous to the facts and law at issue in the current case.

Policy Questions

Policy refers to questions/arguments about what your argument will mean for future sets of fact—these often involve hypothetical questions. Students tend to be intimidated by these questions. Do not be. The fact is that policy questions are your friend and typically they are asked because the bench follows your argument and is considering how it will affect the nation. An advocate who is caught off-guard by a policy question is an advocate who has not thought through his/her arguments and/or does not really understand them. You know your arguments. This about what logical questions about your arguments are likely to follow and be prepared to answer them. To do so, consider the big picture implications of your argument—how will your position affect society?

5. OPEN THE ARGUMENT AND GIVE A ROADMAP

At the outset of your presentation you are expected to beginning your oral argument with an opening typically consisting of three components: greeting and announcement to the court; introduction of co-counsel; and summary of issues that are being presented in the case at bar. The purpose of the purpose of this opening is to introduce yourself and your teammate and to frame the relevant issues for the judges.

There are certainly other ways to approach the opening but in general, openings should: (a) identify who on your team will address what issue, (b) makes clear what you are asking the court to do—what remedy do you seek? (c) makes clear why this case is important—reminds the bench why it took the case in the first place. (d) identifies without being specific your reasons or your arguments. It should be noted that the first speaker for Petitioner is typically expected to provide or to offer to provide a brief recitation of the key facts of the case. All four speakers may wish to include any key facts in their roadmap if calling attention to such a key fact will help advance your case and/or help frame the issue for the bench.

Typically, after the judges have arrived in the room, the first speaker should take his or her outline and immediately go to the podium to await a signal for when he can begin. At the Supreme Court, the oral argument always begins with the statement by the Chief Justice: "Now we will hear case number _____ titled _____. Counsel, you may begin when ready." At lower court levels, this does not apply, and the judges may only ask if you are ready or inform you that you may begin.

After the judges have acknowledged you, the first student attorney for the Petitioner/Appellant should respond by saying. "Chief Judge (or Justice), your honors, May it please the court. My name is _____, and I along with co-counsel _____ are arguing this case on behalf of _____ in this case of _____. The issue I address today is whether _____. My co-counsel is addressing the issue of _____." You may vary this, of course, by introducing co-counsel and his issue at the same time, but for the most part, be sure you get the basics down.

Next, before proceeding with your main argument, you should give a brief overview (a roadmap) of your key points. This lets the court know where you are going with your argument, what to expect, and how your argument unfolds. Typically, it is the major point headings from your outline, so remember not to have too many issues because that is a signal to the court that there is no way you can get through everything. You will usually select the two to four key points you are using to provide a quick summary. It also assists in helping you make transitions from one section to another. Students frequently make the mistake of spending too much time on the overview and not moving quickly enough to the substance of the argument. Openings should be short (30 seconds give or take), they should not be overly dramatic, and they should provide the bench with a clear idea of the path down which you plan to take the bench—hence the name.

If you are the first speaker for the Petitioner/Appellant, you have a unique role because you are the first person to speak. As such, you need to ask the court whether it would like a brief summary of the facts after you have given your roadmap. This helps the judges familiarize themselves with the case at bar. Some judges prefer you ask the court whether they would like a brief recitation of the facts; still others prefer that you give the fact summary without asking. Keep the overview of the facts short and cast it in a light that is most favorable for your client. Most student-attorneys find that they do not have time for more than four to five salient points—you should spend no more than 30–45 seconds on this section. You should not mislead the judges about the facts, but identify those key facts that are most important for your case.

Occasionally, when the first speaker for the Respondent/Appellee gets up to speak, she may want to clarify some facts before proceeding with the main points of the argument. This is especially true if opposing counsel has misrepresented key facts. Do so quickly, and then return to the argument. You do not need to ask the court for permission to do so.

6. EFFECTIVE QUESTION ANSWERING

Question answering is one of the most difficult tasks to perform in oral argument. You need to learn to USE questions to make your points as well as to damage the opposing side's case. You need to resist the tendency to (a) appear annoyed by being interrupted by a question, (b) never appear as if a question is beneath you (although they frequently are about basic matters you have long since dismissed as irrelevant), and (c) swat away questions as if they are insects swarming over your head. Here are some strategies to assist you with answering questions effectively.

- When a question starts—STOP talking. Smile or nod, and act like you want the question and appreciate it. Listen carefully. Take your time and answer it completely.

- Never refuse to answer a question. This includes hypothetical questions and even if a question concerns your teammate's issue. If that occurs and you are the first speaker for your side, you might say "I will answer that question and later my co-counsel will speak to that issue in greater detail." If the question concerns your next argument do NOT say you will "get there later." Go there now.

- Never ask if you have satisfactorily answered a question.

- Do not assume that every question is hostile—some are neutral or in your favor.

- Answer questions directly. If a question can be answered "yes" or "no" at the outset do so and then, if needed, explain your answer. You might pause before explaining your answer to see if it appears necessary to elaborate.

- Use questions to advance arguments. Show how a question ties in with your argument.

- End, if possible, with a provocative point you want to discuss. This may invite questions and allow you to control what is discussed.

- In answering questions, a good approach is to respond first with a yes or no, then follow up with something like: "Your Honor, that question can be answered in two ways. First, _____ (this might be directed right at the question and what they want to hear). Second _____ (this should be related directly to one of your core arguments about the case or the cases).

- Incorporate the facts, case law, and issues related to policy into your answers.

- If asked question that may call you to unduly speculate or really lacks an answer, you may wish to answer along these lines:

  > "Your Honor, I do not know if the amount of money one pays an occasional babysitter is interstate commerce, what we do know is that the sale of the firearms *in this case* did constitute interstate commerce and as such can be regulated by the Congress."

7. KNOW WHAT TO CONCEDE AND WHAT TO FIGHT ABOUT

Advocates should be aware of the weaknesses of their arguments. This means knowing what points your opposing counsel will likely raise and how to defend against these attacks. It also means knowing what points you are better off conceding than fighting about. Not every advocate and not every judge is ready or willing to acknowledge that certain points might or should be conceded. These doubters may assert that concessions are inconsistent with a zealous defense. There is much to be said for this position—after all your role is that of serving as an advocate for your side. At the same time, however, it is important not to confuse willing a battle with winning the war. If you concede small points you are more likely to control the direction of the round and have it fought (and decided) on your terms and not your opponent's terms. What is more, some judges will be impressed by your candor and by your understanding of both your issue and appellate advocacy in general. Consider, for example, the following two real life antidotes which make our position. First, I had the distinct pleasure years ago of watching the Chief Justice of the United States, John Roberts, preside over a law school moot court final. In his capacity as chief justice of the round, he asked one of the advocates if the court ruled for opposing counsel on a specific point "would your side lose?" The advocate thought for a moment and said "yes" and then explained why her side should win that point. During feedback, Chief Justice Roberts praised the student for her answer which he said made clear that she understood the issues before the bench and because she did not waste time trying to convince the bench about a difficult position which was unnecessary. The lesson is: know what to concede and what to fight about. Second, I have a friend who has had experience defending the state in free speech cases. I asked her "how do you win when strict scrutiny is applied?" Without hesitating, she answered "you convince the court not to use strict scrutiny." The lesson is that if you cannot win under a standard do not even try—focus your efforts on points that you can win. To know what to concede and what not to concede give some thoughts to the key facts that are relevant to your arguments as well as to how you would apply possible legal tests. Practice rounds in which you both concede and do not concede points and see how they go. If you find yourself unable to overcome certain facts or lines of argument which are not fatal to your position then consider adjusting your strategy accordingly.

8. DEALING WITH JUDGES AND TIME-KEEPERS

Raising issues with judges and time-keepers may be intimidating. You may feel uncomfortable speaking up about rule violations or correcting judges if they misstate the facts. It is important to be direct but differential when dealing with judges and time-keepers but that does not mean that you cannot assert yourself. For example, if a judge asks a question based on a flawed understanding of the facts in the record, it is wholly appropriate to respond by directing the judge to the corrected fact in the record by giving the page number. If a judge ask a question that is beyond the record, rather than conceding you do not know the answer, explain that the information the judge seeks is beyond the scope of the closed case provided and continue with your argument. Similarly, if a judge is trying to enforce a policy that contradicts the rules governing them competition, explain the correct rule and direct them to the tournament director. In many competitions, participants are assigned whether they are petitioner or respondent prior to going to the room. When you arrive, the judges may try to reassign sides. You can deferentially explain that the tournament director has already informed you of which side you were to argue and ask the judge to check with the tournament director. It's okay to say "I think we have already been assigned sides. If we need to change, we need to check with the tournament director who told us we would be arguing these sides." Finally, it is important to make sure you inform the time-keeper how many minutes each advocate will argue for. Feel free to clarify with them how they will be signaling your remaining time and if it appears they are not giving the correct time, ask them between arguments to clarify the amount of time each speaker is allotted and how they are signaling remaining time.

9. REBUTTAL

There are competing approaches to rebuttal. This chapter draws from several of these approaches. At the outset, it is worth nothing that rebuttal, if done properly, can win a round. But a rebuttal gone wrong can be an ugly thing that costs an advocate points if not the round itself.

Approaching Rebuttal

Be aware of the tendency to use rebuttal to only criticize the opposing position rather than providing a reason to vote for your opposition. Rebuttal is best approached as a simple reminder of why your side is correct and why it should prevail. A good rebuttal highlights the weaknesses of the opposing side, while making your strengths clear. Do not merely restate your side's argument. The most difficult rebuttals can be when the other side's arguments were hard to follow. Pay attention to what was argued by opposing counsel and be clear about what point you are rebutting. In those instances you may wish to address points the bench made to the other side.

The Right Tone

Rebuttal should be viewed as just another part of the larger conversation you are having with the bench. Take care not to appear angry or to insult the other side or the bench. At the same time, you will need to signpost to the bench errors made by opposing counsel or flaws in their argument.

Length of Rebuttal

Rebuttals are either two or three minutes in duration. There are pros and cons of both approaches. If facing a team that you know tends to be very aggressive and/or known for embellishing facts/case law to suit its purposes, a three-minute rebuttal can be useful. It can also be advisable if a bench is not asking a lot of questions and you wish to speak for less time in your opening presentation. Three-minute rebuttals may be advisable if you tend to speed up as the clock ticks down. If you do not feel confident with your rebuttal skills a three-minute rebuttal may serve to accentuate this weakness and thus is to be avoided. A two-minute rebuttal should allow you to hit two points, without running out of points to make.

How Does a Rebuttal Proceed?

You do not need to reintroduce yourself. Begin with "May it please the Court" and then either provide a roadmap for your two rebuttal points or just launch into your first point without identifying both points. The idea behind the roadmap is so judges can take you to the second point if it is more salient to the bench and, in the event that time runs out during your first point, to ensure that the judges know that you know both issues. The idea behind no roadmap is to save time and to ensure that you control the direction of rebuttal.

In What Order Should Points Be Made?

There are different perspectives on this. A federal judge once told me "too many litigators hit the most last point made by respondent first regardless of importance." His suggestion was to rank your points and make them in order by importance. Another approach, embraced by one of the very best moot court coaches ever, is to discuss your own issue the most so if there are any questions it is on the subject you know the best.

10. CLOSING STATEMENTS

As with many aspects of moot court, there are different approaches to conclusions. You likely need to find what suits your style by trying different approaches. You should plan to have at least two—a 30-second conclusion and a 5-second conclusion. In these conclusions remind the bench of your position and the remedy you are requesting. For example, here is a short conclusion: "Your Honor, in conclusion, Respondent asks that the decision of the lower court be AFFIRMED and that petitioner NOT be issued a new trial." Or, for example, "Your Honor, because the police lacked a warrant the search violated Petitioner's 4th Amendment rights. Petitioner, therefore, asks that the

Court REVERSE the decision of the court below and order that the evidence in question be excluded from any new trial."

CHAPTER 6

Moot Court as a Classroom Activity

INTRODUCTION

Moot Court is a valuable experiential learning activity and can be included in a broader course about law, legal reasoning, logic, or communication, or it can be taught as a course on its own. When approaching a moot court class, it's important to remember that you are teaching the students both about the relevant legal principles for the case they will be arguing and teaching them about effective tools of communication. As you take on these dual roles, you might have the students discuss their reading and their understanding of the law to help them get accustomed to putting their thoughts into words. Unlike the competition setting, in the classroom setting, students can take on different roles, being an advocate or a judge. This improves their argumentation by requiring them to think about the issue from multiple perspectives. In this chapter, we review some best practices that can help make moot court successful in the classroom setting or in a structured team practice setting.

PREPARING STUDENTS FOR ORAL ARGUMENT

As we have noted previously, the first step in preparing for oral argument is to read the case that students are arguing. It can be helpful to do so as a group with the emphasis being on ensuring that everyone understands the assignment (e.g., who your side represents), and the facts. As a group, discuss what key issues stand out and why they are important. When this is done, you might discuss what oral argument means; again, making certain students understand their role in the process and the goal of oral argument. When this is complete, have the students familiarize themselves with the most relevant issues and case citations. It is probably impossible for any individual to read all of the cases cited in the sample briefs early in the term. Instead, divide the cases so that everyone is responsible for reading and preparing a summary of selected cases; deadlines for these briefs should be set and they might be shared by the group. Throughout the term, students can go back and read additional cases as they prepare their arguments. The instructor might decide that members who miss these deadlines will be denied access to other students' work until they have completed their assigned briefs. It is important to have clear lines of communication with students so they know what their assignments are and when they are expected to complete them.

At your next class meeting, or two, review what people have written and begin to discuss what issues or cases are most important to the case. After this, you might assign particular legal principals to members for more in-depth study. All principals are likely to be of importance, and no one can know what principles judges will ask about; however, certain principles may be more salient than others. Thus, certain issues may emerge as "main" principles. Do not assign all of the main principals to one person and consider assigning at least two persons to "main" principles. After students have begun researching the key legal principles, students should discuss those principles and begin brainstorming how they will address certain key issues (e.g., aspects in the facts, or a precedent that seems to work against your argument). You should facilitate discussions about what legal doctrine they think applies and strategies for persuading judges that the doctrine supports the students' side. Help them think strategically about their strongest arguments and encourage them to use a persuasive tone that invites engagement from the judges. You might also discuss fallback positions for how to argue the case if the court does not accept the students' favored application of legal tests or doctrines.

Students should begin drafting their outlines to use to guide their arguments. While we know that the ultimate course of the argument is determined by the judges' questions, the student's outline can help them think carefully about the logical construction of their argument. Encourage them to follow the IRAC format discussed in previous chapters and make sure they support their key arguments with legal doctrine. It might be helpful to suggest students start with two main points and to try and support each point with at least one case. You may want students to turn these outlines in so you can review them— this can be done as a written submission or as part of a discussion in office hours. You may decide to encourage them to treat their outline as their own notes and as such, can follow their own personal speaking style.

It is helpful to require students to start participating a mock-moot court, taking turns answering questions or raising points that the judges or the other side will raise, early in the term. The longer students go thinking about their arguments without actually responding to questions, the more likely they are to become intimidated by the possibility of facing questions. If they begin answering questions from the outset, the question/answer pattern of moot court will be their "normal." One strategy that might help ease students into thinking about responding to questions is to have the students divvy up the most common questions raised by the arguments so different people are prepared to discuss different key ideas with the class.

Another important tool in preparation is to have students think about how to distinguish cases that may hurt their argument. Instead of letting students assume that the Court will simply overturn unfavorable precedent, encourage them to think about ways those unfavorable cases differ from the case at bar. Have student brainstorm how to distinguish the facts of harmful precedent from the facts of the case at bar. Remind the students that their goal should be providing the court with a reason, or legal cover, to ignore precedent that might harm their side.

PREPARING THE COURT FOR ORAL ARGUMENT

For moot court to succeed, judges need to understand their role in oral argument. This may be complicated if only because students may be more aware of trial courts than appellate courts and, as a result, they do not truly understand or appreciate what appellate judges do or how they function. It will be important to discuss how oral argument will proceed and what is expected of judges in oral argument. Whether you divide the class up so that some students are judges and some are advocates or all students are required to be both the judge and the advocate at some point, it will be important to remind them that their approach and preparation will be different for each of their roles. It will also be important to help student-judges understand how important their role is both during the oral arguments and after the arguments have concluded. Some student-judges may be reticent to vigorously question student-lawyers; others, in classes where judges produce graded work such as legal opinions that are due after oral argument, may think that their real work begins after oral argument. This is a mistake. Some will ask too many questions and act almost more like a prosecuting attorney than as an appellate judge. Remind them to ask questions but be respectful of their fellow judges and also that the advocates should do most of the speaking not the judges. Being a competent judge in moot court requires working hard and long; it cannot be achieved in a short time-span.

Once the judges have a good sense of what is expected of them, how things will proceed, and what their roles or duties are, the judges might begin to discuss the case. When the students are judges rather than advocates, their focus should not be on what is right or wrong or what should or should not be but rather it should be on what has happened, what issues are, and where the judges ought to look for answers. Judges will need to be familiar with the cases and key legal issues as well. Because it will be difficult for any individual to read all of the cases cited in the sample briefs, the judges might divide the cases in such a way that everyone is responsible for reading and preparing a brief summary of some select number of cases. As with the lawyers, it may be helpful to set deadlines for these briefs. Students who miss these deadlines should expect to be denied access to other students' work until they have completed their assigned briefs. It is not necessary that the judges divide up the issues in the same way as the lawyers. Judges need to look beyond how specific cases connect back to the facts of this particular changes and instead they should concern themselves with how their decision in this case will fit into the bigger picture.

Leading up to oral argument, the judges should meet to discuss issues that are emerging as well as what may be the relevant doctrine or precedent. Because this is an academic assignment, the judges might work together to identify and understand these issues as they emerge. Because they are a court, the judges would do well to be neutral when explaining precedent to fellow judges and to avoid dividing themselves into voting blocs or forming a consensus on how the case should be decided until after oral argument. The court should use the time before oral argument to identify key issues, perhaps even forming consensuses about what issues are important and identifying questions it wishes the lawyers to address. Some courts may decide to divide responsibilities in this area so that certain judges take the lead on asking certain questions. Others will allow things to develop over more informal lines. Regardless of your path, good questions will be essential to the development of an enlightened and lively session. Correspondingly, judges should use the time leading up to moot court to develop questions they will ask the lawyers in oral argument. Judges might set goals for producing a set number of questions. These might be collected by your facilitator, or even the chief justice, and checked to ensure that they are appropriate to the simulation and free of mistakes or errors. This will enable judges to avoid wasting time on questions that are misplaced or error-laden. Students might find it helpful to examine the types of questions that are frequently asked during the deliberations of appellate courts—in particular a court concerned with national issues such as the U.S. Supreme Court.

SUCCESSFUL STRATEGIES FOR JUDGES HEARING THE ORAL ARGUMENT

In a good oral argument, judges engage lawyers in an informed discussion about the case. For this to happen, the court must be prepared. Judges might come to oral argument with a memorandum that summarizes the issues and whatever questions they might have. Judges might consult this memorandum as argument ensues. The previous subsection discussed strategies to use to prepare for oral argument. This subsection will discuss strategies to employ during oral argument.

The key to a successful oral argument from the court's perspective may be the quality of the questions asked; thus, as we have indicated, preparation is important. Being prepared, however, is not enough. Judges need to develop a questioning style or a manner of inquiry with which they are comfortable and which is appropriate to the exercise. Whatever the specific style or manner judges develop, they should strive to be vigorous questioners, while at the same time not so vigorous so as to be unnecessarily intimidating or so vigorous so as to close your ears to what is being said in response. A key to critical thinking is the ability to listen and reflect upon what you hear; do not sacrifice that for the "thrill" of firing questions at a machine-gun-like pace. Your purpose is to ask questions, not grandstand or torture the lawyers. Judges, therefore, are advised to maintain a degree of civility and decorum in their questioning as well as their interactions with their fellow judges. While debate and disagreement are an acceptable, even desired, part of moot court, the exercise itself is not meant to be personal. One strategy for ensuring a harmonious court may be for the judges, just prior to oral argument, to emulate the U.S. Supreme Court's tradition of shaking hands and wishing each other luck during the proceedings to come. For moot court to succeed, participants must believe that the court is fair and unbiased. It is crucial, therefore, for judges to keep their pre-oral argument discussions a secret from the lawyers lest it appear that the court's mind is already decided. In addition, because the court needs to appear impartial, judges should treat lawyers, friend or foe alike, in an equal fashion. Judges should behave in a judicious manner; they should not scream at the lawyers or insult them—they should be polite and respectful.

Another key to a successful moot court is that participants engage in a type of suspended animation. It is important that the judges, especially the chief justice, be firm, yet fair. The court must not allow the lawyers to show disrespect for the court by failing to acknowledge its legitimacy or powers insofar as they go. Judges need to portray a sense of sobriety about their duties, and, if possible, they need to project a degree of gravitas. This is hard to teach. It can, however, be enhanced by manner, how one carries oneself, and perhaps one's attire. The point is that the judges, if they wish to be taken seriously and to have the lawyers and the audience suspend their disbelief, need to take oral argument seriously and to exude a high level of respect for each other and their classmates. To achieve such, courts might develop informal rules that will govern their behavior. These might include not allowing the lawyers to witness disagreements among the judges. It might also be advisable to insist that the lawyers rise when addressing the court and that they preface all remarks with the traditional phrase, "Your Honor, May It Please the Court." The judges should not refer to each other, or the lawyers, by first names and insist that if a lawyer and a justice speak simultaneously, the lawyer yield the floor (so to speak) to the justice. Some courts may elect to develop a dress code for oral argument to add to the authenticity of the simulation. In fact, in tournament competition, attorneys are judged in part on proper dress and respect for the court.

Having a chief justice can go a long way to making a court a success.[1] In oral argument, the chief justice presides; by using a gavel, if one is available, or a stern look, if one has one, the chief justice can help to maintain order and keep a sense of decorum. The chief justice may act as a type of unofficial spokesperson for the court when it comes to communicating its concerns or select questions to the lawyers in a fashion that is both dignified and impartial. The chief justice can help to keep discussion from stagnating or being dominated by the court's most outspoken or assertive members.

SUCCESSFUL STRATEGIES FOR THE COURT'S CONFERENCE

When moot court is over, the judges will likely render some opinion, written or otherwise, that settles the dispute and explains the court's rationale for its decision. Ideally, the court will not vote immediately at the conclusion of oral argument, in front of the lawyers, but instead retire to discuss the case, in secret, among themselves in the presence of their facilitator. At conference, the court should debate the merits of the different sides, address whatever issues or concerns its members have, consider case law or the needs of the nation, explore the existence of whatever consensus might exist on the issues before it, and hold a vote on the merits of the case. If possible, the court should arrive at a consensus for the rationale for its decision that it will later disclose to the lawyers. This process can be accomplished in one session but will likely require more than one meeting. However handled, there are certain strategies that can serve to improve conference.

The chief justice should preside over conference. This involves keeping discussion moving, putting issues on the agenda for consideration, ensuring that members who wish to participate are afforded the opportunity, and recording the results of any votes taken. A good chief justice can boil complex issues down to understandable

---

[1]   If your court is a federal appeals court this would be a chief judge rather than a chief justice.

terms. This ability may be more innate than taught; however listening carefully to what members say is a good start. Chief Judges should pay attention to any key assumptions made, any legal doctrines at hand, and, if dissent exists, any common area that may exist between the different sides. It may be beneficial for the chief justice, every so often, especially before a vote is taken, to summarize the views of the different sides in a fair and comprehensive manner. To do so, it may help to keep a record of the proceedings. The chief justice should keep such notes; however, it may be beneficial to ask that one of the associates also keep track of debate.

The conference should operate according to a clear set of rules, addressing matters such as what will determine the order in which judges will speak or vote, whether to set a time limit for discussion, and, if there will be a majority opinion, how the court will handle its assignment. In addition to operating according to some rules of procedure, judges might consider observing similar rules of decorum to those used in oral argument. This would include no name calling, no outbursts, no profanity, and no fisticuffs. Judges should be encouraged to take the conference seriously and not view it as irrelevant or a tiresome waste of time.

CURRICULUM DEVELOPMENT

As a practical matter, it might be helpful to develop rubrics for the various tasks you are asking the students to complete. A moot court class can require a lot of emotional and intellectual effort, as students may be reluctant or overwhelmed by the task they are trying to complete. Breaking this task into manageable parts with clear expectations from the outset may help you as the instructor provide the students with reassurance and lessen the enormous task of grading their speaking exercises on top of their written work. It is advisable to have rubrics for case briefs, for practice rounds, and for the final simulation. Students can also observe and produce feedback for their colleagues to help the instructor get additional feedback and to give students the opportunity to view the arguments from yet another perspective.

Using a different case for each class can allow students to repeat the moot court class for credit across multiple semesters. Different programs have a different approach to this. Some programs allow students to take the same one-hour moot court class each year because the legal reading and writing the students will do will cover different issues each year. Other programs allow students to earn three hours for their first moot court class, where they are also learning the basic mechanics of how oral arguments work. Then they allow students to follow up with a one-hour practicum each year to allow for the different legal arguments. That being said, the academic rigor of moot court cannot be understated. Not only do students learn valuable research and communication skills, but to engage in the question and answers necessary, they must be experts on their issues. This requires them to spend countless hours reading and thinking about precedent and legal doctrine.

CONCLUSION

This chapter has offered a variety of strategies to guide lawyers and judges through moot court. We discuss in detail how legal teams and the court should function prior to and during oral argument. In the case of the court, we also discuss how it should function during its conference, and we offer tips to assist in the administration of the court. Instructors of mooters need to bear in mind two additional matters of significance. First, the purpose of oral argument is to allow lawyers the rare ability to take part in an enlightened dialogue with the court about the law and the immediate case. For judges charged with the task of interpreting the law, moot court offers the opportunity to question talented lawyers about how to decide important legal questions whose resolution will have an impact upon the nation. Second, the purpose of moot court itself is to allow "mooters" the opportunity to do more than learn about the law or the judicial process.

Lessons for your students about critical thinking and logic, leadership, and working within a group abound; they are yours for the taking.

CHAPTER 7

The Moot Court Tournament

American justice is adversarial: the "truth" will emerge, it is believed, by using a process of attorneys competing with each other. Since the process of answering questions and reasoning through moot court competition allows the students to experience how the adversarial process operates, nearly all American law schools require students to compete in moot court. Schools which are members of the American Bar Association (ABA) are *required* to send at least one team to a national competition. The ABA feels that competition will sharpen students' ability and motivation to practice law. Moot court competitions additionally stimulate students' desire to prepare for "court" and sharpen their critical thinking and communication skills.

COMPETITORS

Nearly every law student will experience moot court; undergraduate students can also benefit from moot court competition. There is no other program which can provide adequate opportunities to sharpen an undergraduate student's abilities at persuasive speaking, research, and logical reasoning. While the traditional class is graded solely on a final exam, final exams do little to improve the true skills that will most benefit undergraduates in whatever career they choose.

In business as well as legal settings final exams are non-existent. However, throughout nearly all business and legal settings, individuals communicate verbally in a concise logical fashion with prepared

127

research and information to back up their positions. Undergraduate students significantly benefit, therefore, from participation in these moot court competitions.

The undergraduate student should be prepared for a significant time commitment. It has been the experience of the authors that the minimal time requirement to prepare for a tournament is at least 50 hours of concentrated effort. Those students wishing to advance significantly might spend up to 200 hours doing research and preparing their oral argument. Moreover, the competition itself usually lasts over a two-day time period. However, few students leave the competition without feeling a sense of accomplishment and learning after the completion of the competition itself.

THE CASE

Moot court problems use a "case" in order to challenge the competitors. The "case" is a simulated or actual appellate court decision. In the moot court case, a trial court has made a decision which is then appealed to an intermediate appellate court. Usually, the moot court case is an appeal from the intermediate appeal court to a Supreme Court either of the United States or a fictional state.

The intermediate appellate court usually cites cases as precedent to support the position that it took in making its decision.

Also included in the decision is a *dissent*. A dissent is at least one of the justices at the intermediate court disagreeing with the holding of the majority. The dissent will also include case law which lends support to their dissent. These cases form the core group of research that a competitor has to use in order to formulate an argument.

Competitions can either use an open or closed format. An "open" case is one where the competitors may use any decided court opinion as precedent to support the competitor's position. With literally millions of cases to search from, the "open" case poses the challenge of refining research and presenting case law which will be persuasive and authoritative to the judges.

The "closed" case is one where the competition rules do not allow the competitors to use any other cases besides those cited in the intermediate court opinion and dissent and any of those listed with the instructions for the competition itself. The "closed" case does not place such a premium upon research but rather upon reasoning and the ability to use the cases provided to them.

Nearly every case tries to have an even balance to it. That is to say neither the petitioner nor the respondent has a clear advantage based upon the positions taken in the case. However, nearly all problems have some bias contained within them. It is nearly impossible to find an evenly balanced appellate court decision. As a result, usually one side has the "law" on its side and the other has equity.

Finding the right argument on each side is essential in order to exploit the bias that is present on either side of the case. Further, this balances out in the end since all competitors are required to argue both sides of the case in competition.

JUDGES

Judges generally come from four basic groups of individuals: 1) lawyers; 2) judges; 3) law students; and 4) university or law school faculty.

1) *Lawyers*—the vast majority of judges in a moot court competition come from the legal community in and about the area where the competition is being held. The time commitment associated with being a judge can be significant. Generally, judges will be required to review the information prior to coming to the competition and then spend hours at the competition itself. Obviously, with the pressures of billing time, lawyers are reticent about volunteering their efforts along these lines. Moreover, many of the lawyers who do attend the competition may not be experienced advocates. Although nearly every attorney has experienced moot court in the law school setting, very few have actually

experienced presenting oral arguments in front of a panel of judges in a real appellate courtroom. As a result, screening by the competition coordinator is important to ensure that the most experienced lawyers are present for the competition.

2) *Members of the Judiciary*—many state and federal judges are willing to invest time in the education of students. As a result, a number of judges volunteer their time and experience and various moot court competitions. This is invaluable since the role that they play in the legal community is the same as they would play at the time of the competition itself. Giving this real-world experience is of great benefit to the competitors themselves.

3) *Law Students*—many undergraduate moot court competitions are held at law schools. Because law students have recently experienced moot court competitions, they make excellent judges for moot court. Moreover, their fresh understanding of the law is also beneficial to the students who will have judges who have recently studied the area of law in which the setting is placed.

4) *Faculty*—undergraduate moot court competitions are generally organized and managed by faculty from various undergraduate colleges. Thus, calling upon their colleagues for assistance in judging is a common practice.

Generally moot court competitions are structured where there are preliminary rounds with a number of undergraduate schools participating. Because a vast number of rounds are needed, usually only two or three judges are present for the preliminary rounds. (Elimination rounds usually have panels of at least three judges). This makes appealing to each particular judge all the more important.

SCORING

Scoring at various law school and undergraduate moot court competitions varies somewhat from one tournament to another. Judging guidelines for the American Moot Court Association (AMCA) tournaments are included next. A sample judging form is included at the end of this chapter. Obtaining a judging form and judging information in advance of any tournament is strongly recommended. While each competition uses scoring guidelines which are unique to that competition, the authors have surveyed most of the competitions offered and have found that the four areas outlined next are addressed in some manner.

Here are the rules set out for judges in the AMCA competitions. These guidelines outline the criteria by which a competitor may be judged.

The judging form contains specific areas to be evaluated as well as specific points within each area upon which judges are instructed to focus. Four areas are generally evaluated by judges: The first is knowledge of the subject matter, the second is response to questioning, the third is forensic skill, and the fourth is courtroom demeanor. Each of these areas is important for the competitors to master.

I.   KNOWLEDGE OF SUBJECT MATTER

- Demonstrates thorough knowledge of the record
- Directs the Court to important points in the record
- Clearly identifies and focuses on the central constitutional issue
- Understands relevant constitutional doctrines and applies them clearly
- Demonstrates thorough knowledge of the cases in the Table of Authorities
- Provides case citations to support arguments

- Only uses cases outside the Table of Authorities solely to the extent that they are quoted and cited within the official cases.

II. RESPONSE TO QUESTIONING

- Does not evade the Court's questions and answers questions clearly
- Answers questions with authority, identifying relevant rules and/or case names
- Fits relevant questions into overall analysis and presentation
- Makes clear transition back to argument after answering a question
- Listens carefully to the Court's questions
- Answers questions directly, starting with "Yes, Your Honor" or "No, Your Honor"
- Addresses questions posed by the Court to opposing counsel
- Uses questions to advance an argument by connecting responses to larger issues

III. FORENSIC SKILL

- Demonstrates proper respect and courtesy toward the Court and opposing counsel
- Projects an image of professionalism in appearance and presentation
- Begins presentation with "May it please the Court," stays within the time limits, and ends with a specific conclusion
- Maintains eye contact and talks to the Court in a conversational manner rather than reading from notes

- Uses correct pronunciation and grammar, uses appropriate vocabulary, and avoids distracting "ahs," "ums," or "ers"
- Speaks in a conversational but formal style, with good inflection and clear voice
- Exhibits a professional stance at the podium and uses gestures effectively and appropriately for appellate argument

---

IV. COURTROOM DEMEANOR

- Provides brief overview or "road map" of argument
- Presentation is well organized and focused on the constitutional question certified by the Court
- Clearly distinguishes central from marginal issues
- Arguments are clear and direct
- Central issues are clear to the Court when the advocate finishes
- Respondent does respond to the constitutional and legal arguments presented by petitioner
- Petitioner, in rebuttal, addresses and rebuts the constitutional and legal arguments presented by respondent
- Petitioner does NOT introduce new constitutional or legal issues in the rebuttal

Tournament Skill Components

The following are strategies the competitor may consider when preparing for competition. Each topic the competitor will be scored upon is addressed.

1.   Knowledge of the Subject Matter

Knowledge of the law is perhaps the single most important area in which the competitors can show their skills. Knowledge is achieved through appropriate research and study of case law and the moot court problem. Obviously, being familiar with all the cases cited in the problem is essential in order to prevail at any competition. One should be familiar with all of the facts in every one of the cases that is cited in the moot court problem as well as the issue presented in each case and the holding of each one of those cited cases. Moreover, the skilled moot court competitor will work in details of these cases so that one may present his or her knowledge to the judges. One separator in this area of the competition is the ability to identify useful points within supporting cases and apply them to the facts at hand to either support or distinguish this controversy with those for which a prior court decision is contained within the record.

2.   Forensic Skills

Forensic skills are essential to a good moot court argument. One must show confidence and use a correct iambic pentameter. Reading one's argument should be forbidden. Also important is to look each of the judges in the eye. Unlike public speaking, where one tries to look just above the eyes of the crowd, in moot court, one should look directly at the judges, especially when answering their questions. Moving eye contact from judge to judge is also essential so that they can feel that you are paying attention to them and are speaking directly to them.

It is important to keep in mind that an appellate argument should be like a conversation. Unlike a trial with a jury, an advocate should not look to command the room. Rather, deference to the court should be the order of the day. This is an opportunity for the advocate to discuss issues with the panel and help those judging understand their position on the issues.

Most important of all with forensic skills is the concept of enjoying yourself. One should make the judges feel that you are comfortable with your argument and also make the judges feel good about the questions that they ask. *Never* let the judges believe that the competitor believes that the question or issue being raised by a judge is stupid.

3. *Answering Questions*

The ability to carry on a conversation with a judge by answering the questions being posed to them is essential to a high score. Answering questions should be done directly to the judge posing them. If at all possible, the competitor should answer the question by citing a case or a statute. That is, giving the court an example of how there is case law which supports the competitor's position and how that answers the judge's question. By doing so, the judge knows that they asked an appropriate question that is cited with case law and supported by that position. Moreover, it shows the knowledge of the law of the competitor. Finally, in answering a question, one should also give a policy argument. That is, one should show why it is that the question being posed would have either a positive or negative effect (whichever is appropriate) on the state of the law and/or society. In essence, the competitor should provide a picture to the judge as to how the effect of the question being posed would affect the law or people in general. This strategy of giving someone a case and a picture generally has the effect of high scores at competition.

4. *Courtroom Demeanor*

Organization and respect for the court are critical in this area. Competitors should have a clear theory of the case, have a roadmap which makes their path easy to follow, and is direct in making these points.

The appearance of the competitor is always important. While the concept of relaxed dress has become more prevalent, courts have not adopted this philosophy. As a result, men should be dressed in suit and tie and should make a conservative appearance. Ladies should always dress in appropriate attire as well. The focus should be on the words of the competitor. Distracting dress takes away from that focus.

One should not stand still nor wave his or her hands about in wild gestures. Rather, simple and appropriate hand movement is always essential to a high score.

THE WRITTEN BRIEF AND ORAL ARGUMENT

Many competitions will require submission of written briefs in addition to oral argument. This is closer akin to the competitions offered at law school. In law school, moot court competitions always require a written brief that is scored and weighed in conjunction with a competitor's oral argument. When arguing in front of an appellate court, the written brief is usually more important than the oral argument. Most appellate court decisions are decided upon by the attorney's briefs. It is rare that an oral argument will turn an appellate court decision. However, the forensic skills and legal arguments that a litigator uses at the trial court level are the same as developed in moot court. There, the ability to make and present a legal argument can sway a judge to one position or another.

At the undergraduate level, many competitions offer some form of competition involving a brief. At the American Collegiate Moot Court Association National Competition, a separate competition involving briefs is offered to competitors. The drafting of the legal brief itself is then scored separately. While one competitor may prevail at the briefing level, it is disconnected from the oral argument in terms of the competitor's scores. Other competitions link both brief and oral argument together weighing the two portions of the competition (brief and oral argument).

Generally, briefs are presented either as petitioner or respondent. They follow the rules of court associated with the U.S. Supreme Court or, if the competition is unique to a state, then to the state Supreme Court.

STRUCTURE OF THE TOURNAMENT FOR ORAL ARGUMENT

Most competitions require two competitors to make a team. That is to say that each team consists of a first and second speaker. The two speakers' scores are then totaled and compared with a combined score of the opposing team. The team with the higher aggregate score of both competitors is said to have "won the round."

Most tournaments are structured with preliminary rounds and elimination rounds. During preliminary rounds, the competitors are randomly paired. The competitors generally have to argue both petitioner and respondent. As a result, a minimum of two preliminary rounds is always recommended for a tournament, requiring that every competitor must face a petitioner's and a respondent's side of the argument. Scores are then tallied based upon the competitor's performance in each of the rounds. Each competition uses a variety of methods of scoring teams. Most use this head-to-head method to determine who won the round. The team then moves on to the next preliminary round. The second preliminary round is scored in a similar fashion, and then each team is evaluated based upon the number of ballots or rounds it has won. Those competitors who have won both of their preliminary rounds have a "2–0 record." Teams that have won a preliminary round and lost a preliminary round have a "1–1 record." And obviously, those teams that have lost both their preliminary rounds have a "0–2 record." In AMCA competitions, each judge's ballot counts as an individual win or loss, thus increasing the number of decisions and reducing the chance for ties.

Concern comes when teams with the same record have to be compared to each other. For example, if more than one team has won both its preliminary rounds, then they both have a "2–0" record or have won four ballots. As a result, the way these "ties" are broken may be based on a number of factors. These may include strength of schedule or the aggregate number of speaker points. In the next section is the scoring sheet which has been used at various moot court competitions. Obviously, the greater the number of preliminary rounds, the less likely ties will occur. As a result, all AMCA sanctioned events have three preliminary rounds.

THE ELIMINATION ROUNDS

Once teams have been ranked by record in the preliminary rounds, a finite number of teams advance to the elimination rounds. During the elimination rounds, each team's total aggregate speaker points are compared to their opponents. That team with a greater aggregate number of speaker points prevails and moves on to the next elimination round. Elimination rounds continue until one final team is crowned the winner.

Power Protect

Many competitions will rank those teams that have moved from the preliminary rounds into the elimination rounds. The higher-ranked teams are generally paired against the weaker teams. This is called "power protect." Each team is given a rank based upon first, its win-loss record. Those teams with a "3–0 record" are all considered to be higher ranked than any team with a "2–1 record." Then each of the teams with the same records is ranked according to the total aggregate speaker points that it has received in the preliminary rounds. As a result, the highest ranked team will be one with a "3–0 record" and the highest strength of schedule or most aggregate speaker points from the preliminary round. This highest-ranked team will then compete against the lowest rank.

Trophies are awarded to those teams who prevail at competition. However, other trophies are also generally awarded for individual performance of the competitors. While each moot court "team" consists of two competitors, many times an individual competitor will show significant skill during the competition. The individual's total speaker points are aggregated among the three preliminary rounds. Those competitors with the top ten total aggregate speaker points from the preliminary rounds are generally awarded "orator awards" for their individual performance.

The following table is the official judging ballot used at the American Moot Court Association's national tournament. This same score sheet is also used at the many regional tournaments leading up to the national championship.

Table 5.1—Judging Ballot

TEAM NUMBER _____

AMERICAN MOOT COURT ASSOCIATION

OFFICIAL BALLOT

Round (circle):	Prelim I	Prelim II	Prelim III
Round of Sixteen	Quarter	Semi	Final

RANGE OF SCORING

POOR	FAIR	AVERAGE	GOOD	EXCELLENT
Below 60	60–70	70–80	80–90	90–100

CONTESTANT NAME _____

NAME: _____

SCORE (1–100 per category)		SCORE (1–100 per category)
_____	KNOWLEDGE OF SUBJECT MATTER:	_____
	Preparation on facts, law, and record; reasoning, organization; full use of time; etc.	
_____	RESPONSE TO QUESTIONING:	_____
	Responsiveness to judges; authoritativeness; ability to think quickly and well and return to argument; etc.	
_____	FORENSIC SKILLS:	_____
	Manner which is relaxed, confident, believable, poised; eye contact; ability to speak without reading notes; grammar; vocabulary; inflection; etc.	

CONCLUSION

Tournaments are the culmination of the full moot court experience. Benefits believed to be attributable to participation in moot court include: improved communication skills, enhanced critical thinking abilities under duress, improved legal research and writing skills, enhanced self-confidence and poise, and enhanced acceptance rates into law school.

One of the greatest benefits of undergraduate moot court is practical preparation for law school. Since the moot court experience will be repeated as part of continuing legal education, it is an invaluable tool in preparing students for their future.

CHAPTER 8

Brief Writing for Moot Court

In the previous chapters you have seen how to become an effective moot court orator. While development of oral argument skills is an essential part of being a successful mooter, understanding how to write a cogent brief is similarly important. A brief is a written version of your legal argument. Many moot court events, from undergraduate to law school, hold a written par to their competitions. In law school competitions, it is typical for the written brief to be scored in conjunction with the oral argument portion. Becoming a strong mooter requires development of oral, as well as written, argument skills.

This chapter will explain strategies for writing briefs for moot court. The chapter will detail three aspects to writing strong legal briefs: (1) moot court-specific brief writing tips, (2) legal writing tips (including citation strategies), and (3) general writing suggestions. After reading this chapter, we believe you will be well on your way to crafting excellent moot court briefs.

MOOT COURT BRIEF WRITING TIPS

Brief writing strategies for moot court are very similar to brief writing tactics in general. Whether you are writing a brief for a moot court competition, or, a brief to a court as a practicing lawyer, some techniques will be the same. In the last two sections of this chapter we will detail these more general, and cross-cutting, strategies for brief writing. In the first section of this chapter, however, we will address concerns specific to the moot court brief writing process.

Know the Rules

Every moot court brief writing competition will require participants to submit their briefs in accordance with competition rules. It is absolutely paramount that you understand what the governing rules are for your respective brief writing competition. Is there a page limit? Does the font have to be in a certain form? What sections of the brief are required to be submitted? What legal citation format is required? Typically, brief writing competitions will specifically delineate these rules.

As an example, the American Moot Court Association (AMCA) governs undergraduate moot court competitions and holds a brief writing competition as a part of its national tournament. These briefs must comport to rules, including document structure and style. For example, the brief is not to exceed twenty pages, must use Times New Roman and 12-point font, and be submitted in PDF format.[1] The rules also specify which parts of the brief are required to be submitted (e.g., Summary of Argument, Table of Contents, etc.).[2] These rules will specify the appropriate format for your brief and it is folly to ignore them; do so at peril.

Brief writing rules will also tell you how your brief will be scored. Understanding the constituent parts for grading will allow you to focus your attention on those portions of the brief writing competition that are most important. For instance, the AMCA brief writing competition is graded on a 100-point scale with various portions ranging from 10

---

[1] *See* https://storage.googleapis.com/wzukusers/user-28362831/documents/5bcf1b7 e00f6b4TA4pCb/Brief%20writing%20competition%20rules_2018.pdf.

[2] This chapter will not go through a detailed analysis of every section of a brief that needs to be submitted. Look at the rules of the competition to see which parts need to be included. To the extent certain parts of the brief merit more precise guidance, the section on legal writing below will detail these tips and strategies.

to 15 points.[3] In contrast, the scoring can be quite different in law school. For instance, the *Hunton Andrews Kurth* Moot Court National Championship held for law students similarly grades on a 100-point scale. However, teams' scores are a combined function of oral argument scores and brief writing scores.[4]

A final note regarding the rules is the amount of assistance a participant can have in preparing the brief. It is important to keep this rule in mind as you do not want to run afoul of this rule as it can cause a team to be disqualified for inappropriate assistance. As an example, for the AMCA undergraduate brief writing competition, the rules state clearly that "no outside assistance from attorneys or faculty" can be utilized in the brief writing process.[5] The Kurth Championship states that "[t]eam members may not, during the brief writing process, discuss the problem with *anyone*."[6] The point is, for both competition reasons, and ethical concerns, it is exceedingly important for you to understand how much assistance you can obtain in the brief writing process. Certifying to the competition that you have not had any assistance, when you have in fact had such assistance, can be a disqualifying violation and cost you dearly in the tournament. Proceed with caution.

Division of Labor

Another consideration for writing briefs for moot court is the division of labor between yourself and your partner. Practicing lawyers are often the sole author of written briefs. It is possible that these attorneys might have distinct sections for which they are responsible within a group, but many times lawyers will draft the briefs themselves (or, review the written work of another author). In moot court, it is always the case that you will have a partner. As a result, writing a brief takes coordination with them.

---

[3] *See, supra*, note 1.

[4] *See* http://www.law.uh.edu/blakely/mcnc/2019/2019%20Championship%20Rules_Final.pdf.

[5] *See, supra*, note 1.

[6] *See, supra*, note 4, at 3 (emphasis added).

Moot court teams are typically divided between one person who handles one legal issue (Issue X), while their partner is expert in the second issue (Issue Y). Because both individuals are contributing to the moot court process, writing a brief will require coordination with one's partner. Take time to discuss with your partner who will be preparing each section of the brief. It is likely the case that Issue X specialists will draft the Issue X legal arguments in the brief (and Issue Y specialists draft the Issue Y arguments). However, briefs are comprised of several parts (e.g., Summary of Argument, Table of Contents, Table of Authorities, etc.). Because there are distinct sections beyond the actual legal arguments that each team member will make, it is important to identify early who will be responsible for these other sections of the team's brief. Perhaps one person is particularly adept at legal citation; if so, it would make sense for this individual to handle the Table of Authorities. Perhaps the other team member is skilled at document formatting; this individual could handle format compliance review. Whatever the respective skillset each member brings to the team, the point is to structure your development of the brief with these in mind and to coordinate with your partner to achieve the best possible brief writing score.

Plan Effectively

An essential element to writing effective legal briefs is to plan your time writing the brief. Crafting good, written legal arguments takes time. The process of brief writing from start to finish includes several layers. These brief writing steps require care and precision, and therefore, time. Do not wait until the last minute to begin composing a brief. This tactic is highly inadvisable. You need to plan the brief writing process.

As noted above, after you have familiarized yourself with the various portions of the brief that need to be submitted consistent with the competition rules, you should chart out a "backwards calendar" for the various stages of writing the brief. For instance, it makes sense to meet with your partner early in the process and identify the various parts of the brief for which each person will be responsible. Once you have this structure in place, then both of you can work backwards from the date that the brief is due, specifying goals for when each constituent part of the brief is to be finished. As you move forward (and closer in time) to the due date, each part of the brief is finished and can be connected together to form the finished product. Be sure you leave enough time for editing the brief and correcting any mistakes you might find. Editing is crucial to good writing; be sure you leave enough time to edit your written work before you submit it to the competition.

Let us make one clear, and perhaps obvious, suggestion about this backwards calendar. The Table of Authorities and Table of Contents for your brief should be finished last. Why last? The reason for doing so is that the brief will undergo revisions. As these revisions are made, cited cases may be cut (or added), and substantive text may be cut (or added). When these alterations occur, they potentially change the page case cites and arguments are on within the body of the brief. As a result, modifying the Table of Authorities and Table of Contents as you write is simply a waste of time; do so when you are finished writing the body of the brief.

Carefully planning the brief writing process with your partner can ease a great deal of anxiety. Those who are most concerned and stressed about the brief tend to be those who wait until the last minute to compile the brief. In the context of undergraduate moot court, it is often the case that students are taking several classes at once, have busy lives, perhaps even a job or two, and therefore do not have a great deal of "extra" time to write a written brief. Indeed, the AMCA brief writing competition has a due date in mid-December. Students are usually in final exam season at this point, which is already a stressful time period. Starting early and coordinating with your partner can alleviate anxiety associated with the brief writing process.

LEGAL WRITING TIPS

Now that you have an understanding of the processes used in composing a written brief, we turn to address legal writing tips and strategies. The purpose of this section is not to be a full, all-encompassing review of how to write like a lawyer. There are many, many books devoted exclusively to the nuances of legal writing, and it is useful to turn to these resources for a longer treatment. Instead, we wish to give some practical tips on effective legal writing that can make your brief standout from the rest.

Have a Theme

Themes matter. If you represent an individual who has sued the government for violation of your client's civil rights for excessive police force, your theme of the case will be quite different than if you are the government responding to such a lawsuit. As the plaintiff, a theme about individual liberty and metaphors which cradle the Bill of Rights are apt; in the alternative, a theme of governmental necessity to protect the public against lawlessness can be appropriate.

No matter the factual situation of your respective moot court case problem, the point is to be sure that your theme runs throughout your brief. Humans are drawn to storytelling; in writing a brief, you are the storyteller. Tell a story where your client is the protagonist and stands triumphant at the end of the brief. As former Justice Antonin Scalia and Bryan A. Garner note in their excellent book on legal argumentation, "[d]esign the entire writing—from the statement of questions presented to the conclusion—to bring out your theory of the case and your principal themes. . .[y]our purpose is to bring the court to a certain destination; the brief should be designed and built to get there."[7]

Be sure your theme runs throughout the brief, including the summary of argument and argument sections. It is fairly typical for young law students and lawyers to be concerned with making strict step-by-step legal arguments. This concern is important, but it is not the only one. The legal elements in your case are the scaffold upon

---

[7]   Antonin Scalia and Bryan A. Garner, *Making Your Case: The Art of Persuading Judges* 59 (2008).

which your theme can be stretched. Do not ignore moments where driving home a legal conclusion can also drive home your theory of the case.

Outline Your Arguments

The argument section of your brief is where you place substantive legal arguments. The argument section needs to be a tight explanation of the legal reasons why you should win. Writing an effective legal argument section requires planning.

The best way to plan your legal argument section is to outline your argument. Take time to meticulously plan the argument so that it flows from one logical point to another. This argument form is often known as tautological argumentation. In other words, the sheer logic of your argument requires a certain result, namely, your client winning their case.

With moot court, it is often the case that you will have already created an outline for your oral arguments. As noted, AMCA's brief competition has a deadline in mid-December. Students have already been to competitions for their oral arguments by this point. As a result, their oral argument outlines can serve as a rough outline for the brief writing component. Do not believe, however, that you can merely take your oral argument outline, put it into full-sentence format, and call it a day; this tactic will likely leave you without a full written brief. However, the argument structure you adopt for oral argument can often be converted to a general written brief outline and serve as the bedrock for your brief.

You also want to think about the implications of your legal arguments and build them in to your written brief. There is no reason to play "hide the ball" with the "court" in brief writing competitions. In other words, pretending that difficult counter-arguments do not exist to your main arguments is silly. If there is a particularly difficult counter-argument that can be made by the other side in responding to your brief, then address that difficulty in the body of your brief. A touch of honesty can go a long way in representing that you have carefully considered the ramifications of your argument and give credence to the seriousness with which you have considered the main arguments in your brief. Outlining your arguments will assist you in thinking about these countervailing arguments. And, in the written brief, as opposed to oral argument, you will have the time and space to address such points which can hurt you and help your opposition.

Logically Orient Your Arguments

Effective brief writing also requires you to logically orient your arguments around your overriding theme. Logically orienting your arguments can be viewed in two forms: (1) formatting considerations and (2) structural considerations. Let's take a look at these two concepts.

Formatting your arguments in a logical fashion means the actual presentation of the arguments. For example, which argument should you make first? There are two schools of thought on this approach. The first approach is to lead with your strongest arguments. The idea here is to present those arguments which can win the case outright at the start. Crush the opposition out of the gate, and the court will not need to worry about your less-than-ideal arguments later. The second approach is to draft an argument structure that is the same as the opposing party. For instance, if you are the Respondent on a brief, go section by section the same as the initiating brief (from opposing counsel) to effectively counter the arguments made by the other side.

Given that moot court is different than real lawyering, many brief writing competitions actually permit teams to choose which side they will brief. For example, the AMCA brief writing competition allows teams to select whether they wish to write a brief for the Petitioner or the Respondent. In this case, you are not actually responding to a "real" brief (if you are the Respondent). As a result, using the second formatting suggestion above does not make much sense. Accordingly, we recommend using the first formatting suggestion: lead with your strongest arguments first.

In addition to formatting considerations, you also want to think about the structure of your arguments. In this facet to brief writing, you should adhere to the standard method of legal reasoning of IRAC (Issue-Rule-Application-Conclusion). In Chapter 5, we discussed this general theory of legal reasoning in detail. A short example here, however, will demonstrate how this method applies to brief writing.

Assume you have a fact pattern involving whether the police have conducted an unlawful search. In order for there to be an unlawful search, there must first have been a search, and, that search must have been conducted in an unreasonable manner under the Fourth Amendment. Without going into great nuances of constitutional law here, just accept that whether a search has occurred for the purposes of the Fourth Amendment requires application of the *Katz* test (*see United States v. Katz*, 389 U.S. 347 (1967)) and the trespass test (*see United States v. Jones*, 565 U.S. 400 (2012)). The *Katz* test states that a "search" occurs when an individual has both a subjective expectation of privacy (in whatever was searched) and an objective expectation of privacy that society would deem reasonable. The trespass test states that a "search" has occurred for the purposes of the Fourth Amendment when the government engages in a trespass against one's personal effects. If either test is satisfied, there has been a "search" under the Fourth Amendment. And, if there's a "search" under the Fourth Amendment, the government needs a warrant (based upon probable cause), unless, one of the exceptions to the warrant requirement applies. If these rights are violated, then the evidence cannot be used in a criminal prosecution against an individual (pursuant to the exclusionary rule announced in *Mapp v. Ohio*, 367 U.S. 643 (1961)). Given this very general example, you might structure your arguments on behalf of a criminal defendant on this issue (or, a plaintiff in a civil rights lawsuit) in the following manner:

I.   The Overzealous Government Officials Violated Mr. Defendant's Fourth Amendment Rights.

   a.   The Government Conducted a "Search" of Mr. Defendant.

      i.   Mr. Defendant Had Expectations of Privacy.

         1.   Mr. Defendant Had a Subjective Expectation of Privacy.

         2.   Mr. Defendant Had an Objectively Reasonable Expectation of Privacy.

      ii.   The Government Committed a Trespass Against Mr. Defendant.

   b.   No Exception to the Warrant Requirement Exists in This Case.

   c.   Because There Was No Warrant, the Evidence Gathered by the Government Cannot Be Used.

In this example, we can see the ISSUE (whether the government violated the defendant's Fourth Amendment rights?). Then we methodically announce the guiding RULE(S) that will define our legal inquiry (contained in (a) and (b)). We then APPLY the rules announced to the facts of our case ((a)(i) *et seq*.; (a)(ii); (b)). Finally, we specify the CONCLUSION to be drawn ((c); the evidence must be excluded). While this is a very general and basic example, and you would of course fill in these points with a richer legal analysis, the illustration demonstrates how to structure written arguments using the IRAC method. Moreover, it also demonstrates how we can stylistically phrase our argument headings in such a manner as to comport with our theme: the government has overreached and violated the personal liberty of an individual.

Citation Concerns

Another facet to legal writing that distinguishes itself from writing in general is the usage of legal citation. Brief writing competitions will undoubtedly score a brief on citation format. Poor legal citation can be an obvious error that stands out to brief graders and cause you to lose easy points with your moot court brief. The brief writing competition rules will tell you which citation system to use. Typically, brief writing competitions will use the "*Bluebook*."[8] Some will use the *ALWD Citation Manual.*[9]

Before delving into legal citation tips, the author of this chapter would note that there is at present a strong debate within legal academia about the utility of strict legal citation form. This criticism is not unfounded as legal citation in the *Bluebook* (the most utilized citation system) has grown into a massive document that spans well over 500 hundred pages of citation rules. As former Circuit Court of Appeals Judge Richard A. Posner as noted, "It is a monstrous growth, remote from the functional need for legal citation forms, that serves obscure needs of the legal culture and its student subculture."[10] The University of Chicago School of Law has gone so far as to create its own citation system known as the *Maroonbook*.[11] Debates about how many spaces exist between punctuation marks based on the total number of letters in the abbreviated thing (whatever it may be) ignore the fundamental precept of citation theory: can the reader easily understand and look up whatever is cited? The author of this chapter only points out this debate so students reading this book can perhaps think creatively about better citation systems as they enter their legal education (and save us from the avalanche of rules imposed by systems such as the *Bluebook*).

---

[8]   *The Bluebook: A Uniform System of Citation* (20th ed. 2016).

[9]   Coleen M. Barger and Association of Legal Writing Directors, *ALWD Citation Manual: A Professional System of Citation* (6th ed. 2019).

[10]   Richard A. Posner, *The Bluebook Blues*, 120 Yale L.J. 850, 851 (2011); *see also* Richard A. Posner, *Goodbye to the Bluebook*, 53 U. Chi. L. Rev. 1343 (1986).

[11]   *The Maroonbook: The University of Chicago Manual of Legal Citation* (Vol. 86 2018).

Notwithstanding the above commentary, legal citation in moot court briefs is a "hate the player, not the game" situation. Whether a mooter likes it or not, undoubtedly brief writing competitions will require students to adhere to one of the more (in)famous systems of legal citation (like the *Bluebook*). The process of using these systems can be daunting to a young student. Here are some tips when it comes to legal citation:

1.   Find the citation manual—and use it.

     Do not "wing it" with legal citations. If the competition calls for the *Bluebook*, get a copy of it and use it with care. Luckily, in moot court competitions, the type of material cited is fairly common (e.g., court cases, statutory provisions). As a result, utilize the back flap of the *Bluebook* (it contains quick reference guides for typical material). This approach can reduce the time spent fumbling through the tome of rules.

2.   Look at other winning briefs.

     Some competitions will publish past winning briefs. These briefs can be used as a guide as you draft your brief. What worked in the past is likely to work today, so see if there are examples of past winning briefs. For example, if you are an undergraduate competing in the AMCA brief writing competition, *see* the 2019 national winning brief of Yana Gagloeva and Liam Sidebottom (Respondent) on the AMCA website.[12]

3.   Be accurate with legal citations.

     If you cite an authority for a proposition, be sure that authority actually represents the proposition in the manner you have cited. In real court, inappropriately citing a case for a proposition can be easily demolished by opposing counsel, as well as potentially draw the ire

---

[12]   Found at https://www.acmamootcourt.org/national-brief-writing-competition-champions.

of the judge(s). In moot court, you do not have "real" opposing counsel, especially in the brief writing stage. However, it is distinctly possible that the grader of a brief is familiar with the cited authority, or, might actually take the time to look it up. If so, and you have improperly cited an authority, you can be in for a world of hurt with point deductions. And, if you've been caught once wrongly citing something, your credibility is diminished in the eye of the grader (not something you want). So, be precise and honest in your citations.

4.   Don't use unnecessary string citations.[13]

String citations are a series of citations to authorities for a singular proposition. These can clutter a brief and make your brief difficult to read. For example, let's say in your research you have found seven cases that stand for proposition "X." Unless there is a need to demonstrate how a variety of courts have ruled on an issue (for instance, there is a circuit court of appeals split on the matter), stringing together a list of seven cases for a single proposition is wasteful to the reader's time. Think to yourself: "would three, or two, or even one citation do the trick here?" Listing repetitive precedent, for example, will generally not make your authoritative statement any more authoritative than fewer citations, but it can make the brief harder to read for the grader.

5.   Keep your references consistent.

This suggestion is less a legal citation tip than a general legal writing tip, but is still quite useful. In legal pleadings, the parties can take on various names. For example, the criminal defendant could also be the "Appellant" below (the person who filed the appeal to

---

13   This concept can be found in Scalia and Garner, *supra*, note 7, at 99.

the intermediate appellate level), and the "Petitioner" (the person petitioning for review before the U.S. Supreme Court). Of course, they are also a person with a name (Mr. Jones, for instance). Regularly referring to parties by their various names and titles can only serve to confuse a reader. Pick one. If you represent Mr. Jones, then call him that. If you represent the government against Mr. Jones, call him the Petitioner (theoretically this de-personalizes the person, though it isn't clear this tactic actually works). Whatever "citation" or reference you choose for parties, stick with it. Your brief (and grader) will reward you.

Having detailed tips and strategies applicable to legal writing, and the related issue of citation concerns, we now turn to general writing tips.

GENERAL WRITING TIPS

By now you should discern that writing an effective legal brief requires a great deal of care in crafting your work. Attention to essential elements of legal writing, logical analysis, and citation are crucial to scoring well on a moot court brief. In the concluding section we will detail some general writing tips that can assist mooters in constructing persuasive, winning briefs.

Writing Generally

Before we detail specific tactics and techniques that can improve your writing, we need to take a step back and think more theoretically about writing. *Why do we write?* It seems straightforward enough a question, but the unthinking nature of how we communicate with the written word leads to problematic tendencies. These "bad habits" only serve to skew our intended statements and also constitute obstacles to conveying ideas. In the time of emojis and cellphone thumbstrokes we have only hastened these tendencies. And in that process, we have cultivated a spasmodic, staccato vernacular that misguides our intended meanings. In daily life this phenomenon is a problem; in legal writing it is devastating for the advocate.

George Orwell long ago detailed similar problems with the English language. As Orwell noted, "the slovenliness of our language makes it easier for us to have foolish thoughts."[14] It can be added to this statement that slovenliness in our language makes it harder to convince others we are right. This problem is acute when it comes to legal argumentation. If a judge (or, brief grader) cannot understand your argument, how can you convince that individual your legal conclusion is right? We endeavor here to provide a few suggestions for general writing that will serve brief writers well.

Write Clearly

A well-written brief is easier to read and easier to understand. If the point of the brief is to articulate why your side should win (and the other should not), losing your audience with tortured language and sentence structure only hinders this effort. Be clear, brief, and succinct in your writing. As Orwell notes, "[n]ever use a long word where a short one will do."[15]

Clear writing seems foreign to lawyers, who often appear to believe bonus points are awarded for the number of letters used in a word. For example, let's say you represent a person who has sued for damages when their neighbor's cat bit them. You could say, "Neighbor's mammalian quadruped then took a lacerative chomp on Plaintiff's arm." But this is absurd. Just say, "the cat bit Mr. Plaintiff." The essence is the same; the wording is not. The latter is clearer. There is no need to put on an air of pretension. The reader will not score you higher for it.

When thinking about writing more clearly, also be attentive to the rhythm of your language. This effect is most obvious with the spoken

---

[14] George Orwell, "Politics and the English Language," in Th*e Collected Essays, Journalism, and Letters of George Orwell, Volume IV*, at 128, (Ian Angus and Sonia Orwell eds, 1968).

[15] Orwell, *supra*, note 14, at 139.

word. Assuredly you have found yourself nodding along during a speech or conversation at some point in your life. Those who are considered the best orators in history understood the importance of rhythm. Paragraphs should take someone on a journey through an idea. And, like any journey, there are movements, sometimes sharp, sometimes smooth, but always leading to a final destination.

Writing should be the same journey. Avoid monotonous sentences that read like a training manual. At the same time, do not write with a frenzied style where each sentence is orthogonal to the next. The point is to find the rhythm that matches your legal analysis. Some sections of briefs will require a slower pace, refined and elegant to match the ethereal nuance of a novel question of law. Other sections, however, are more punctuated; the legal test is clear, the precedent is clear, and the result is clear. Becoming expert at this type of writing takes practice, but it is feasible to learn these techniques and apply them even to legal writing.

Dispense with Legalisms

The law, by its very nature, looks backward. In common law system (like the United States), *stare decisis* dictates adherence to precedent, which requires lawyers look to the past. This doctrinal mechanism of review is all well and good, but because the law looks backward it can cling to jargon that has no place in the present.

Legal writing is replete with examples of adherence to phrases, many Latin, that misdirect a reader's focus from the sentence at hand. Some aspects of legal writing cannot escape these phrases. For instance, *stare decisis* (as I used earlier) is not going away any time soon. Nor, frankly, should it. It is much simpler to say "*stare decisis*" than to express the concept of "let the decision stand." However, other phrases are obsolete and unnecessary. If there is a common English word equivalent, drop the legalism and go with the current vernacular. Some examples will help here.[16]

The legal phrase "case *sub judice*" is often used, yet, it simply translates to, "this case." Why go with the outdated Latin form? Similarly, legal writing often contains the phrase, "in the event that," when one could simply say, "if." And perhaps the biggest bugaboo of this chapter's author is the word, "said." For instance, "said contract states. . ." Just say, "*the* contract states. . ." The word "the" is fewer letters and does the task of serving as an appropriate article. Why try to sound smart instead of being smart?

This chapter is not meant to serve as an exhaustive list of all the problematic usages of outdated legal phrasings. What we hope, however, is this serves as a caution to you: if you're going to use an old phrase or Latin, is it really necessary to do so?

Get Rid of Passive Voice

Passive voice is problematic in all modern writing, including legal writing. For whatever reason, writers prefer to minimize the punch of their sentences by throwing the action in a sentence away from the reader's attention. This phenomenon is not new, as Orwell even denounced it in his seminal essay on the English language.[17] Students, however, appear to have embraced it more since Orwell's time.

Passive voice, in general, should be avoided. There is a time and place for it in the English language. If a writer wants to center the reader's focus on the thing affected by the action at issue, then it makes sense to use passive voice. Most of the time, however, we want to highlight the action at issue. Returning to our scenario of the cat that bites neighbors, consider the following example:

---

[16] The first two examples come from Bryan A. Garner, *Legal Writing in Plain English* at 44–45 (2013). The book is an excellent guide to improving legal writing.

[17] Orwell, *supra*, note 14, at 139.

Passive Voice: My client was bitten by the cat.

Active Voice: The cat bit my client.

In this example, we would want to use the active voice. The entire dispute revolves around someone's pet (the cat) causing injury to your client (through the bite). We want to draw attention to action of the cat. Using the active voice provides the necessary focus.

Here's another example. Let's say your opponent has filed a motion to reconsider a previously decided matter. You, of course, won the first motion (congrats!). You want the court to reject the motion for reconsideration and adhere to the previous ruling. Two ways exist to state the prior history in the case:

Passive Voice: The previous motion for summary judgment
                  was denied by this court.

Active Voice: This court previously denied the motion for
                  summary judgment.

In this example, we again want to use the active voice. We want to point out to "this court" that it has already denied the motion in question. The court took the action in question, and we want our focus to be on the court's behavior, not the previous motion. In other words, we want to demonstrate that the court has already considered the issue once, and there is no need for duplicative consideration. Putting "the court" as the point of action demonstrates only further (and contrary) action will provide the relief sought. Courts do not like to re-do work they have already done. So the focus on "the court" is appropriate in this instance. And, the sentence is shorter to boot.

These examples are fairly basic, but hopefully give you pause when writing your brief. With rare exceptions, it is inadvisable to use the passive voice. Get rid of its use, and your briefs will be clearer to your grader.

Edit, Edit, Edit

After you have written your brief, there is one last effort to make: editing. There is no such thing as good legal writing without editing. Perhaps there is a time and place for stream of consciousness writing. James Joyce and Jack Kerouac were proponents of this writing technique. Joyce and Kerouac were not, however, lawyers writing briefs to a court. Putting aside the utility of such an approach for literary purposes, when it comes to legal writing (and really, almost any writing) one must be diligent in editing.

Editing does not simply mean correcting spelling errors, or, grammatical mistakes. These corrections are important and indeed necessary. However, good editing requires more than fixing the basic problems and requires a sincere effort to carve away extraneous words and phrases to induce clarity. Think to yourself: can I say what I have said here using less words, shorter words, or less-arcane language? If the answer is "yes," then do it. Get rid of the fat and down to the meat of your ideas.

The ability to effectively edit takes practice; one does not become a terrific editor overnight. And, good editing means spending serious time reflecting on your writing. While difficult, there are concerted means to improving one's editing. Here are a few tips for doing so:

1. Put the brief down and go back to it.

    Once your brief is finished, put it down and don't look at it for a day (you'll have plenty of time since you've constructed a backwards calendar and are ahead of the deadline!). When writers stare long enough at their computer screen and the words they have put onto it, they tend to miss errors. This phenomenon makes sense. If you constantly see something, and repeatedly scan past something, you are less apt to notice any deficiencies in that thing. The same approach happens with writing. So, put the brief down, and do something else. Go back to the brief the next day and take a look at your writing with fresh eyes.

2.   Consult writing guides.

There are several good sources for improving one's writing, and legal writing in particular. Some of those sources are cited in this chapter. Look at these texts for supplemental instruction in writing. One additional source that is a "classic" on writing is William Strunk, Jr. and E.B. White's *The Elements of Style*. There are several editions of the book; find one and use it. The book has served several generations well in learning to write more effectively, and, efficiently. Whatever guide you choose, be sure you invest time using it and improving your writing.

3.   Read your brief aloud.

This chapter's author will often discuss with a student their writing and will say to the student, "Does this sentence make sense to you?," followed by reading it aloud. The student invariably will say, "no; I didn't notice that." For whatever reason, when people write, they have a voice in their head, but that voice may miss errors in language. A tactic that can combat this problem is to read your writing aloud and listen to the text, if you will. If you read a statement in your brief aloud, and it does not make sense to you, rest assured it will likely make no sense to the person who will read it. So, read the brief to yourself and catch these errors. It will serve you well in the editing process.

CONCLUSION

In this chapter we have discussed how to write an effective moot court brief. Good brief writing takes time and effort. There is no substitute for hard work in this domain. Understanding the rules for the brief writing competition, and developing a reservoir of writing skills from which you can draw can seem difficult. The good news, however, is that writing is a skill that can be improved over time. Devote some time to this endeavor, and you are well on your way to composing an award winning brief.

CHAPTER 9

Conclusion

Moot court can be a transformational activity. Each of the authors of this book have seen remarkable student growth through participation in a moot court class and/or competition. This is true for many reasons.

1) Moot court provides for hands on learning. In this activity, students perform the tasks of an attorney including legal research and writing, and preparing and present an oral argument. Regardless of major or career path, each of these components of legal work provide a number of critical skills which can be used in nearly any profession.

2) Moot court is a High Impact exercise. As colleges and universities increasing emphasize the importance of High Impact Practices (HIP) such as faculty/student research collaborations and internships, moot court provides an occasion to participate in a meaningful HIP learning activity and build necessary skills that employers and law schools value. Further, the experience you will gain in moot court will likely be more hands on than a typical internship experience, as many internships will not offer you the opportunity to write and present their own arguments.

3) Moot court improves communication skills. Whether fair or not, and regardless of where your academic journey leads you, people will always judge you by the way you speak and the way you write. Fortunately, moot court will benefit you in both areas.

4) Moot court provides a host of other soft skills. These include enhanced critical thinking abilities under duress, improved legal research and writing skills, enhanced self-confidence, and poise. All of these may translate into enhanced acceptance rates into graduate schools and law schools.

5) Public speaking can be scary. Polls indicate that public speaking is the greatest fear of most Americans (even above heights and snakes which came in two and three).[1] 40% of survey respondents indicated a fear of speaking in front of others.[2] In fact, studies found that public speaking ranked even higher than death on the list of fears.[3] The good news for you, as readers of this text, is that this is a fear that can be overcome. Moot court will force you out of your comfort zone. It will put you in situations where you not only have to speak in front of others but also need to be able to think quickly and respond to questions. Through practice and experience, you will come out a much more comfortable and confident individual after having participated in moot court.

6) Moot court will make you a better writer. In each written activity you do as part of this process, from basic case

[1] https://www.washingtonpost.com/news/wonk/wp/2014/10/30/clowns-are-twice-as-scary-to-democrats-as-they-are-to-republicans/?utm_term=.ae9cc48ba013.

[2] http://time.com/89814/how-to-overcome-fear-of-public-speaking-and-give-a-great-presentation/.

[3] Dwyer, Karen & Davidson, Marlina. (2012). Is Public Speaking Really More Feared Than Death?. Communication Research Reports. 29. 99–107. 10.1080/08824096.2012.667772.

brief summaries to full blown appellate briefs, you will learn to read and focus on what is important in the law. Having to adhere to strict formatting and page limits will force you to boil down complex legal arguments to the essentials. The chapters contained in this book will teach you to write effectively, concisely, and persuasively.

7) Moot court is an excellent team building activity. Much like organized intercollegiate sports, this activity will help you learn to work with a partner and as part of a larger team. The ability to work well with others is useful in whatever career you choose. And, being part of a team which supports and cares for each other is a special feeling you will remember long after the competition has ended.

8) Moot court will help you prepare for law school American legal education relies principally upon the Socratic method of instruction: law students are required to arise upon demand and recite the facts of a case or to expound upon a legal doctrine while under the duress of probing inquiries of the law faculty. While requirements will vary from school to school, most American law schools still require that students participate in at least one moot court. Many law schools offer a series of moot court opportunities and organized competitions for students to enhance and demonstrate their legal and forensic skills. Undergraduate moot court thus prepares you for both the law school classroom and law school moot court.

9) Moot court can help you decide on a career path. Moot court is as close to a law school experience you can have as an undergraduate student. Many of the students the authors have worked with over the years have gone on to law school and eventually careers in the law.

However, many students also competed in moot court only to find that law school may not have been the right course for them. It is much better for you to find this out about yourself now, rather than after you spend three years and tens (or hundreds) of thousands of dollars to prepare for a career you don't love.

10) Moot court opportunities are rapidly growing. American undergraduate moot court tournaments have steadily grown in numbers over the past twenty years. Undergraduate competitions are presently organized throughout the nation by the American Moot Court Association (AMCA). Nearly 500 teams compete in AMCA sanctioned each year and that number continues to grow. There has never been a better time to put the skills you learn in this book into practice.

Bottom line—while moot court has all of the benefits listed above, it should also be fun. Make the most of this experience and enjoy the journey.

Important Legal Terms

Advisory Opinions: One of the Brandeis Rules. The Supreme Court is limited to actual cases and controversies and will not issue an opinion that advises government agents or branches as to the legality of a hypothetical government action.

Affirm Precedent: To uphold a prior decision or judgment. Often occurs when an appellate court sustains on appeal an opinion rendered by a trial court or a lower appellate court.

Amicus Curiae: Latin for "friend of the court." A legal brief submitted to a court on the behalf of a party who is not a direct party to a legal proceeding but who will likely be affected by the proceeding and thus has an interest in how it is resolved.

Appeal: To formally challenge the legal validity of a court decision. An appeal to a criminal verdict does not question whether a judge or jury made mistakes as far as reviewing evidence and determining facts go per se. Rather, an appeal questions the process through which the court rendered its decision. For instance, did the court err in how it interpreted the law, or in how it selected a jury? Other appeals may ask if a law or policy of the state violates some higher body of law such as the Constitution.

Appellant: The party to a case who lost in a lower court and appeals that decision to a higher court. The appellant would be the first to speak in oral argument before an appellate court.

Appellate Courts: A court that rules on challenges to the validity of decisions made by lower courts. Appellate courts do not decide questions of innocence or guilt. Instead, they judge whether lower courts erred in how they applied or interpreted the law or how they followed rules of legal procedure.

Appellee: The party to a case who won in a lower court. The appellant would be the second to speak in oral argument before an appellate court.

Applied Challenge: A challenge to a single application of a law to facts.

Apply: In legal terms, to make relevant to or be governed by. Often this has the effect of limiting the state. For instance, the decision to apply the free press clause of the First Amendment to the states means that the states were not to enact laws or adopt policies that restricted the freedom of the press.

Brandeis Rules: A summary of U.S. Supreme Court rules, doctrines, and traditions found in a concurring opinion written by Justice Louis Brandeis in the case of *Ashwander v. TVA* (1936). The Brandeis Rules summarize the types of opinions that the Court will not issue as well as the types of cases that the Court will not decide. They represent the Court's efforts to limit its own powers of review. Under the Brandeis Rules, the Court will only decide cases that involve a controversy and for which the parties have standing. The Court will not decide political questions, it will not rule in cases that are moot, or which can be remedied in another fashion, nor will it issue advisory opinions, or declaratory judgements.

Circuit Split: When different circuits are in direct disagreement.

Civil Law: A specific series of rules and regulations that are meant to guide human behavior and settle disputes among individuals. The civil law, which dates to the Roman Empire, is legislature-made law and is presented in a legal code which, if strictly followed, would decide disputes just as the legislature intended.

Common Law: A loose collection of legal decisions that, taken together, form precedent for future cases. The common law, which dates to medieval England, is judge-made law and does not appear in any code.

Concurring Opinion: An opinion written by a judge who votes with the majority in a case but does not necessarily agree with the majority's rationale or methodology or all of its conclusions. A concurring opinion may be used to offer an alternative approach to similar cases in the future as was the case in Justice Robert Jackson's concurring opinion in *The Steel Seizure Case* (1952). A concurrence may also be issued to emphasize what a majority opinion does not do, as was evident in Justice Harry Blackmun's concurring opinion in *NLC v. Usury* (1976).

Controlling Precedent: The court decision from the past that is most relevant to how a subsequent court should decide a legal question. A controlling precedent would dictate how a court engaging in *stare decisis* would decide a current legal issue.

De Facto: Of or by fact rather than law.

De Jure: Of or by law.

De Novo: Latin for starting anew. Under this standard, an appellate court can substitute its own conclusions about whether the court below correctly applied/followed the law. This relates to questions of law rather than questions of fact.

Declaratory Judgments: One of the Brandeis Rules. The Supreme Court will not advise persons of their rights. The Court will only rule on real cases and controversies when individuals have filed suits or have been brought to trial by the state.

Defendant: The party to a case who is sued, or who is arrested and charged with a crime.

Dicta: Ideas expressed in a court opinion that are not essential to the decision rendered in that specific case. These often include a judge's view of a subject in general. The singular of **dicta** is **dictum.**

Discretionary Functions: Actions taken by government officials which are matters of judgment rather than requirements of the law. Such functions are not susceptible to writs of *mandamus*. They would include decisions about taxes or whether to veto a specific bill.

Dispositive Fact: The key or most important fact in a case.

Dissenting Opinion: An opinion written by a judge who does not vote with the majority. Dissents focus on the aspects of the majority's reasoning that the dissenter believes are wrong. Some dissents offer alternative approaches for how similar cases may be decided in the future.

Distinguish Precedent: To argue that the principle established by or the holding of a past decision is not controlling in a current legal controversy. This is done by demonstrating that a key aspect of the past case, such as the facts, is different from the facts of the present case. A common motivation for **distinguishing** is to avoid a precedent that, if applied, would damage an argument. Another motivation for distinguishing is to avoid breaking new legal ground by overturning precedent. Distinguishing allows a court to chart a new legal course without reversing any precedent. The court would simply find that the precedent and the present case were significantly different and, thus, the new ruling did not overrule the past ruling because they did not address the same issue(s). In *Alden v. Maine* (1999), for instance, the Supreme Court limited the ability of citizens to sue states under federal statutes. In *Garcia v. SAMTA* (1985), the Court had affirmed a federal law that allowed citizens to sue a local transportation authority. Rather than reverse *Garcia, Alden* differentiated the facts of the two cases. Because *Garcia* involved a local agency and *Alden* involved a state, the Court reasoned its decision to limit Congress's ability to enable citizens to sue state governments did not necessarily limit its ability to enable citizens to sue local governments. A key point to keep in mind with respect to distinguishing is that the force or breadth of the precedent is not lessened with respect to the facts from which it was derived, or to future cases that raise the same facts.

Doctrine: A set of principles that guide behavior. For instance, the Doctrine of Selective Incorporation provided a method for determining which liberties found in the Bill of Rights applied solely to Congress and which of these liberties applied to state and local governments.

Doctrine of Mootness: One of the Brandeis Rules. The Supreme Court will not decide a case if events have rendered its opinion no longer needed.

Doctrine of Ripeness: One of the Brandeis Rules. The Supreme Court will typically not issue a ruling unless the case is ready to be decided. All other legal or administrative remedies must be exhausted. It is possible, however, in cases of emergency or when time is short, such as in *Bush v. Gore* (2000), that the Court will take the unusual step of deciding a case before a lower court is finished with its deliberations.

Doctrine of Standing: One of the Brandeis Rules. The Supreme Court will not address a case unless the plaintiff can illustrate a real legal claim or right and that he or she is personally affected by the case.

Due Process of Law: Refers to legal processes or procedures that treat individuals in a fair manner.

Equity: The traditional power of judges at the common law to, in the name of fairness and justice, offer relief to party in instances when the law does not prescribe any remedy.

Ex Parte: Latin phrase meaning "on the side of" or "on the application of." Often associated with requests from one side, such as a prisoner, for an appeal to a specific policy or a specific public act.

***Ex Post Facto* Law:** Latin phrase meaning "after the fact." A law that retroactively makes a certain action a crime, or retroactively increases the penalty that an individual convicted of a specific criminal act would face. Traditionally, to be deemed *ex post facto,* a law must be penal in nature; however, the Supreme Court, in *Fletcher v. Peck* (1810), held that a civil law that has a similar "effect" as an *ex post facto* law might in fact be considered to be an *ex post facto* law.

Extend Precedent: When a court interprets precedent to apply to a different set of facts or to achieve a result unintended by the court that issued the original precedent. For example, *Eisenstadt v. Baird* (1972) extended the Supreme Court's decision in *Griswold v. Ct* (1965) by recognizing a general right of marital reproductive privacy to promulgate a more general right of reproductive privacy that protected all persons.

Facial Challenge: A claim that a statute is always unconstitutional.

Federal Courts of Appeals: Federal appellate courts created using Congress's powers under Article III of the U.S. Constitution. There are 13 federal courts of appeals. These courts settle most federal appeals. Eleven of the courts of appeals serve multi-state regions known as circuits. The other two circuits exist to hear appeals that involve federal bureaucratic agencies or patent disputes and contract lawsuits filed against the United States.

Federal District Courts: Federal trial courts created using Congress's powers under Article III of the U.S. Constitution. There are over 600 federal district courts; each one serving a specific state. The number of federal district courts per state is determined by population.

Good Faith: The presumption that a party acted in a manner it believed was legal and/or the presumption that a claimed interest on the part of the state is genuine and not *post-hoc*.

In re: Latin phrase meaning "in the matter of."

Join the Judgement: When a Justice joins the outcome but not the rationale of an opinion.

Join the Opinion: When a Justice joins both the outcome and the rationale of an opinion.

Judicial Deference: The act of yielding to or accepting the judgment of another party.

Judicial Notice: The authority of courts to accept certain facts by way of common knowledge without the need for specific evidence.

Judicial Review: The power of courts to find a law or policy invalid.

Jurisdiction: A court's authority to rule on a specific case or issue.

Legal Brief: A written summary of legal arguments that is submitted to a court by or, most commonly, on behalf of a specific party to a legal proceeding.

Legal Conclusion: A conclusion about the law based on the facts of case. E.g., the police needed a warrant because there was no exigent circumstances to prevent obtaining a warrant.

Legal Facts: The events that transpired between individuals, groups, or states that lead to a judicial proceeding. E.g., the police entered the home without a warrant.

Legal Precedent: A decision that influences how future cases that raise similar questions will be decided. A legal precedent becomes a part of the law that is reapplied when courts engage in *stare decisis*.

Legislative Courts: Special courts created using Congress's powers under Article I, Section 8 of the U.S. Constitution. Legislative courts provide technical expertise on specific subjects such as taxes, immigration, or military issues. Judges on such courts typically serve fixed terms.

Limiting Precedent: When a court revises existing precedent so that it still has the force of law but means less than it did in the past. In *Casey v. Planned Parenthood of Southeastern Pennsylvania* (1992), for instance, the Supreme Court reaffirmed that abortion was a right protected by the U.S. Constitution. At the same time, *Casey* altered existing precedent under *Roe v. Wade* (1973) to expand both when the state could restrict access to abortion and the types of limits the state could place on women seeking to procure an abortion. In doing so, the Court narrowed the breadth of the *Roe* decision.

Majority Opinion: A formal or written opinion that presents a verdict in a court case and explains the rationale behind the majority's decision. Most commonly associated with appellate courts.

Mandatory Opinion: A majority opinion of the Supreme Court of the United States.

Martial Law: The absence of civilian law in favor of rule by military authorities.

Narrow Opinion: An opinion that is focused solely on the issue at hand and does not overturn any precedent or decide or address any extraneous questions. An opinion that is "narrow" seldom recognizes any new rights or affirms any sweeping government powers. For that reason, it is often the choice of a court that would prefer to keep its opinions limited in scope and reach.

Overbreadth: A regulation of a basic liberty that is too broad or too restrictive; one that goes beyond the government's needs or interests and restricts the people's rights in a way that is excessive.

Overturn Precedent: When a court rules that a past legal decision is no longer valid or correct. In doing so, the court reverses the past decision and replaces it with a new one. The Supreme Court's decision in *Brown v. Board of Education* (1954), in forbidding racial discrimination by state or local governments, repealed its previous ruling in *Plessy v. Ferguson* (1896), which had allowed the state to discriminate on the basis of race.

Per Curium Opinion: An unsigned opinion of the Court. Often issued because there was no one single or true author of an opinion.

Persuasive Opinion: A non-Supreme Court opinion or a plurality Supreme Court opinion. One that is not mandatory but rather the deciding body must be persuaded to follow or apply it.

Petitioner: The party who requests a court to issue an order or an injunction.

Plaintiff: The party to a case who sues or brings charges against another party.

Plurality Opinion: An opinion of fewer than five Justices that settles an immediate controversy, but does not set precedent because it lacks a majority of the full Court.

Political Question Doctrine: A Brandeis Rule. The Supreme Court will not decide questions that constitutionally are delegated to the political branches of the federal government. These include questions relating to Indian tribes, the validity of the enactment process of constitutional amendments, dates and duration of hostilities, questions relating to the Guaranty Clause of the U.S. Constitution, and foreign relations. For more on this doctrine see *Baker v. Carr* (1962).

***Prima Facie* Evidence:** Latin for "on its face." Refers to evidence, that unless rebuked, is strong enough upon which to draw a legal conclusion or fact.

Real Legal Controversy: One of the Brandeis Rules. The Supreme Court will not decide "friendly lawsuits" between parties who are merely curious about the law or cases that do not involve a party who has been wronged by another party. There must be a real issue or dispute involving an imminent danger presented.

Remand: To send a case back to a lower court for further proceedings in keeping with the higher court's ruling. When a court does this it sets aside (or **vacates**) the lower court's ruling.

Remedy: What the moving party is requesting of the court.

Respondent: The party who opposes the request of a petitioner.

Rule: A broad declaration of precedent to guide future cases. E.g., there is a right to counsel.

Ruling: Answers a specific legal issues such as whether to affirm or reverse a lower court.

Slip Opinion: A written opinion that is published on-line but is temporary. A slip opinion issue by the Supreme Court is the first edition of an opinion to be posted on the Court's website. Slip opinions remain on-line until all of the opinions for a full Term are published in bound form. Slip opinions lack pagination and if there are discrepancies between the print edition and the slip opinion the former typically prevails.

Standard of Review: There is more than one use of this term. One concerns the level of deference that a court provides to a lower court when reviewing its decision. For example, *de novo*. The other refers to different levels of judicial balancing tests. For example, strict scrutiny, intermediate scrutiny, or rational basis review.

Stare Decisis: Latin for "let the prior decision stand." This term refers to when a court decides a case or answers a legal question in the present in accordance with how it was decided in the past.

Statute: A law enacted by a legislature.

Statutory Interpretation: When judges read and give effect to statutes by applying them to the cases before them. An example is *Smith v. U.S.* (1993).

Summary Judgement: A judgement entered by a court in favor of one party without a full trial.

Trial Courts: A court that determines whether accused parties or persons are guilty or innocent of the charges against them. This is known as "trying facts."

Vacate: To set aside a lower court ruling.

Writ of *Certiorari:* Latin phrase for "to make more certain." Judicial order that instructs a lower court to send up the records of a specific case for review by a higher court. If the U.S. Supreme Court issues a **writ of *certiorari***, it is agreeing to consider the appellant's case on appeal.

Writ of *Habeas Corpus:* A Latin phrase meaning "you have the body." There are several different *writs* of *habeas corpus*. They include court orders to free a prisoner who has been unfairly or illegally jailed, and a court order to a jailer bring a detained party before a court for due process.

Writ of *Mandamus:* Latin phrase for "we command." A court order instructing a government official to carry out some nondiscretionary function. Such would include delivering commissions or performing a nationwide census.

Major Electronic Publishers[1]

Today, students studying the law have numerous electronic choices to peruse. Depending on the resources of your library, there should be multiple sources of electronic material that you may have access to for doing your research. It is not necessary that you learn all of them, because you will quickly find that some materials are replicated within each of the databases. Instead, we suggest you experiment with the different sources to see what works the best for you, and then learn to become a professional at searching that database. Access to a certain data source is based on what your library has acquired.

The two major electronic publishers—LexisNexis Academic Universe and Westlaw—grew up in the 1970s as a response to a need attorneys had to access the most recent information available. Both of these of these organizations have transformed and grown radically, so that today they constitute the leading sources of commercial on-line legal databases. Each emphasizes U.S. law (including case law, statutes and regulations, legal texts, news, and other information), but within the last decade, both have increased their data for international and comparative law. Both are a "fee-based" service—you have to be a subscriber. Depending on the subscription service that your university or college has, you may or may not have access to some types of databases that are available to commercial users.

---

[1]   The authors recognize Adam Whitten who was a co-contributor to this appendix.

LexisNexis Academic Universe

LexisNexis Academic Universe is another online legal source, provides news databases and law-related information from around the world.[2] As a division of Reed Elsevier Inc., it is part of a mega-publishing company that includes other publishers such as Matthew Bender and Martindale-Hubbell. Material is updated daily, and it uses a search engine that relies on terms and connectors (Boolean search) and natural language (Freestyle), as well as a template that takes you through a guided search so you can tailor your research. Most information is provided through clicking on "tabs" specifying the material you need. We suggest that you rely on the "Guided Search" options where you can because this makes accessing the database much easier. Lexis is the law-related research side of the database, while Nexis allows you to conduct research in all major newspapers, journals, magazines and other sources. There is an on-line tutorial that walks you through sample searches according to the material you need to find.

Westlaw

Westlaw is part of the West Group, which is a traditional publishing source and is well known for having developed the case reporter system that we use today. West Group was the first to develop the "key number" system, which allows you to find core legal issues and concepts through a "headnote" classification. The Canadian-based Thomson Corporation bought the American company in 1996. With Westlaw you can search using terms and connectors (also known as Boolean search strings), a template that guides you through the process, or with natural language called the WIN system (Westlaw is Natural). Before beginning your searches, you need to specify what directories you want to access. After you do this, the program takes you through a search through the utilization of point & click methods or pull-down

---

[2]   Please note that some universities are moving to another Lexis-Nexis product called NexisUni. See here for a comparison of the two databases: https://www.lexisnexis.com/pdf/academic/nexis-uni/nexis-uni-faq.pdf.

menus. Westlaw also maintains an on-line tutorial that is helpful. We suggest you complete it before beginning your research.

LegalTrac

LegalTrac maintains almost a million articles from legal publications beginning in 1980, including academic law reviews, law journals, and materials from commercial publishers. You may use the "Subject Guide" search, which provides all the different substantive areas where you can search. Under each subject heading you will then find a set of articles that correspond to your subject area. You can then search within the different subject headings to suit your needs. LegalTrac also allows you to do a "relevance" search which relies on word variations in combination or alone. For example, say you wanted to research euthanasia, you might also search on physician-assisted suicide or right-to-die. LegalTrac allows you to take those word variations into consideration. You can also search on key word terms, rather than depending on the "subject" headings that you are given. Finally, under more advanced procedures you can search on combinations of items to help make your search more specific. Thus you can search by key word, journal or title name, author, or abstract to help you more quickly identify articles that are appropriate for you.

Legal Information Institute

This free, web-based resource is operated by the Cornell Law School and began in the 1990s to give comprehensive information about a broad range of legal issues. It also provides useful links to other legal reference resources, including non-legal sources that help with researching policy issues. The site also provides access to law reviews, abstracts, and full text articles, and professional information relevant to both law students and lawyers. The website also provides comprehensive information about the workload of the federal courts. It provides federal and state materials including U.S. Supreme Court opinions, state statutes, federal regulations, and state codes. You search for sources by key word or by topic listings that are provided. You should be sure to look through the search tips before beginning to do searches on the website because there is a great deal of information. Also included is a gallery of all U.S. Supreme Court Justices throughout history with short biographical sketches as well as a useful glossary of legal terms.

CourtListener

This free service has three-million plus legal opinions from federal and state courts and it has a RECAP archive. It also has many Supreme Court oral argument audio recordings, and some from state courts. One unique database it has is info on judges from federal and state courts including the background, legal accomplishments, and critical opinions that have been decided.

CAP API

The Caselaw Access Project was built by digitizing the Harvard Law School Library and Ravel (now owned by LexisNexis and listed below). It has broad usage available for free covering 6.5 million unique cases from 1658 to 2018. There are some limits on access so check those before beginning your project.

LoisLaw

This is a paid fee (subscription service) that runs off a web-based search engine and includes case laws, statutory law, constitutions, administrative law, court rules, and state materials. It also has limited access to U.S. and foreign legal publications. You need to rely on a subject index and provide key word search delimiters. This is typically only available at law schools.

Versuslaw

A fee-based service on the web that allows access to federal and state case law, legislation, and codes. The materials are somewhat limited but provide basic information. You can search in a full-text format or by using terms and connectors (Boolean search strings). Unless you are an undergraduate at a school that has a law library, this will probably not be available to you.

Quicklaw

Subscription-based online service that provides case law, primary and secondary legal materials, and other resources relevant for doing legal research on the United States, the United Kingdom, Canada, and the Commonwealth. There is also a general collection of treaties and international laws of all jurisdictions arranged by subject. There is also a wide variety of legal communication materials, including electronic newsletters analyzing specific issues, attorney and legal profession directories, and book reviews. Information is arranged through topic, so you have to use it according to subject and key word database. Law schools may have this resource, so if you are an undergraduate enrolled at such an institution, see if you can get access to it.

Fastcase

Fee-based online service that provides case law, primary and secondary legal materials, and other resources relevant for doing legal research in the United States. You can search in a full-text format or by using terms and connectors (Boolean search strings).

Casemaker

Fee-based online service that provides case law, primary and secondary legal materials, and other resources relevant for doing legal research in the United States. You can search in a full-text format or by using terms and connectors (Boolean search strings).

Casetext

Fee-based online service that is low cost and has all federal cases and statutes, and all state cases and statutes beyond the trial court decision. It identifies cases that have been overruled and provides links to cases being cited in the case you are reading. It also has a Black Letter Law database that has well-settled points of law. It also has CARA, an artificial intelligence program which lets lawyers upload documents, such as briefs or complaints and does searches tailored to what is being researched.

Ravel Law

Like other fee-based data sources, Ravel contains published cases, from every state and federal court from an extended time period and has comprehensive coverage of unpublished cases after May 15, 2015. Prior to that, coverage of unpublished cases is broad but *not* comprehensive. It uses Boolean and natural language, and you can limit searches by jurisdiction. What makes Ravel unique is that it provides visual representations of case citation frequency so you can see connections between cases and the way in which cases are being used.

Things Someone Should Have Told You (but Probably Didn't)[1]

1. Wear business attire, but be sure you are comfortable in the shoes and clothes you choose because you may have to walk distances to reach your scheduled "courtroom." Do not wear something for the first time to a competition or simulation. Be sure you know whether it is too tight, scratches, rubs, pulls, or whatever before you have to wear it for several hours!

2. As a general rule, courts tend to be conservative, so dress and look appropriate. The rule of thumb is, if you were a criminal defendant before the court, how would you want the judge and jury to perceive you? It is not fair, but you can be judged based on what you are wearing. When in doubt, ask your coach or professor about whether something is appropriate.

3. Keep hair and jewelry out of your way. Things that rattle on your body when you move or hair that gets in your eyes not only distracts you but the panel as well and diminishes your effectiveness by diverting attention from your argument.

4. Do not eat a big or greasy meal one to two hours prior to your presentation.

---

[1] The authors recognize Adam Whitten who was a co-contributor to this appendix.

5.   Have antacids, headache medicine, or cough drops with you in case you need them.

6.   Take a watch (that does not beep) with you in case the bailiff does not have one. Take water with you into the room if none is provided, and if it is permitted. If not, go to get a drink before you enter the room. Take something to write with, something to write on, and a copy of the record with you.

7.   Turn off all cell phones.

8.   Use the bathroom before the round and limit fluid intake, especially those drinks with caffeine, an hour before your presentation.

9.   Arrive at the "courtroom" at least 5–10 minutes early before your scheduled argument time. If the courtroom is empty, go in and sit at the appropriate counsel table.

10.   Petitioner/Appellant sits on the left (as you are facing the bench), and Respondent/Appellee sits on the right. Be sure to put your names on the chalk/dry erase board, along with the number of minutes each person will be speaking (include rebuttal times if you are the Petitioner/Appellant).

11.   Be sure to inform the bailiff about rebuttal time when he or she arrives. Ask the bailiff about time cards and in what increments the time cards will be given. You may also want to ask if the bailiff will stand up when time is up.

12.   Ask the bailiff whether the judges are going to give you feedback immediately following the round in person, or whether the judges give comments only on the score sheet.

13.   When the bailiff brings in the judges or the judges arrive on their own, stand up and stay standing until you receive a signal (nod) to sit down from the bench (typically the judge that has been designated as the "Chief Justice". The Petitioner should proceed directly to the podium and wait for another signal or statement from the judge to begin.

14. Be sure that you do not know the judges or have a conflict of interest. When in doubt, have the bailiff check with the persons who are running the competition or simulation to be sure that the round can proceed.

15. When it is your turn to speak, go directly to the podium, place your notes on it, and await a signal or statement from the judge. Step back a couple of paces from the podium to let the judges know that you are awaiting their sign.

16. NEVER talk to your co-counsel while opposing counsel is presenting—write notes if you have to communicate. *Do not make faces either*—you look unprofessional when you do that! If opposing counsel speaks during your presentation, simply ignore them and keep being persuasive.

17. At competitions, NEVER identify what school you are from. If you are asked by the judges or the bailiff, inform the judges that you were instructed not to tell by your coach or professor.

18. In general, just take brief notes to the podium. If necessary, you may step back to your table during argument to get something (brief, copy of statutes, etc.).

19. Be yourself! Do not speak in a phony style or voice.

20. Do not be afraid to make concessions or indicate there are things that you do not know if you do not know them.

21. If you have tough questioning, do not give up. Hang in there and emphasize what you do know. Make a mental note that you will be more prepared the next time.

22. Do not tell the panel you are unprepared, cannot answer questions, or make excuses for why you are not performing well. Keep emphasizing the key points about your client's case.

23. If judges ask the same question, it means that they did not like your answer the first time. Be wary of simply reiterating what you said

before. Try to clarify it, or address more directly what the panel is asking for.

24. Never make things up that are not in the record or make up cases that do not exist. You might get away with it, but if you do not, and they bust you for it, you will most definitely get points lowered.

25. If there is a "hypothetical" the bench asks you about, try to show why the hypothetical does not apply, or how the rule you are suggesting could account for that hypothetical. Always remind the court what the issue is before the court and keep your focus on that. Do NOT get hung up on the hypothetical, answer it and move back to your argument.

26. Have fun with this! Oral argument should be an adrenaline rush, not an assignment from purgatory. Smile and enjoy the chance to show off how much you have learned.

27. Be confident, but not cocky and arrogant, about your argument. Remember to always look like you are winning and to use your best advocate tone of voice to persuade the court that you believe in your client's case.

28. Make sure you use all your time and use it effectively. If you are in the middle of answering a question and time is up, be sure to say: "I see my time is up. May I finish my response?" Briefly summarize, but keep it brief!

29. When you are done, say "Thank you, your honor(s)" and sit down.

30. In competition rounds, you should leave the room immediately and wait close to the room for the judges to bring you back in to give you a critique. Tournament directors at competitions will tell judges how long judges have to give you a critique. If the judges are going too long, be polite, and let the bailiff know that you need to go to your next round so that hopefully the bailiff will inform the panel. Always keep an eye on your time and get to the next round as soon as possible.

31. In all rounds (but this typically only happens in medal or final rounds), when the judges stand, you should stand and stay standing until the judge leaves the room or comes down to greet you.

32. At the end of the entire round of argument, stand up and walk over to shake the hands of your opponents. Always be gracious, no matter how difficult or nasty the round may have been.

33. If the judges are giving you feedback in the round, sit quietly until they do so. If not, thank everyone including opposing counsel for their time, gather your materials and leave the room. Do a quick check to be sure you have not left anything.

34. DO NOT discuss your round with others in the hallway. Wait until you have privacy and can speak where you cannot be heard. You can never know who might be listening.

Common Boolean Terms and Connectors

Both LexisNexis Academic Universe and Westlaw rely on Boolean connectors for doing full text searches. You will find when you access the sources that there is a menu that can walk you through the search. This sheet is more of a quick reference guide to give you an idea of most commonly used terms.

LexisNexis Academic Universe	Terms & Connectors
and	and
or	or
phrase	" "
in the same sentence	ws
in the same paragraph	wp
with n terms of (n = 1–255)	w/n
but not	and not
root expander	!
universal character	*

Citations, Title, Source, Author, Text, Date functions done through the pull-down menu and not done in conjunction with full-text search as the case with Westlaw.

Westlaw	Terms & Connectors
and	&
or	(leave a space)
phrase	" "
in the same sentence	/s
in the same paragraph	/p
preceding within sentence	+s
preceding within paragraph	+p
with *n* terms of (*n* = 1–255)	/*n*
preceding within *n* terms of (*n* = 1–255)	+*n*
but not	%
root expander	!
universal character	*

Fields

Citation	CI ( )
Title	TI ( )
Source	SO ( )
Author	AU ( )
Text	TE ( )
Date	DA (Aft 00/00/00 mm/dd/yy and Bef 00/00/00) mm/dd/yy

Internet Legal Resources[1]

Source	Web Address	Materials
Justia	*https://www.justia.com/*	General site containing multiple sources
FindLaw.Com	*www.findlaw.com*	General site containing multiple sources
Legal Information Institute	*http://www.law.cornell.edu*	Cornell Law School data source for federal and state laws
The Oyez Project	*https://www.oyez.org/*	Multimedia archive of U.S. Supreme Court cases, including recordings of oral arguments
SCOTUSBlog	*https://www.scotusblog.com/*	Blog managed by Supreme Court practitioners covering current and past cases; provides timelines and links to case documents, as well as articles on current cases
Google Scholar	*https://scholar.google.com/*	Case law from all federal and state courts; academic articles
The Founders' Constitution	*http://press-pubs.uchicago. edu/founders/*	University of Chicago Press links to important Constitutional documents and materials

---

[1] The authors recognize Adam Whitten who was a co-contributor to this appendix.

195

Source	Web Address	Materials
govinfo	*https://www.govinfo.gov/*	Provides free public access to official publications from all three branches of the Federal Government
U.S. Supreme Court	*https://www.supremecourt.gov/*	Full text of opinions, rules, includes briefs & oral arguments
Federal Courts	*https://www.uscourts.gov/*	Gateway to all federal courts and opinions—official site
State Courts	*https://www.ncsc.org/*	Gateway to all state courts and opinions—official site
Library of Congress	*http://www.loc.gov/*	Gateway to government publications & lists of text-based sources for research-official site
U.S. Code	*http://uscode.house.gov/*	Full text of U.S. codes—official site
Congress.gov	*https://www.congress.gov/*	Full text of federal bills from the 93rd Congress to the present
Congressional Record	*https://www.congress.gov/congressional-record*	Official U.S. site to *Congressional Record*
Code of Federal Regulations	*https://www.govinfo.gov/app/collection/CFR*	Complete text of current Code of Federal Regulations
Federal Register	*https://www.federalregister.gov/*	Official site of the *Federal Register*
Regulations.gov	*https://www.regulations.gov/*	Website for official public comments during notice and comment period when adopting new regulations
The U.S. Government's Official Web Portal	*https://www.usa.gov/*	U.S. official website that contains numerous government publications & law sources
U.S. State Department	*https://www.state.gov/*	Access to resources for international laws

Source	Web Address	Materials
State & Local Government on the Net	*http://www.statelocalgov.net/*	Gateway to state & local government websites
Law Library Resource Exchange	*http://www.llrx.com*	General site containing multiple sources

How to Brief a Case

Before briefing the case, read over it and focus on the substantive and procedural issues. What started the conflict, what action is being sought? What policy issues are at stake? Think about the type of proceeding (e.g., appeal from a summary judgment, judgment after trial, etc.) and the type of relief sought (e.g., damages, injunction, etc.). Be efficient in reading cases and writing briefs. This does not mean "skimming" a case, but it means recognizing which information should go where in your brief. Develop a system for quickly and precisely marking the case so that important passages are easily identified in a concise and accurate manner.

Remember that preparing briefs improves your legal reasoning skills. Briefs synthesize cases into basic points so you can quickly access information. Briefing requires that you study the essential facts and reasoning from the court's opinion and succinctly express them in your own words. This helps you develop a critical facet of legal reasoning—the ability to put complex matters into simple form. Use the court's terminology only if it helps you understand the case or there is a specific standard, test, or rule the court is articulating. Try to use your own language as if you were explaining it to a friend and avoid legal-ease. This enhances your understanding of the case. Remember, it is not a typing exercise but an exercise in critical thinking!

The first three or four briefs are the hardest—taking you about two hours at first, and about 45–60 minutes for the next few after that.

Eventually briefs will take only 20–30 minutes (depending on the length of the original or the excerpt). You are thinking and writing in a completely different way, using words that you may have never heard before. As you are more comfortable speaking and understanding the language, identifying issues, and moving quickly through sections, you will become more adept. If you come across words you do not understand, be sure to use an on-line legal source or *Black's Law Dictionary*.

Structure is essential to your briefs because it allows you to organize the arguments, so set your briefs up with the **facts**; **issue**; **reasoning**; and **holding**. Pay attention to the concurring and dissenting opinions so you can fully understand the case.

Facts

(7–9 sentences) A synopsis of the key case facts that deal with the conflict and how it came about. Structure this in a logical sequence of events. While some cases conveniently summarize the facts at the beginning, some cases require the facts be drawn from the entire opinion (including the concurring and dissenting opinions)! The facts are a short statement of the events and transactions that led to the initiation of the legal action. Some of the "facts" may be in dispute, and you should note this. Be sure to note which facts are *relevant*. Think about how it adds to understanding the case. Do not judge which facts are relevant until you read over the entire case, as the ultimate determination may turn on something that seems insubstantial.

Identify the role played by each party where relevant, and indicate whether they are the "plaintiff," "defendant," "appellant," "appellee," "respondent," or "petitioner," but also associate them by the name as it may appear in the title of the case. Bear in mind that the party presently seeking something from the court may not be the plaintiff and that sometimes only the cross-claim of a defendant is addressed. Confusing the parties can ruin your analysis and understanding. Be sure you know "who's suing whom" and pay attention to what laws are in conflict, or how different parties are relying on the same law but reaching different interpretations. Where possible cite the law in a way that you will remember it (memorizing numbers from statutes is often a waste of time).

Issue

(1–2 sentences) A statement of the legal question answered by the case. For clarity, the issue is best if put in the form of a question with a "yes" or "no" answer. The issue is simply the rule of law handed down. Though the complexity of case issues varies, a concise, single-sentence question should sum it up. If a case presents more than one issue, express each issue separately in a single-sentence question, and number each issue accordingly (issue 1, issue 2, etc.).

The problem is discerning what is *the* issue raised in the case. A case will say it raises and then answers several questions. Typically, there are only one or two such questions before the court. A question or statement not central to resolving the controversy is addressed in language known as *obiter dictum* or "remarks by the way." Dicta are comments not necessary for the final disposition of the case, but such observations clarify and explain something about the appropriate rule of law. While you may incorporate this in the brief, do not place it with the issue. To find the issue, ask *who wants what* and then ask *why that party succeeded or failed to get it.* Then take the "why" and turn it into your "yes" or "no" question.

Reasoning

(3–12 paragraphs, but this will vary substantially according to the number of issues and case complexity) ***This is the most important section of your brief and you should spend most of your time on it.*** Note which justice is the author of the opinion, and think about the policy and legal issues at stake in the court's decision. What are the policy ramifications of a decision to favor one party over another? What rule of law is being clarified? Why is the court adopting one interpretation over other potential interpretations? How does the court reconcile the present decision with prior case law? Pay attention to the case law on which the court relies. You should try to follow the I-R-A-

C form discussed in the chapters of this text, identifying the RULE and the APPLICATION in the reasoning section. What legal rules does the Court use to favor one party over another? Be sure to quote that case law into your RULE section to show the court's interpretation. How are cases distinguished that contradict the present decision? What cases are pivotal and most important? Create links between the interpretation and the decision to favor specific reasoning. What rule of law does the court favor and why? Then how does the Court apply this rule to the specific facts of this case? What key facts of this particular case make the Court's decision result in this particular outcome?

The rule and application the most difficult parts to do, and you should go through the Court's opinion paragraph by paragraph. After each one, try to synthesize what was presented into a summary sentence. Only refer to cases that are critical to the court's decision because numerous cases will be cited. You want to highlight only the most important ones. You do not have to put the citation to the case, but try to put the year with it to keep track of how precedent has developed over time.

Holding and Decision

(5–7 sentences) A succinct explanation of the rationale for the decision that tells you who wins and loses, and why, including the concise rule of law in two sentences. What is the general principle of law which the case illustrates? In distilling the reasoning, always include an application of the general rule or rules of law to the specific case fact. Bring to light the court's implicit justifications and reasons for the rule, the policy issues, and those critical factors that ultimately shape the case outcome. Be careful in selecting the rule of law. Cases typically present more than one legal ruling. How to find the decisive rule of law? If a particular legal ruling is only a step in the court's overall argument, then most likely it is not the decisive rule of law. A rule of law is decisive when the final conclusion or statement of the law determines why one party wins over the other.

Concurring & Dissenting Opinions

(5–7 sentences per opinion) A summary of the main points that compares and contrasts how and why the author of the opinion agrees, disagrees, or would like to clarify key points with the majority opinion. Confine the points to critical differences between the opinions that will help you remember strengths and weaknesses about the majority opinion. Remember that concurring and dissenting opinions are written because there is something "left unsaid" or "misrepresented" in the majority opinion.

Sample Case Brief[1]

Masterpiece Cakeshop v. Colorado Civil Rights Commission,
584 U.S. ___ (2018) (7–2)

Facts: Jack Phillips, the owner of Masterpiece Cakeshop, refused to make a wedding cake for Charlie Craig and David Mullins who were about to be married. Phillips argued he could not make the cake because it would compel him to use his artistic talents to express a message with which he disagreed and requiring him to do so would violate his religious beliefs. For him, decorating cakes is a way in which he expresses himself and honors God, and it would be against his religion to make cakes for same sex marriages which he sees as a sin. Craig and Mullins filed discrimination charges with the Colorado Civil Rights Division saying Phillips' actions violated the Colorado Anti-Discrimination Act (CADA), §§ 24–34–301 to –804, C.R.S. 2014 which prohibits discrimination based on sexual orientation in public accommodations. The Administrative Law Judge found for Craig and Mullins, the Colorado Civil Rights Commission (CCRC) affirmed, as did the Colorado Court of Appeals.

Issue: Did the CCRC err in rejecting a cake shop owner's reasons for declining to make a wedding cake for a same-sex couple thus violating First Amendment of rights of expression and free exercise? YES

---

[1] The authors recognize Victoria Magallanes and Jordan Hyden who were co-contributors to this appendix.

Issue [framed differently]: Can the state require a baker (under a state public accommodations law) to provide a product which violates his religious beliefs? NO

Reasoning: (Kennedy) Gay persons and same-sex couples have the same civil rights protections under law, but religious objections to the practice of same-sex marriage is protected expression. The Colorado law prohibiting disparate treatment against gay persons or same sex couples in public accommodations must be applied neutrally toward religion. Phillips' artistic expression and his sincerely held religious beliefs means that forcing him to do so violates fundamental principles of the First Amendment.

Supreme Court jurisprudence has evolved since 2012 when Phillips refused to serve Craig and Mullins. Same sex marriage has only more recently been settled (see *U.S. v. Windsor*, 570 U.S. 744 (2013) and *Obergefell v. Hodges*, 576 U.S. ___ (2015)). Even though there were other similar cases like Phillips before the CCRC, it was reasonable for Phillips to act as he did. The CCRC should have been neutral, but instead was hostile, in their treatment toward Phillips' religious beliefs. The commissioners' comments disparaged Phillips' religion and were inappropriate. In three other cases, bakers had objected when customers wanted anti-gay messages, refused customers, and the CCRC upheld the bakers' refusals. This creates concerns about fairness.

Concurring: (Thomas & Gorsuch concurring in part & concurring in judgment) address speech issue left open by SCOTUS. Conduct is not protected speech just because it expresses an idea, it depends on whether it is "intended to be communicative". Creation of a custom cake is expressive because of consultation Phillips does with client. Putting a "disclaimer" message out, or the fact that the bakery is "for profit" held out to the public does not matter. The state cannot compel the message.

Concurring: (Gorsuch and Alito concurring) address application of Employment Div. v. Smith (1990) peyote case which held a neutral and generally applicable law will usually survive a constitutional free exercise challenge, BUT if government fails to act neutrally or acts in a hostile manner toward religious freedom it must satisfy the strict scrutiny standard and show a compelling government interest that is narrowly tailored to achieve that interest (*Church of Lukumi Babalu Aye, Inc. v. Hialeah* (1993) animal sacrifice case). Case here protects both. CCRC not neutral—it upheld the decision of 3 bakers who refused baked goods with anti-gay message (customer alleged it was a sincerely held religious belief to be anti-gay marriage). Focusing on a protected category (religious freedom, gay persons) does not help solve issue. Atheist might want an anti-gay cake, and heterosexual customer might want a gay cake, it was the kind of cake, not the kind of customer.

Concurring: (Kagan and Breyer) Agreed with the majority that Phillips had not been treated with neutrality by the CCRC. Disagrees with the majority that the CCRC violated the law by treating the cases of Phillips and Silva (the other baker who refused to provide baked goods because of anti-gay messages) differently. Questions turns on the protected status of the person seeking access to the good or service.

Dissent: (Ginsburg and Sotomayor) Commission's comments about Phillips' religious views nor handling of bakers refusing to make cakes with anti-gay messages means Phillips should win. Phillips never gave evidence that objective observer would see wedding cake as conveying message or that observer understands message as bakers. Jack (man who wanted cake with anti-gay message) case and Masterpiece are quite different because Jack requested cakes with particular text inscribed, Craig and Mullins were refused the sale of any wedding cake at all-turned away before any specific cake design discussed.

Holding: The Colorado Civil Rights Commission was hostile in its application of the CADA when balancing the sincerely held religious beliefs of a baker (who refused to provide a wedding cake to a same sex couple) with the states interests in protecting access to public accommodations. CCRC actions and statements against the baker were viewpoint discrimination and violated principles of neutrality toward religion under the First Amendment as incorporated to apply to the states under the Fourteenth Amendment Due Process Clause.

Quick Checklist for Oral Argument

- Do you have an outline of your argument reduced to 1–2 typed pages that sketches the key points of your case?

- Do you and your partner each have the most current copy of your arguments to share with each other?

- Do you have a copy of all the cases, including the citations, year, and court for the cases you rely on for your argument in case you need to provide them to the judges?

- Do you have a copy of the record (that is the most recent update of the case problem) so you can refer to it if called upon to do so?

- Do you have your key cases summarized in "mini-briefs" on note cards so you can refer to them during arguments?

- Have you gone over your case with co-counsel, discussed how to handle rebuttal, and divided the time for speaking?

- Do you have paper, pen, notepads (sticky notes) to take notes on your opponent's case so you can respond directly to points that are made?

- Do you have a timer (typically on your cell phone) so you can be sure the timekeeper is keeping accurate time?

- Do you have all contact info for the tournament in case you need to reach out regarding questions or clarification about an issue related to the competition? (where possible have the cell phone numbers of other teammates, your coach(es), and the tournament organizers)

Sample Moot Court Cases

Each year, the American Moot Court Association (AMCA) publishes a case on its web site for the upcoming competition season. Each case contains two issues and is generally based on current legal controversies. What follows are two examples of these cases.

The first hypothetical, *Kedesh College v. A.R.H.* was used in the 2015–16 academic year. This case looked at free exercise and equal protection challenges in regard to the rights of an undocumented immigrant. This is the full case that was used in competition, including the case hypothetical, supporting cases, and statutes.

The second hypothetical, *William DeNolf v. State of Olympus*, is an edited version of the case used in the 2017–18 academic year. This case has been condensed to reduce the number of supporting cases and has no statutes included. This example is more suitable for use in a classroom exercise or more condensed argument setting.

Each has been used in multiple competitions throughout North America and has been thoroughly vetted to ensure accuracy and balance.

IN THE SUPREME COURT
OF THE UNITED STATES

No. 2015–2016

Kedesh College and A.R.H., Petitioner

vs.

United States, Respondent

On Writ of Certiorari to the Court of Appeals
for the Fourteenth Circuit

ORDER OF THE COURT ON SUBMISSION

IT IS THEREFORE ORDERED that counsel appear
before the Supreme Court to present oral argument on the
following issues:

1.   Whether the Fair Education Act violates the rights of Kedesh
College under the Free Exercise Clause of the First Amendment of the
United States Constitution.

2.   Whether the Fair Education Act violates A.R.H.'s right to equal
protection of the law as applied to the Congress of the United States
through the Fifth Amendment of the Constitution.

PUBLISHED OPINION

IN THE UNITED STATES COURT OF APPEALS

FOR THE FOURTEENTH CIRCUIT No. 01–76326

KEDESH COLLEGE AND A.R.H., APPELLANTS

vs.

THE UNITED STATES, APPELLEE

United States Court of Appeals for the Fourteenth Circuit

Before, Chief Circuit Judge, K. MAURY, and J. MART, and J.C. ARVIN, Circuit Judges.

OPINION BY MAURY, Chief Judge

I

(A)

Factual Overview: Statutory Grounds for the Appeal

Kedesh College and A.R.H. appeal the decision of the District Court for Western Olympus, which AFFIRMED the constitutionality of the Fair Education Act ("the Act"). See Appendix I. The federal district court had jurisdiction under 28 U.S.C. §§ 1331 and 1343(3), and our jurisdiction rests on 28 U.S.C. § 1291. Because of the factual overlap, the district court consolidated the two cases. All parties have stipulated that they accept this consolidation. The facts are not in dispute.

(B)

Factual Overview: Undocumented Persons and Federal Higher Education Law in America

Both the Department of Homeland Security and the Pew Research Center estimate that nearly 4% of the population of the United States (between 11 and 12 million) is undocumented. The Pew Research Center estimates that every year, 65,000 undocumented persons graduate from high school in the United States. The National Immigration Law Center places the percentage of undocumented persons living in the United States who graduate high school and/or attend college in the United States between 5% and 10%, whereas the percentage of corresponding documented persons or citizens is about 75%. According to the Institute of International Education, there are nearly 900,000 nonimmigrant international college and graduate students who are legally enrolled in American colleges and universities. This represents about 5% of the 20 million students enrolled in colleges or universities in the United States. The nonimmigrant international college and graduate students contribute $24 billion to the United States' economy annually. Only 28% of these students qualify for any scholarships or financial aid in the United States. There are no requirements that these students stay in the United States after receiving their education and the majority, as required by federal law, return to their home countries after graduation.

(C)

Factual Overview: Undocumented Persons and the Labor Force

It is estimated that over 5% of the labor force in the United States is undocumented (about 8 million people) and that 30% of the immigrants in the United States are undocumented. According to the Congressional Budget Office ("CBO") and the Social Security Administration ("SSA"), undocumented persons pay billions of dollars in taxes every year. The SSA estimates that 10% ($300 billion) of the Social Security Trust Fund comes from undocumented persons. Yet, few are eligible to receive social security benefits. The CBO has stated that "[o]ver the past two decades, most efforts to estimate the fiscal impact of immigration in the United States have concluded that, in aggregate and over the long term, tax revenues of all types generated by immigrants—both legal and unauthorized—exceed the cost of the services they use." The fiscal impact of undocumented persons on the United States is inversely related to the level of education of each person. According to an estimate of the National Resource Council, immigrants—excluding children—without a high school diploma will cost the nation about $31,000 each, whereas more educated immigrants will produce a lifetime net fiscal gain of $105,000 each.

(D)

Factual Overview: The Enactment of the Act

In 2006, Congress enacted the Fair Education Act ("the Act"). It was signed into law by President George W. Bush. The Act, which forbids any public or private college or university operating in the United States to accept any undocumented person, took effect on January 1, 2015. Previously enrolled students were exempt provided that they graduate by December 2014.

The Act's sponsors, Senator Shelton Morgan (D) and Representative Kevin Poush (R), asserted that the Act is necessary to efforts to preserve the resources and the benefits associated with higher education for the children of documented persons and to ensure that those who benefit from higher education give back to the United States and that it would encourage and promote lawful residency.[1] The Act's stated goal is for there to be no undocumented persons enrolled in any public or private college or university by the end of 2014. The Act, which would disincentivize illegal immigration to the United States for educational purposes, does not forbid foreign students legally in the country from seeking degrees in the United States.

The Act set up an enforcement mechanism that required each college and university, private or public, to submit proof that its students are legal residents or citizens of the United States. Cognizant of the need for flexibility in enforcement, the Act requires the president of each university to execute the law in a manner that he or she deemed "reasonable and appropriate."

---

[1]   Senator Morgan and Representative Poush's respective positions on religion are not part of the record.

(E)

Factual Overview: Deferred Action for Childhood Arrivals (DACA)

After his party lost control of the House of Representatives in 2011, President Barack Obama explored a strategy of using his executive authority to affect immigration and education policies without the need for new legislation. In June of 2012, the Obama Administration, in an effort to increase the number of undocumented persons attending college or university, announced a policy of Deferred Action for Childhood Arrivals ("DACA"). See Appendix II. Under DACA, which is administered by the Department of Homeland Security ("DHS") certain undocumented persons who came to the United States as children are eligible to attend college or universities without fear of deportation. The President and its supporters hailed DACA as "a sensible, compassionate, and fair alternative to the Act." DACA expressed sympathy for persons who did not intend to break the law, have known no other home, speak no other language and have been productive members of society. The deferred action designation does not change an immigrant's legal status; it creates guidelines for prosecutorial discretion that would apply to persons who qualify if they are in or not currently in removal proceedings. Critics of DACA, who favor more comprehensive immigration reform, have noted that DACA itself established certain criteria that may exclude specific individuals often for no fault of their own. For instance, applicants must maintain continuous residence in the United States, beginning June 2007. This means that a child of immigrant parents whose family left the country for any period of time can be deemed ineligible for protection under DACA. While there are exceptions to DACA, it precludes many undocumented persons from attending college or university in the United States. The President hailed the action as "a step away from the heartless one-size-fits-all approach to immigration and education reform embraced by so many on the other side of the Capitol." The White House stressed that the action, which was taken by the Secretary of the DHS, is constitutional.[2] The United States took the position that colleges and universities will be considered in compliance with the Act if they follow the criteria set forth in DACA.

(F)

Factual Overview: Federal Law and Paying for College Costs

Federal law places obstacles in the way of undocumented persons attending college or university in the United States. The 1965 Higher Education Act, while it allows the states to offer financial aid to undocumented persons, does not permit undocumented persons to receive federal financial aid. Some states forbid public colleges and universities to offer aid, grants, work study support, or scholarships to undocumented persons. The Illegal Immigration Reform and Immigrant Responsibility Act of 1996 allows states to charge undocumented persons in-state tuition so long as the same opportunity is offered to legal residents. It also allows states to refuse to offer undocumented persons in-state tuition rates. Thirty-three states forbid state colleges and universities from offering undocumented persons in-state tuition rates, while eighteen states allow undocumented persons who attended primary and secondary schools in that state to pay in-state tuition rates.[3] Such tuition is more affordable than out-of-state tuition rates. Several states have enacted legislation to limit the ability of undocumented persons to attend public universities and colleges. These efforts have ranged from total bans to policies that only allow undocumented persons to apply to lower-tier state colleges and universities.

---

[2]   There is a challenge to this authority that has been brought by the Speaker of the House against the President. That challenge is separate from this lawsuit and issues related to executive power are not before this court.

[3]   According to the National Immigration Law Center, states allowing undocumented persons to pay in-state tuition include: California, Colorado, Connecticut, Florida, Illinois, Kansas, Maryland, Minnesota, Nebraska, New Jersey, New Mexico, New York, Oklahoma, Oregon, Olympus, Texas, Utah, and Washington. Estimates show that the majority of undocumented persons living in the United States live in these states.

(G)

Factual Overview: Undocumented Persons and Higher Education in the State of Olympus

Olympus is a state of one million legal residents (800,000 citizens and 200,000 non-citizens who are in the country legally) and an estimated 50,000 undocumented persons—10,000 of whom are under the age of 18. Of these 10,000 individuals, 8,500 attended public primary or secondary schools. The remainder attended private schools (1,000) or were home-schooled (500). Olympus includes five state universities, and ten state colleges that are scattered throughout the state. In-state tuition is anywhere from $5,000 to $10,000 cheaper per year, depending on whether a student attends a state university or state college and whether one seeks to obtain an undergraduate or graduate degree. All five of the public universities offer doctoral programs and each has a law and medical school. The state has a community college system, with one campus for each of its twenty counties, and ten private universities and twenty private colleges—half of which have a religious affiliation. Prior to 2014, all persons were eligible to attend college or university in Olympus. Between 2000 and 2014, about 10,000 undocumented persons attended both public and private colleges and universities. They were eligible for in-state-tuition rates, and private aid, work-study support, or scholarships. See Appendix III for a detailed summary of Olympus education laws.

The Olympus State Department of Education ("ODOE") estimates that half of undocumented persons who graduate from college in Olympus remain in the state immediately after graduation. The majority of those who stay in Olympus continue to work and pay taxes in the state. Very few end up in jail or on public assistance. The majority of undocumented persons who leave upon graduation return to Olympus in less than ten years. With respect to American citizens who attend a public college or university in Olympus, half remain in the State immediately after graduation. Very few nonimmigrant international college students remain in Olympus immediately after graduation. This is because most have to return to their country of citizenship as part of the condition of their visa to study in the United States. Of the legal residents who attend and graduate from a public college or university school in Olympus, three quarters return to the State in less than a decade.

According to Immigration and Customs Enforcement ("ICE"), Olympus's experience with undocumented college students is fairly typical. Simply put, while experiences may vary from state to state, in the United States overall about half of its citizens who graduate college stay in the state where they earned their degree immediately upon graduation, while about three-quarters leave and then return to that state within a decade. About half of the undocumented persons who attend college or university choose to stay or return to the state in which they earned their degree. The number of documented and undocumented college students does tend to fluctuate by region with the largest numbers being in the largest cities.

(H)

Factual Overview: Kedesh College and the Fair Education Act

Kedesh College is a small, private, non-profit, nondenominational religious college located in central Olympus, in the City of Knerr. The College draws its name from the biblical city of Kedesh, which is known as a city of refuge or sanctuary. The school's motto *"But let all who take refuge in you be glad; let them ever sing for joy. Spread your protection over them that those who love your name may rejoice in you. For surely, O LORD, you bless the righteous; you surround them with your favor as with a shield,"* is found in *Psalms 5:11 and 5:12*. Kedesh College was founded in the mid-twentieth century, and is especially known for assisting immigrant communities. This is due largely to the background of the school's founders, each of whom immigrated to the United States to avoid persecution.[4] Its faculty and students must sign a nondenominational

---

4   The school was founded by Kris T. Bonillas, a Quaker who immigrated from Mexico; Mita Dezwall, a Hindu who immigrated from India; Bruno Merten, the son of Latter-Day-Saint missionaries, who emigrated from China after his parents were arrested for distributing religious materials to the masses; Yebby Ring, a Jewish immigrant from Poland whose ancestors had fled

statement of faith as a condition of their employment with or enrollment in Kedesh College. Students are also expected to perform a minimum of 512 hours of charitable work in their home and local communities as a condition of receiving their degrees.

Kedesh College receives about 5,000 applications annually.[5] It aggressively seeks applicants from all walks of life, both from America and around the world. As a part of their application, applicants are required to write separate essays on the significance of Kedesh College's statement of faith, and detailing how they envision carrying out the motto of the school upon graduation. Although Kedesh College considers other factors for admission, its President, Dr. Bobby Bronner, stated that these two student essays are the "most important part" of a prospective student's application.

Kedesh College symbolically accepts 511 or 512 students in each incoming freshman class. The average grade-point-average ("GPA") for the past four incoming classes has been 3.05, which is on par with the average GPA of public universities in the United States.[6] While Kedesh College receives a relatively small pool of applicants compared to top-tier private schools, its acceptance rate is similar to that of schools in the Ivy League,[7] and is much lower than the average acceptance rate of four-year universities overall.[8] Its graduation rate has

---

Communism and pogroms; and Janet Zahorsky, an immigrant from Czechoslovakia whose ancestors were Catholic and who had fled the Eastern Bloc before the Soviet Union was dissolved.

[5]   Kedesh received 4,518 applications for the class of 2015, 4,987 applications for the class of 2016, 5,391 applications for the class of 2017, and 5,104 applications for the class of 2018.

[6]   A study published in 2010 found that the average GPA of an incoming freshman attending a public university was 3.0 while incoming freshmen attending private universities had an average GPA of 3.3.

[7]   Kedesh admitted 512 students to the class of 2018, out of an applicant pool of 5104 prospective students (10.0% acceptance rate). Kedesh's acceptance rate was higher than that of Ivy League powerhouses Harvard (5.9% of 34,295 applicants) and Yale (6.26% of 30,932 applicants), lower than Dartmouth (11.5% of 19,235 applicants) and Cornell (14% of 43,041 applicants), and on-par with the University of Pennsylvania (9.9% of 35,788 applicants), as well as other prestigious non-Ivy League schools such as Duke University (10.7% of 32,506 applicants).

[8]   According to data published by the College Board in 2013, only 2% of four-year institutions with open admission had an acceptance rate of less than 25%. By contrast, 50% of

risen over the past ten years from 68% in 2004 to just below 80% in 2014.[9] Each year, the College accepts a small number of new students to fill vacancies left by students who are unable to continue their education.

In addition to its roughly 2,000 students, Kedesh College also employs 42 part- and full-time faculty members, and about 200 administrators and staff. Although Kedesh College is a relatively new educational institution, it already has an endowment of more than $10 million, thanks to the contributions of its growing alumni population (approximately 20,000 graduates). Seventy percent of Kedesh College graduates report being "somewhat active" or "very active" in the College community during the first ten years after their graduation.

Kedesh College accepts undocumented persons, offers in-state tuition for qualified students who graduated from a primary or secondary school in Olympus, and offers several privately endowed scholarships which are awarded to non-citizens. Under the College's founding document, at least one scholarship is designated to a deserving undocumented person. Although Kedesh College is an independent institution, it works in partnership with organizations around the world to bring students from poor and often war-torn nations to study at Kedesh College for free. Kedesh College encourages all prospective students to visit campus during one of four "Exodus Weeks," held on campus twice in the fall semester, and twice in the spring. During this time prospective students and their families meet with faculty and staff, stay in the dorms, sit in on classes, and participate with current students in community service projects, often in local immigrant communities. Although prospective students may arrange independent visits outside of an "Exodus Week," the College has a strict no-outside visitors policy for the final eight weeks of each semester, so that students can focus

---

four-year institutions with open admission issued acceptance letters to at least 75% of their applicant pool.

[9]   The average graduation rate for four-year universities in the United States was just under 60%, according to statistics published by the National Center for Education Statistics in 2014.

on their academic and community service pursuits. Kedesh College does not allow outside groups to rent space on campus or use any of its facilities.

During his testimony at congressional hearings regarding the Fair Education Act, Kedesh College President Dr. Bobby Bronner asserted that the proposed changes were "unfair, unconstitutional, and un-American." He spoke at length about Kedesh College's religious mission, and argued that the law would inhibit it from acting upon its motto, and founding purpose, by preventing the College from expressing and demonstrating love and acceptance to students from undocumented families. After the Act was passed and signed, Kedesh College announced it would continue to accept and offer financial support, including in-state tuition rates, to qualified undocumented persons. Kedesh College filed a lawsuit in federal district court seeking a permanent injunction restraining the United States from enforcing the Act. In the suit, the College asserted that the Act violates its rights of free exercise and of freedom of association under the First Amendment. Kedesh College does not assert an independent free speech claim. Judge D.R. Fair disagreed, and denied the College's request. Kedesh College appealed to this Court.

(I)

Factual Overview: A.R.H. and the Fair Education Act

A.R.H. is a native of Japan who has lived in the United States since she was six-months-old. A.R.H., who is not an American citizen, is not currently in removal proceedings. She was born March 17, 1997. Her parents, whose names are being withheld, came to the United States prior to the birth of A.R.H. to study as international students at Olympus State University. After graduation, A.R.H.'s parents each obtained a work visa. Not before too long, A.R.H.'s mother discovered that she was pregnant. At her husband's insistence, A.R.H.'s mother traveled back to Japan to give birth to their daughter. An orphan with no living relatives, A.R.H.'s mother stayed with her husband's family until A.R.H. was six-months-old. A.R.H.'s mother did not like her in-laws, and as soon as her husband would consent and they could afford it, she returned to the United States to join him. The couple visited Japan twice with A.R.H. to visit her father's family. Each visit was in the summer and each lasted more than three months. Soon after their second visit, when their daughter was three years old, A.R.H.'s father died in an automobile accident. A.R.H.'s mother, who still had a work visa, stayed in the United States past the visa's expiration. When A.R.H. was ten, her mother married an American citizen. A.R.H.'s mother believed that as a result of her marriage, she and her daughter were American citizens. A.R.H.'s mother and her new husband paid all of the taxes that they owed. The couple spent their summers in Canada where they had a cabin on a lake. They often stayed for more than three months at a time when visiting Canada.

A.R.H. is a devoted daughter and a terrific student. She only speaks English, has no recollection of her grandparents (who spoke only Japanese) or her aunts and uncles (who speak limited English), and does not identify herself as Japanese. A.R.H. attended public school in Olympus and graduated from Knerr High School in June 2014. She planned to start college in the fall of 2014.

A.R.H. and her mother did not realize that A.R.H. is not an American citizen until she began applying to colleges. After discovering her status, A.R.H. applied for DACA. She also applied to Kedesh College because it accepted undocumented students. The College accepted A.R.H. and offered her a scholarship reserved for undocumented persons. A.R.H. was notified of her acceptance and scholarship in May 2014. In June 2014, DHS informed A.R.H. that her DACA application had been denied for two reasons: "(1) she had left the country on more than one occasion for more than ninety days at a time and thus failed to continuously reside in the United States, since at least June 15, 2007; and (2) she was convicted of multiple misdemeanor offenses for underage drinking and "cow-tipping."

On July 7, 2014, President Bronner notified A.R.H. that under the Act, and as a result of Judge Fair's ruling, the College could not honor its offer. A.R.H., who is not currently enrolled in any college or university, filed suit against the United States on the grounds that the Act violated her right to equal protection of the law under the Fifth Amendment. The case was assigned to Judge Fair who denied A.R.H.'s request for a permanent injunction. A.R.H. appealed.

(J)

Factual Overview: Consolidating the Lawsuits and Standard of Review

Kedesh College was joined in the instant appeal by A.R.H. We do not review the material facts. We review the substantive merits of the constitutional arguments raised below. The parties have stipulated to the aforementioned facts. All issues raised are questions of law, not fact. The standard of review on appeal is *de novo*. We AFFIRM the ruling of the district court.

II

KEDESH COLLEGE'S FIRST AMENDMENT CLAIM

The First Amendment provides that "Congress shall make no law respecting an establishment of religion, or prohibiting the free exercise thereof; or abridging the freedom of speech, or of the press; or the right of the people peaceably to assemble, and to petition the Government for a redress of grievances." U.S. CONST. amend. I. Kedesh College contends that the Fair Education Act unconstitutionally burdens its ability to exercise a religious practice at the heart of its institutional mission. Kedesh College also argues that its First Amendment right to association is implicated by the Act, but does not assert that this infringement rises to the level of an independent constitutional claim. The district court concluded that the Act was immune to a free exercise challenge under *Employment Division. v. Smith*, 494 U.S. 872, 886 (1990), and that the "hybrid-rights" exception in *Smith, see id.* at 882, is illogical and mere dicta. Because we ultimately conclude that, post-*Smith*, the Act does not violate Kedesh College's Free Exercise rights—either standing alone, or in conjunction with another protected constitutional right—we affirm the judgment of the district court, but for very different reasons.

(A)

Level of Constitutional Scrutiny

The Act applies to all universities, sectarian or nonsectarian, and there is no scheme of exceptions or other evidence suggesting that the Act pre-textually targets religious universities. Neither party disputes that the Act applies to Kedesh College, or that some textual ambiguity or exception in the statute would permit Kedesh College to continue admitting undocumented students. The Act, although it is a neutral law of general application, requires that Kedesh College *must* change its current practices in a way that conflicts with the core religious and institutional mission of the College.

We are bound by *Employment Division v. Smith*.[10] In *Smith*, the U.S. Supreme Court reviewed an Oregon criminal statute, which at the time, attached criminal penalties to the sacramental use of peyote by adherents of the Native American Church. *Id.* at 874. The Court declined to apply strict scrutiny, holding that the statute was a neutral law of general applicability, which was not directed at religious

---

[10]   Although *Smith* controls federal Free Exercise claims against federal and state action, it is possible that certain congressional actions may be subject to strict scrutiny under the Religious Freedom Restoration Act of 1993 (RFRA), or the Religious Land Use and Institutionalized Persons Act of 2000 (RLUIPA). See *Thomas v. Anchorage Equal Rights Comm'n,* 165 F.3d 692, 697 n.4 (9th Cir. 1999); *see Grace United Methodist Church v. Cheyenne,* 451 F.3d 643, 661 (10th Cir. 2006). The Supreme Courts of Mississippi and Tennessee held prior to *Smith* that free exercise claims brought under their state constitutions trigger strict scrutiny review, even if the law is neutral and generally applicable. Seven states—Alaska, Massachusetts, Minnesota, Olympus, Washington, Wisconsin, and Vermont—have followed suit since *Smith*. Four states—Kansas, Maine, Montana, and Nebraska—apply heightened scrutiny to free exercise claims arising under their state constitutions, while California and Michigan have hinted that they would reject *Smith* when reviewing state constitutional claims. Although the RFRA, the RLUIPA, and state precedent evince a deep-seated disagreement between Congress, the Supreme Court, and nearly one-third of the states over the proper protection appropriate for free exercise claims, we need not wade into this thicket because Kedesh College does not raise a free exercise challenge under the RFRA or RLUIPA, and state constitutional provisions have no effect on the force of federal laws.

practices, and thus did not violate the Free Exercise Clause. *Id.* at 886 n. 3, 890.

Smith itself does not state the precise level of judicial scrutiny that attaches when a neutral law of general applicability is challenged on free exercise grounds. *Id.* at 886 n. 3. Our sister circuits are divided on that question, either employing rational basis review, *see Grace United Methodist Church v. City of Cheyenne*, 451 F.3d 643, 649 (10th Cir. 2006), or finding such laws immune to free exercise challenge *in toto*, *Parker v. Hurley*, 514 F.3d 87, 105–107 (1st Cir. 2008). Here, Kedesh College urges us to apply a different standard—strict scrutiny—because the Act implicates "not the Free Exercise Clause alone, but the Free Exercise Clause in conjunction with other constitutional protections[.]" *Smith*, 494 U.S. at 881. We address each point in turn.

(B)

Sincere Religious Belief and Substantial Burden

In order to prevail on its First Amendment claim, either an independent Free Exercise Clause claim or a hybrid claim, Kedesh College must first demonstrate that the Act substantially burdens its ability to act upon a sincere religious belief. Kedesh College more than meets this burden.

We must tread carefully when considering the sincerity of a plaintiff's religious belief. *See Smith*, 494 U.S. at 897 (O'Connor, J., concurring in the judgment). Fortunately, in this case, there is no question that Kedesh College's religious beliefs are sincere. While Kedesh College's founding documents and statement of faith are not part of the record before us, the parties agree that the College—although a self-identified "non-denominational" institution—was founded for religious purposes. These purposes include a core mission to express and demonstrate tangible acceptance, support, and identification with those who are unaccepted, downtrodden, and foreigners in an unfamiliar land. The school's motto, admission and scholarship policies, and its legacy of involvement in local immigrant communities for more than fifty years, only serves to confirm that these beliefs are sincerely held.

See Salvation Army v. Department of Community Affairs, 919 F.2d 183, 194 (3d Cir. 1990).

Likewise, we find that the Act burdens Kedesh College's ability to act upon this sincere religious belief. Although the record does not suggest that the Act was *intended* to stifle religious conduct, there is little doubt that under the plain language of Section 2 of the Act, Kedesh College is no longer free to act as it has for more than 50 years. Kedesh College may neither admit nor enroll undocumented persons into its student body, nor confer any degree or other student privileges upon such persons. The education of undocumented persons is a key aspect of Kedesh College's religious and educational mission. Thus this burden is not "incidental." *Cf. Smith*, 494 U.S. at 878. Kedesh College is not free to "operate its religious education program in another area" because the Act's prohibition applies to all colleges and universities, both public and private, under the jurisdiction of the United States without exception. *See Grace United Methodist Church*, 451 F.3d at 655 (citation omitted). Kedesh College may keep its religious convictions, or its identity as a private, four-year, degree-granting American college. It cannot have both.

(C)

Free Exercise Analysis Post-Smith

Not all burdens on religion are unconstitutional. While the district court was of the opinion that a neutral law of general application cannot violate the Free Exercise Clause, citing to *Parker v. Hurley*, we agree with the Tenth Circuit that the better reading of *Smith* is that neutral and generally applicable congressional enactments may impose even substantial burdens on religious practice, so long as they are rationally related to a legitimate state interest. *Grace United Methodist Church*, 451 F.3d at 649.

The Act is a neutral and generally applicable law, and the interest behind it—conservation of scarce resources, as a matter of federal immigration policy, for the higher education of children of documented persons—is "so dominant[,]"that our inquiry into

Congress's reasoning is necessarily a narrow one. *Arizona v. United States*, 132 S. Ct. 2492, 2501 (2012); *see Mathews v. Diaz*, 426 U.S. 67, 82 (1976). Congress's stated intent reflects a political judgment that is not only well within the plenary power of Congress, but is neutral with respect to the religion of all affected undocumented persons and educational institutions. *Arizona*, 132 S. Ct. at 2501, 2511 n.1. It is not an "illegitimate" interest. *Cf. United States v. Windsor*, 133 S. Ct. 2675, 2693–96 (2013). Nor is it irrational for Congress to conclude that prohibiting the children of undocumented persons from attending public or private colleges or universities will conserve scarce resources. *See Mathews*, 426 U.S. at 82–83. Thus, the Act survives rational basis review under *Smith*.[11]

(D)

*"Hybrid-Right" Analysis post-*Smith

The hybrid-rights exception finds its genesis in *Smith*, which distinguished the facts before it from prior cases where a neutral, generally applicable law implicated "not the Free Exercise Clause alone, but the Free Exercise Clause in conjunction with other constitutional protections[.]" *Smith*, 494 U.S. at 881.

While *Smith* suggested that the Supreme Court previously applied strict scrutiny to hybrid-rights claims, no currently published circuit court decision has applied strict scrutiny to a hybrid case post-*Smith*. *Parker v Hurley*, 514 F.3d 87, 98, (1st Cir. 2008). The Ninth Circuit decision in *Thomas v. Anchorage Equal Rights Comm'n*, is the closest to such a holding. *See* 165 F.3d 692, 714–17 (9th Cir. 1999). That ruling was subsequently withdrawn *en banc* and thus is not currently published. It was withdrawn *not* because the logic was flawed or disavowed, but because the underlying controversy in that case was not ripe. Thus, while it cannot be cited as precedent, we find *Thomas* instructive because the logic is persuasive, and our present issue is ripe. It is worth noting that the First, Third, Tenth, and D.C. Circuits have accepted the theoretical

---

[11] This opinion cites three cases found on the list of Issue 2 cases. Advocates for Issue 1 may cite these cases.

possibility of a hybrid violation of the Free Exercise Clause, although no plaintiff has successfully prevailed on a hybrid claim. *See Parker*, 514 F.3d at 98 & n.11; *Salvation Army*, 919 F.2d at 199; *Grace United Methodist Church*, 451 F.3d at 656. The Second and Sixth Circuits have dismissed the hybrid exception as "illogical" dicta. *See Thomas*, 165 F.3d at 704; *Grace United Methodist Church*, 451 F.3d at 656.

Kedesh College's hybrid-rights claim raises a question of first impression in this Circuit. While we have doubts about *Smith*, we are also not free to ignore its plain language. *See Thomas*, 165 F.3d at 704. *Smith* states that where religious free exercise is substantially burdened by state action, strict scrutiny is appropriate—even as applied to neutral laws of general application—if "other constitutional protections" are implicated. *See Smith*, 494 U.S. at 881. Here, Kedesh College argues that the Act implicates its protected right to free association.

The First Amendment protects the right to association in two distinct, yet occasionally convergent, ways: (1) the right to enter into and maintain "certain intimate human relationships," or private associations, and (2) "a right to associate for the purpose of engaging in those activities protected by the First Amendment[.]" *Roberts v. U.S. Jaycees*, 468 U.S. 609, 617 (1984). Accordingly, we review the facts before us to determine if the Act implicates Kedesh College's right to free association in either sense. If either is the case, we will perform strict scrutiny review.

(1)

Kedesh College's "Intimate or Private" Association" Claim

The Bill of Rights preserves not only individual liberties, but also "certain kinds of highly personal relationships[.]" *Id.* at 618. Although familial relationships are the archetype of these associations, the First Amendment's scope also extends to other relationships which are "sufficiently private to warrant constitutional protection[.]" *La. Debating and Literary Ass'n v. City of New Orleans*, 42 F.3d 1483, 1494 (5th Cir. 1995). In determining whether a given association is "private" in the constitutional sense, courts consider several factors, including the purported association's size, purpose, selectivity, congeniality, and exclusivity, as well as any other characteristics that may be pertinent. *See Roberts*, 468 U.S. at 620.

Kedesh College possesses several factors which support a finding that it is an intimate or private association. Kedesh College is a stand-alone institution, and its student body, faculty, and staff (less than 2,400 persons total) is a great deal smaller than the tens or hundreds of thousands of members of organizations previously before the Supreme Court such as the Jaycees or the Rotary Club. *See, e.g., id.* at 613. The College's incoming class is hard-capped at 511 or 512 new students each year, and agreement with its religious motto and mission is a key component for both admission (student essays) as well as continued enrollment (statement of faith). *See La. Debating and Literary Ass'n*, 42 F.3d at 1497; *cf. Chi Iota Colony of Alpha Epsilon Pi Fraternity v. City Univ. of N.Y.*, 502 F.3d 136, 146–47 (2d Cir. 2007). Finally, the College's high retention rate, coupled with the continued involvement of alumni for years after their graduation, demonstrates congeniality among the members of its community, both past and present.

Kedesh College also possesses characteristics that are not "intimate" in nature. Although agreement with its motto and mission are the most important part of its application, admission is theoretically available for any student who is willing to sign the school's nondenominational, albeit religious, statement of faith. Instead of recruiting internally, Kedesh College actively recruits students from around the globe, in partnership with international organizations. *See Chi Iota Colony of Alpha Epsilon Pi Fraternity*, 502 F.3d at 147. Although its graduation rate is impressive, the non-profit college still undergoes some attrition, and brings in new students each year to fill vacancies left by the students who inevitably leave. Finally, the record does not indicate that Kedesh College hides its existence, or prohibits nonmembers from attending any or all of its internal functions. *Cf. La. Debating and Literary Assn*, 42 F.3d at 1496–97. Rather, it advertises world-wide, encouraging prospective students across the globe to join its community, and hosts four publicly available functions each year with the express goal of bringing in new students.

After considering all these factors, we find that, on balance, the community at Kedesh College does not comprise an "intimate" or "private" association for First Amendment purposes. Notwithstanding the College's relatively small, preset size, and the shared purpose and congeniality among its members, we find Kedesh College's lack of exclusivity to ultimately be dispositive. Kedesh College cannot claim that it is an "intimate" or "private" group, while encouraging as many prospective students as possible to join its community. *See Chi Iota Colony of Alpha Epsilon Pi Fraternity*, 502 F.3d at 147.

(2)

Kedesh College's "Religious Association" Claim

Kedesh College argues that the Act interferes with its "right to associate for the purpose of engaging in those activities protected by the First Amendment." *Roberts*, 468 U.S. at 617. Although this right is most commonly conjoined with a group's free speech rights. Kedesh College does not assert an independent free speech claim. *See id.* at 623. It contends that the Act infringes on its right to associate with like-minded persons, to express and live out their shared religious convictions on the importance of demonstrating acceptance, support, and identification of immigrants in tangible ways.

As an initial matter, we find that Kedesh College is a "religious association," within the first sense of protected associations under the First Amendment. The College is private and religious in nature, and ministering to immigrant communities (specifically undocumented persons) has been a core mission of the College beginning with its founding more than half a century ago. Although academic achievement is clearly an important part of life at Kedesh College, it appears far more interested in its students' religious commitment and their investment in their local communities, rather than their academic performance.

Unfortunately for Kedesh College, its religious commitment is not enough to recognize the College as a "religious association." The Third Circuit previously considered a claim of "religious association," in *Salvation Army*. Ultimately, that court concluded that, because the right to association is a derivative right, "[it] would not expect a derivative right to receive greater protection than the right from which it was derived." *Salvation Army*, 919 F.2d at 199. Because the Free Exercise Clause—standing alone—only affords rational basis review post-*Smith*, a derivative "religious association" right can also be afforded no more than rational basis review. *See id.* at 197; *but see Parker*, 514 F.3d at 98–99.

We find ourselves in agreement with the reasoning of the Third Circuit. It would seem anomalous to us if "corporate exercise received greater protection than individual exercise[.]" *Salvation Army*, 919 F.2d at 199. Even finding, as we do, that Kedesh College is a "religious association," the Act need only pass rational basis review. *See id.* We find that it passes such review.

Because Kedesh College raises no viable companion right, which requires the application of anything other than rational basis scrutiny,[12] our holding today is controlled by *Smith*. Despite the fact that the Act places a substantial and inescapable burden on Kedesh College, the Act passes constitutional muster because it is rationally related to a legitimate state interest. *See Grace United Methodist Church*, 451 F.3d at 649. If the controlling test was different, or if the Court had more fully developed the hybrid-rights exception, Kedesh College might very well

---

[12] Although most hybrid claims involve the rights of association, *see Salvation Army*, 919 F.2d at 198–99, freedom of speech, *Grace United Methodist Church*, 451 F.3d at 656–57, or a core liberty interest protected by the Fourteenth Amendment, *Parker*, 514 F.3d at 94, 101, the Supreme Court in *Smith* did not explicitly define which "other constitutional protections" might trigger hybrid analysis. This led at least one of our sister circuits, in an opinion since withdrawn for ripeness, to apply the doctrine to a claim not rooted in the First or Fourteenth Amendment, *Thomas*, 165 F.3d at 701–02. For reasons discussed in the following section, we need not plumb the permissible depths of *Smith*'s hybrid-right exception because we find that the Act does not violate the Equal Protection Clause.

prevail on its Free Exercise Clause claim. Such, however, is not the current state of the law.

As an intermediate appellate court, we express no opinion on the wisdom of the Act itself, the correctness of *Smith*, or the legal morass that currently confronts practitioners who seek to raise constitutional claims in *Smith*'s wake. Absent further guidance from the Supreme Court, we are compelled to conclude that, under *Smith*, Kedesh College's Free Exercise Clause claim must yield to the will of Congress as expressed in the Act, draconian though it may be.

III

(A)

Federalism Analysis: Congressional Supremacy

A.R.H. challenges congressional action in an area in which Congress enjoys plenary power. The plenary authority of Congress is constitutionally provided for and is well established in the United States Constitution and in Supreme Court jurisprudence. We shall examine those foundations.

We start with the Constitution itself. Art. I. Section 8, cl. 4 provides: "The Congress shall have Power To . . . establish a uniform rule of naturalization[.]" U.S. Const. art. I, § 8, cl. 4. It is from this constitutional provision that Congress has long enjoyed the plenary authority to regulate in the area of immigration and naturalization. *See Arizona*, 132 S. Ct. at 2498. Many opinions of the Supreme Court further this same legal principle. In *Plyler v. Doe*, the Court asserted that all "courts must be attentive to congressional policy[ ]" when evaluating immigration matters. *Plyler v. Doe*, 457 U.S. 202, 224; 224–25 (1982); Further, the Court in *Mathews v. Diaz* held "judicial review of . . . decisions made by . . . Congress . . . in the area of immigration and naturalization[ ] . . . [is] narrow[.]" *Mathews*, 426 U.S. at 82. However, it is the Court's most recent pronouncement in *Arizona v. United States* that makes this point clear. There, the Court held that Congress has significant power to regulate immigration. *Arizona*, 132 S. Ct. at 2498.

Such regulation depends on Congress's responsibility to create laws based upon "searching, thoughtful, rational civic discourse." *Id.* at 2510. This plenary power means that the states are precluded from enacting regulations in a field that Congress is constitutionally empowered to regulate on its own. *See id.* at 2498; 2501. This principle applies where Congress has provided a framework of regulation " 'so pervasive . . . that Congress left no room for the States to supplement it' or where there is a 'federal interest . . . so dominant that the federal system will be assumed to preclude enforcement of state laws on the same subject.' " *Id.* at 2501 (internal citations omitted).

(B)

Federalism Analysis: The Constitutionality of the Fair Education Act

While the facts of the record indicate that deference to the states has created a scenario in which a host of different admittance policies dot the education landscape, it is clear that congressional regulation of immigration policy is so dominant as to preclude any other form of enforcement of those objectives. *Record at 3–4.* Congress has made its sole objective for the Act clear: there is to be "no undocumented person enrolled in any public or private college or university by the end of 2014." *Id.* at 2. Thus, the plenary power of Congress in this matter, while accepting its inconsistent application amongst the states, is unfettered. Congress clearly intended to play a role so dominant as to preclude any other regulation to exist in the same legislative sphere.

In conclusion, congressional superiority in this matter is made clear. The full force of Congress's plenary power stands firm in this case. Because of such power, the Act is a valid exercise of congressional authority and is constitutional, regulating in the realm of immigration and education in place of the states. Thus, A.R.H.'s petition hinges solely on her equal protection claim. In such an analysis, we shall not question the wisdom of the federal enactment, but whether A.R.H. and those similarly situated have been treated so differently as to warrant a ruling in their favor.

(C)

Equal Protection Analysis: An Overview

The aforementioned cases make it clear that in the world of immigration law and policy, it is the unique political prerogative of Congress, not the courts, to make legislative determinations. Therefore, where the court receives a challenge to such congressional regulation, the judicial inquiry into the reasoning of the Congress's decision must be narrow. *See Mathews*, 426 U.S. at 82. This narrow inquiry depends upon the claims of the challenging party. That means that the challenging party, here A.R.H., must challenge the constitutionality of the congressional act by asserting that the line of distinction that Congress has drawn with the Act is based upon reasoning that is invalid. *Id.* at 73–74, 82. But the burden upon the challenging party does not stop there; the party must also assert that the reasoning is not tolerable and that the congressional aim can be met by creating another distinction, or by creating a law with a different aim. *Id.* at 82 ("The party challenging the constitutionality of the particular line Congress has drawn has the burden of advancing principled reasoning that will at once invalidate that line and yet tolerate a different line separating some aliens from others.").

A.R.H. asserts that the enactment of the Act, and its application towards undocumented persons, violates her Equal Protection rights. We do not deny that A.R.H., an undocumented alien living in the United States, is protected by the Equal Protection Clause of the Fourteenth Amendment. *See Plyler*, 457 U.S. at 211–12, 215–16; *see also id.* at 253 (Burger, C.J., dissenting). We affirm this right by reiterating the Supreme Court in *Plyler*, noting that the application of Equal Protection principles is not territorially limited. There, the Court stated "the phrase 'within our jurisdiction' [within the Fourteenth Amendment] was intended in a broad sense to offer the guarantee of equal protection to all within a State's Boundaries, and to all upon whom the State would impose obligations of its laws." *Id.* at 214; U.S. Const. amend. XIV, § 1. While the facts indicate that A.R.H. is an undocumented citizen, it is also made clear that the force of federal law has been exerted upon A.R.H. and her family. *Record 6–7*. She is thus protected by the Equal Protection guarantees inherent in the Fifth Amendment's guarantee of Due Process. See *Mathews v. Diaz*, (1976).

Our reasoning turns on two seminal decisions of the Supreme Court: *Plyler v. Doe* and *Mathews v. Diaz*. These decisions are controlling on the matter of federal regulation of immigration matters and the rights of undocumented persons under the Fourteenth Amendment. Additionally, they are the most relevant to petitioner's case as presented before us. We shall address each in turn.

(D)

Equal Protection Analysis: Plyler and the Right to Higher Education

Echoing the federalism analysis provided, Congress enjoys substantial latitude in creating classifications that "roughly approximate the nature of the problem perceived," and "that [also] accommodate competing concerns both public and private." *Plyler*, 457 U.S. at 216. This substantial latitude affords Congress the ability to legislate, bearing in mind the inability of the state or federal government to remedy every ill presented. *Id.*. at 221 n.1 (Powell, J., concurring). With this authority, the Court has repeatedly held that "[t]he Constitution does not require things which are different in fact or opinion to be treated in law as though they were the same." *Id.* (alteration in original) (internal quotation marks omitted) (citation omitted). Additionally, *Plyler* noted that that there is no fundamental right to education. *Id.* at 221, 223 *(majority opinion)*. Because of "doubts about the judiciary's ability to make fine distinctions in assessing the effects of complex social policies," it has "articulate[d] a firm rule: fundamental rights are those that 'explicitly or implicitly [are] guaranteed by the Constitution.' " *Plyler*, 457 U.S. at 232 (Blackmun, J., concurring) (second alteration in original) (citation omitted). Congress has preserved this reasoning, as it does not provide undocumented persons with a constitutional right to postsecondary education. *Record at 1*.

Plyler recognized a right of undocumented minors to receive an education. But therein lay the distinction: *minor children*. *Id*. at 220. The right of these children to receive an education was recognized because of the vital importance of a primary education. *Id*. at 221, 223 *(majority opinion)*. Such an education furthers primary understanding of our democratic government and is necessary to prepare young citizens to participate effectively and intelligently within that democratic government. *Id*. Without a primary and secondary education, state law created a shadow class of citizens, specifically the minor children of undocumented persons. *Id*. at 218–20.

The interests that preserved the right of minor children to receive primary and secondary education are not applicable to the case at bar. Here, A.R.H. is an eighteen-year-old college applicant. The equal protection analysis conducted in *Plyler* concluded that denial of education to a group of children was an affront to their rights, but again, the emphasis is placed upon the rights of minor children. *Id*. at 220–22. In this case, we can conduct a speculative analysis of the maturity or awareness of A.R.H. in considering whether she should be treated like the minor children of *Plyler*. But again, we reiterate the guiding principle in judicial review of immigration challenges: the judiciary is not equipped to make the necessary "fine distinctions" in order to correct the wisdom of federal law. *Id*. at 232 (Blackmun, J., concurring).

Neither the federal nor the state constitution in this case provides a fundamental right to postsecondary education. *Id*. at 221, 223 *(majority opinion)*. The Court has continuously held that the right of education for undocumented persons is limited to minor children. *Id*. at 220. Thus, we conclude that A.R.H. does not have a viable equal protection claim under the *Plyler* analysis.

(E)

Equal Protection Analysis: Mathews v. Diaz
and Residency Requirements

A.R.H. also argues that the residency requirements, including continuous duration of residency, are impermissible under the Equal Protection clause, in line with arguments proffered in *Mathews v. Diaz*. There the question presented to the Court was "whether the statutory discrimination *within* the class of aliens is permissible." *Mathews*, 426 U.S. at 80.

Mathews made clear "Congress has no constitutional duty to provide all [undocumented persons] with [certain] benefits. *Id.* at 82; at 77–80. The fact that all undocumented persons are protected by the Due Process Clause (and the Equal Protection Clause) does not summarily lead "to the conclusion that all [undocumented persons are to be treated] in a single, homogeneous legal classification." *Id.* at 78. Many laws and provisions are premised upon distinctions between citizens and aliens that are legitimate. Within a class of undocumented persons, there may be a wide-ranging variety of reasons why rights may be contingent upon the strength of ties between undocumented persons and this country. *Id.* at 78–79. That differentiation in treatment, on its face, does not lead to the conclusion that the distinction is "invidious." *Id.* at 80. The *Mathews* Court stated:

> Neither the overnight visitor, the unfriendly agent of a hostile foreign power, the resident diplomat, nor the illegal entrant, can advance even a colorable constitutional claim to a share in the bounty that a conscientious sovereign makes available to its own citizens and *some* of its guests. The decision to share that bounty with our guests may take into account the character of the relationship between the alien and this country: Congress may decide that as the alien's tie grows stronger, so does the strength of his claim to an equal share of the munificence. *Id.*

In *Mathews*, appellees challenged two residency requirements that served as prerequisites to receiving welfare benefits. *Id.* at 82. Recipients had to be a permanent resident or must have continuous residence for a period of at least five years. *Id.* The Court responded by noting that if these requirements were not imposed, then Congress would look to at least limiting the benefits to those who lawfully entered the United States. *Id.* In such a case, unless welfare benefits would be given to "mere transients[,]" Congress would impose *some* durational requirement and such a requirement would be appropriate. *Id.* The distinctions are fine, highlighting the fact that the reasonableness of durational requirements is interchangeable. *See id.* at 82–83. Thus, it is "unquestionably reasonable" for Congress to make eligibility to receive any benefit from the state or federal government contingent upon residency and duration of residency. *Id.* at 83. *Mathews* held that "it is the business of the political branches of the Federal Government, rather than that of either the States or the Federal Judiciary, to regulate the conditions of entry and residence of aliens." *Id.* at 84; *see Graham v. Richardson*, 403 U.S. 365 (1971)). Further, *Graham*, a case favorable to A.R.H., is distinguishable as the current analysis involves the relationship between undocumented persons and the federal government, not their relationship with the state, as was the case in *Graham*. *See Graham*, 403 U.S. at 366–67.

III

Conclusion

Kedesh College and A.R.H. have challenged Congress at its highest ebb of constitutional authority. Because this authority is well-established within the text of the Constitution, and within the jurisprudence of the Supreme Court, their A.R.H.'s challenge fails.

The decision of the lower court is *AFFIRMED*.

DISSENT by J. MART, Circuit Judge

I

Freedom of Religion and of Association

I agree with parts of the opinion of the majority. It is well written and often well-reasoned. Unfortunately, for reasons upon which I will expand, I find myself unable to join with my brethren in their opinion and judgment.

A key reason for my decision to dissent from the holding of this court's opinion is that I fear that its ruling does damage, however unintended, to one of our important and traditional values: freedom of religion. It is a freedom we all share, perhaps one we take for granted, and it was the desire for that freedom that led so many of our forefathers to our shores and, so long as we remain a nation of free religion, one that will continue to beckon others to emigrate to our land.

In my view, the majority misapplies Employment Division v. Smith, 494 U.S. 872 (1990). It errs when it opts to apply a standard other than strict scrutiny. The Free Exercise Clause promulgates one of our most basic and cherished freedoms—that of religious choice—one that calls forth for heightened judicial protection and scrutiny. The appropriate test, therefore, is strict scrutiny. Any application of a lower-level scrutiny to laws such as the one before us today does not award freedom of religion its proper due and results in erroneous rulings such as the one issued today.

Smith noted that "[t]he free exercise of religion means, first and foremost, the right to believe and profess whatever religious doctrine one desires." Id. at 877. Kedesh College was founded under the religious doctrine to assist all people regardless of citizenship by providing them with an education. Everything associated with the school's history, its founding, the number of students it admits, and the selection of its name, and hold religious significance. Kedesh College is even named after the biblical city of refuge or sanctuary.

It is indisputable that the Fair Education Act substantially burdens Kedesh College's ability to act upon a sincere religious belief. *Majority opinion, at 9.* Short of compelling Kedesh College to select one specific denomination, there is no greater infringement on Free Exercise than to bar Kedesh College from accepting undocumented students based upon an asserted interest of saving resources when the facts show the opposite. International students are not a drain on the national economy. In fact, as the facts establish, these students annually contribute $24 billion to the national economy. *Record, at 1.*

The majority concludes that Smith is the controlling case. Yet, Smith is distinguishable from the facts here. In Smith, the Court considered whether a state law criminalizing the use of peyote violated Respondents' rights to free exercise when they were fired and later denied unemployment benefits for their use of peyote during a religious ceremony held at their church. Smith, 494 U.S. at 874. Deviating from long-standing precedent, the Court set forth a new rule holding neutral laws that are generally applicable do not rise to the level of strict scrutiny even if they have an incidental effect on a First Amendment right. *See generally Smith*, 494 U.S. at 878. The Court explained that a hybrid right may exist if another right, independent of free exercise, was also implicated. *Id.* at 882. However, such a right was lacking in Smith. Id. at 881–82.

Here, unlike Smith, we address a federal law with no criminal sanctions. In refusing to apply strict scrutiny in Smith, the Court distinguished its prior precedent by explaining the cases "have nothing to do with an across-the-board criminal prohibition on a particular form of conduct." Id. at 884. On this point, I find Justice O'Connor's concurring opinion in Smith to be of significance. "The First Amendment," she wrote, "does not distinguish between laws that are generally applicable and laws that target particular religious practices." Id. at 894 (O'Connor, J., concurring).

I turn now to the "hybrid-rights" issue. The Ninth and Tenth Circuits correctly interpret the hybrid right discussed in Smith. Thomas v.

Anchorage Equal Rights Comm'n, 165 F.3d 692, 703 (9th Cir. 1999); Grace United Methodist Church v. City of Cheyenne, 451 F.3d 643, 656 (10th Cir. 2006). In adopting the Tenth Circuit's approach that the companion claim under the hybrid right must be "colorable," the Ninth Circuit, in a ruling since withdrawn *en banc* because the issue was not ripe, explained, "In order to trigger strict scrutiny, a hybrid[-]rights plaintiff must show a 'fair probability'—a 'likelihood'-of success on the merits of his companion claim." Thomas, 165 F.3d at 703. Applying that logic to the present case, it is evident that Kedesh College presents a "colorable claim." The majority holds that Kedesh College is not an intimate or private association. *Majority opinion, at 12*. Yet, the facts show, and my Brethren concede, that Kedesh College possesses several factors indicating it is just that. In *Roberts v. United States Jaycees*, the Court noted factors that may be relevant in determining whether an association is an intimate or private including "size, purpose, policies, selectivity, congeniality, and other characteristics that in a particular case may be pertinent." Roberts v. U.S. Jaycees, 468 U.S. 609, 620 (1984). I agree with the majority's analysis as it relates to the College's size, purpose, and congeniality. *Majority opinion, at 12*. However, I am unable to agree with the majority's conclusion that Kedesh College is not "intimate" in nature because of its recruitment procedures. *Id.* All intimate or private associations must recruit externally otherwise the association itself would cease to exist. Recruitment is not the same as acceptance. Kedesh College still remains a private association because it controls who it lets in and students are required to agree and act in accordance with its founding principles.

Whether Kedesh College's claim is evaluated under solely Free Expression or under the hybrid right, the appropriate test to be applied is strict scrutiny. The Act places a substantial burden on the College's central religious belief. *Id.* The United States fails to show that they have a compelling state interest in barring undocumented students from attending college. In addition, the Act, and the decision to affirm it, "trench on the prerogatives of . . . educational institutions" to make decisions for themselves about who to admit into their student bodies.

Regents of Univ. of Mich. v. Ewing, 474 U.S. 214, 226 (1985). Such is their right under the doctrine of academic freedom. *Id. At 226.*

II

The Fair Education Act

(A)

Federalism

The majority holds that preemption principles counsel us to defer to congressional action in this case, because of Congress's plenary power in the area of immigration. *Majority opinion at 13–14.* I respectfully dissent from that conclusion. The Act, however, does not regulate immigration; it regulates education. Education policy is traditionally performed by the states. Of the nation's 7,021 Title VI postsecondary institutions, 2,015 are public. Of these public institutions, the federal government is responsible only for the five service academies.[13] So long as there are no violations of federal constitutional provisions, education is a matter properly left to the states. Here, Congress remedies no such violation.

While it is the prerogative of the federal government to regulate what kinds of students receive *federal* student aid, it is not the domain of the federal government to forbid the states from spending their own education dollars on particular groups of students. Nor is it the domain of the federal government to forbid private, nongovernmental institutions from assisting certain kinds of students. As the majority notes, the facts of the record indicate that prior deference to the states "has created a scenario in which a host of different admittance policies

---

[13] There are 7,021 Title VI institutions. They include: 2,422 two-year-non-degree-awarding colleges or universities; 2,870 four-year-degree-awarding colleges or universities; and 1,729 degree-awarding colleges or universities. Of the 2,422 non-degree-granting two-year Title VI institutions, 359 are public and 2,063 are private (182 of which are non-profit and 1881 are for-profit.) Of the 2,870 four-year Title VI degree-granting postsecondary institutions, 678 are public and 2,192 are private (1,543 are non-profit and 649 of which are for-profit.) Of the 1729 degree-granting two-year Title VI non-degree-granting postsecondary institutions, 978 are public and 751 are private (87 are non-profit and 664 of which are for-profit.) U.S. Dep't of Educ., Nat'l Ctr. for Educ. Statistics, *Common Core of Data (CCD)*, "Public Elementary/Secondary School Universe Survey," 1989–90 through 2010–11.

dot the education landscape." *Majority opinion at 14.* This is as it should be. States function as laboratories for democracy. Within the realm of education, as it intersects with citizenship, state policies have run the gamut from laws limiting the ability of undocumented persons to attend public institutions of higher education to laws enabling undocumented students to pay in-state tuition. The federal government should not be interfering in this traditional state dominion. While Congress may arguably have plenary power in the realm of immigration, *see Arizona v. United States,* 132 S. Ct. 2492, 2501, 2511 n.1 (2012), this grant does not allow it to take over a state domain only tangentially related to immigration. The Act is not a valid exercise of congressional authority, but rather unconstitutionally intrudes upon a matter left to the states.

(B)

The Fifth Amendment and Equal Protection

Another reason for my decision to dissent is that I fear that its ruling also does damage to another of our important constitutional values: equal protection under the law.

Because the Act involves congressional, rather than state, action, we look to the Fifth Amendment. The Fifth Amendment states: "No person shall . . . be deprived of life, liberty, or property, without due process of law[.]" U.S. Const. amend. V. The Supreme Court has held that the Fifth Amendment is applicable to the federal government in much the same way that the Fourteenth Amendment's Equal Protection Clause is applicable to state governments. *Bolling v. Sharpe,* 347 U.S. 497, 498–99 (1954). This is the doctrine of reverse incorporation. Under this doctrine, equal protection principles bind the federal government even though the Fourteenth Amendment's equal protection clause, by its terms, only applies to states. *Id.* This is because "the concepts of equal protection and due process, both stemming from our American ideal of fairness, are not mutually exclusive." *Id.* at 499. In practice, it means that "[w]hile the Fifth Amendment contains no equal protection clause, it does forbid discrimination that is 'so unjustifiable as to be violative of due process.' " *Weinberger v. Wiesenfeld*, 420 U.S. 636, 638 n.2 (1975) (citation omitted).

The majority, relying upon *Mathews v. Diaz*, 426 U.S. 67 (1976), applies the rational basis test. This application is inconsistent with precedent and fails to account for factual differences between *Mathews* and the controlling lines of precedent. The Act is subject to strict scrutiny, which it fails.

In 1954, in a Fifth Amendment case, the Court held that "[c]lassifications based solely upon race must be scrutinized with particular care, since they are contrary to our traditions and hence constitutionally suspect." *Bolling*, 347 U.S. at 497 (footnote omitted). Subsequently, the Court, in several Fourteenth Amendment cases, has held that classifications based on alienage and classifications based on race are to be judged according to the same standard. *See Graham v. Richardson*, 403 U.S. 365, 372 (1971) ("[C]lassifications based on alienage, like those based on nationality or race, are inherently suspect and subject to close judicial scrutiny." (footnotes omitted)); *In re Griffiths*, 413 U.S. 717, 722 (1973) ("Resident aliens, like citizens, pay taxes, support the economy, serve in the Armed Forces, and contribute in myriad other ways to our society. It is appropriate that a State bear a heavy burden when it deprives them of employment opportunities."); *Bernal v. Fainter*, 467 U.S. 216, 219 (1984) ("As a general matter, a state law that discriminates on the basis of alienage can be sustained only if it can withstand strict judicial scrutiny." (footnote omitted)). This is the case because "[a]liens as a class are a prime example of a 'discrete and insular' minority for whom such heightened judicial solicitude is appropriate." *Graham*, 403 U.S. at 372 (internal citations omitted).

It is important to note that the [Supreme] "Court's approach to Fifth Amendment equal protection claims has always been precisely the same as to equal protection claims under the Fourteenth Amendment." *Weinberger*, 420 U.S. at 638 n.2 (citations omitted). In light of case law, the Act should be analyzed under strict scrutiny, as this is the level of scrutiny generally applied in cases regarding discrimination on the basis of alienage. *See, e.g., Bernal,* 467 U.S. at 219; *In re Griffiths,* 413 U.S. at 722; *Graham,* 403 U.S. at 372. For a law to pass strict scrutiny, it "must advance a compelling state interest by the least restrictive means available." *Bernal,* 467 U.S. at 219 (footnote omitted). In the instant case, the government asserts that the Act is "needed to reserve the resources and benefits for the children of documented persons," and that the primary goal of the Act "is for there to be no undocumented persons enrolled in any public or private college or university by the end of 2014." *Record at 2.* Arguably, the government may have an interest in preserving the resources of its programs, and in limiting its expenditures in the furtherance of such preservation. *See, e.g., Graham,* 403 U.S. at 372–73, 374–75. "But a State may not accomplish such a purpose by invidious distinctions between classes of its citizens. . . . The saving of welfare costs cannot justify an otherwise invidious classification." *Id.* at 374–75. This is true even in the case of undocumented persons rather than citizens: "Since an alien as well as a citizen is a 'person' for equal protection purposes, a concern for fiscal integrity is not . . . [a] compelling . . . justification[.]" *Id.* at 375.

Even under rational basis review, the government's reasoning for discriminating against students like A.R.H. is unpersuasive. Rational basis review is not toothless. *See, e.g., United States v. Windsor,* 133 S. Ct. 2675, 2696 (2013); *see also id.* at 2706 (Scalia, J., dissenting); *Plyler,* 457 U.S. at 216. The Act fails for the same reasons that the laws in *Windsor* and *Plyler* failed—the lack of a legitimate interest. *See Windsor,* 133 S. Ct. at 2696; *Plyler,* 457 U.S. at 216. The record illustrates that the United States has no reason to discriminate against undocumented persons other than animus toward such individuals or some desire to earn political points with the voters. Neither qualifies as a legitimate interest weighty enough to deny a person equal protection or due process of the law. *See Windsor,* 133 S. Ct. at 2696. *Windsor* advised that "[i]n determining whether a law is motivated by an improper purpose or animus, '[d]iscriminations of an unusual character' especially require a careful consideration." *Id.* at 2693 (citation omitted). *Windsor* is especially instructive in that it was a Fifth Amendment case that applied equal protection considerations to the Congress. *Id.* at 2696.

(C)

Conclusion

While the majority may be correct in its analysis that neither the federal nor a state constitution provides a fundamental right to postsecondary education, this does not abrogate A.R.H.'s rights to equal protection of the law in a broader sense. Just because she is not guaranteed a postsecondary education does not mean that the government can discriminate against her in the provision of it. "Liberty under law extends to the full range of conduct which the individual is free to pursue, and it cannot be restricted except for a proper governmental objective." *Bolling*, 347 U.S. at 499–500. There is no proper governmental objective here, and thus the Act violates the Fifth Amendment.

I respectfully dissent from the decision of this court.

Issue One Cases

1. *Roberts v. United States Jaycees*, 468 U.S. 609 (1984) https://supreme.justia.com/cases/federal/us/468/609/case.html.

2. *Regents of Univ. of Mich. v. Ewing*, 474 U.S. 214 (1985) https://supreme.justia.com/cases/federal/us/474/214/case.html.

3. *Employment Division v. Smith*, 494 U.S. 872 (1990) https://supreme.justia.com/cases/federal/us/494/872/case.html.

4. *Salvation Army v. Department of Comm'y Affairs*, 919 F.2d 183 (3d Cir. 1990) https://openjurist.org/919/f2d/183/salvation-army-v-department-of-community-affairs-of-state-of-new-jersey-p.

5. *La. Debating and Literary Assn. v. City of New Orleans*, 42 F.3d 1483 (5th Cir. 1995) http://law.justia.com/cases/federal/appellate-courts/F3/42/1483/604698/.

6. *Thomas v. Anchorage Equal Rights Comm'n*, 165 F.3d 692 (9th Cir. 1999) https://caselaw.findlaw.com/us-9th-circuit/1436313.html.

7.   *Grace United Methodist Church v. City of Cheyenne*, 451 F.3d 643 (10th Cir. 2006) http://law.justia.com/cases/federal/appellate-courts/F3/451/643/627360/.

8.   *Chi Iota Colony of Alpha Epsilon Pi Fraternity v. City Univ. of N.Y.*, 502 F.3d 136 (2d Cir. 2007) http://law.justia.com/cases/federal/appellate-courts/ca2/06-4111/06-4111-cv_opn-2011-03-27.html.

9.   *Parker v. Hurley*, 514 F.3d 87 (1st Cir. 2008) https://caselaw.findlaw.com/us-1st-circuit/1387902.html.

Issue Two Cases

1.   *Bolling v. Sharpe*, 347 U.S. 497 (1954) https://supreme.justia.com/cases/federal/us/347/497/case.html.

2.   *Graham v. Richardson,* 403 U.S. 365 (1971) https://caselaw.findlaw.com/us-supreme-court/403/365.html.

3.   *In re Griffiths*, 413 U.S. 717 (1973) https://supreme.justia.com/cases/federal/us/413/717/case.html.

4.   *Weinberger v. Wiesenfeld*, 420 U.S. 636 (1975) https://supreme.justia.com/cases/federal/us/420/636/case.html.

5.   *Mathews v. Diaz*, 426 U.S. 67 (1976) https://supreme.justia.com/cases/federal/us/426/67/case.html.

6.   *Plyler v. Doe*, 457 U.S. 202 (1982) https://supreme.justia.com/cases/federal/us/457/202/case.html.

7.   *Bernal v. Fainter*, 467 U.S. 216 (1984) https://supreme.justia.com/cases/federal/us/467/216/case.html.

8.   *Arizona v. United States*, 132 S. Ct. 2492 (2012) https://supreme.justia.com/cases/federal/us/567/11-182/opinion3.html.

9.   *United States v. Windsor*, 133 S. Ct. 2675 (2013) https://supreme.justia.com/cases/federal/us/570/12-307/opinion3.html.

Appendix I

The Fair Education Act of 2006

The Congress of the United States does hereby enact the following public act:

Section 1: DEFINITIONS. In this act the following terms are employed:

(1) "Undocumented person" refers to a person who lacks the proper legal right to be in the United States of America or any of its territories. Such a person can include a born or naturalized citizen who has renounced his or her citizenship.

(2) "Postsecondary education" refers to the formal education that follows elementary and secondary schooling.

(3) "Postsecondary school" refers to an institute of education, including private or public and for-profit or non-profit, that provides students with a postsecondary education.

Section 2: No postsecondary school shall permit any undocumented person to enroll in, audit, or attend classes after December 31, 2014.

Section 3: Undocumented persons enrolled in, attending, or auditing classes in postsecondary schools prior to December 31, 2014 shall be allowed to enroll in, audit, or attend classes if such is allowed under the laws of the state or territory where the postsecondary school is located. Such persons shall be eligible to receive any postsecondary degree for which they qualify provided that such award occur before January 1, 2015.

Section 4: The president, or equivalent thereof, of every postsecondary school shall be responsible for ensuring that the postsecondary school that he or she serves is in compliance with this law. This includes adopting procedures and mechanisms that he or she deems reasonable and appropriate.

Section 5: Every postsecondary school shall submit proof to the United States Department of Homeland Security that its students are legally entitled to pursue a postsecondary education in the United States and its territories.

Section 6: Nothing in this law shall be construed to authorize a postsecondary school to violate any state, local, or federal law.

Section 7: The Act shall take effect on January 1, 2015.

Appendix II

Summary, with selected excerpts, from the June 15, 2012 Memorandum issued by DHS Secretary Janet Napalitano re: Deferred Action for Childhood Arrivals ("DACA")

A) DACA applies to persons both in removal proceedings and not currently in removal proceedings.

B) To be considered for prosecutorial discretion resulting in deferred action, subject to renewal after two years, an applicant must provide documentary evidence that he or she:

(1) Came to the United States under the age of sixteen;

(2) Has continuously resided in the United States, since at least June 15, 2007 and is physically present in the United States on June 15, 2015;

(3) Is currently in school, has graduated from high school, has obtained a general education development certificate (GED), or is an honorably discharged veteran of the United States Armed Forces or Coast Guard;

(4)   Has not been convicted of a felony offense, a significant misdemeanor offense, multiple misdemeanor offenses, or otherwise poses a threat to national security or public safety; and

(5)   Was under the age of 31 as of June 15, 2012.

C)   No individual should receive deferred action unless they first pass a background check.

Appendix III

Selected Sections of Olympus Education Law

Section 1:   DEFINITIONS. In this act the following terms are employed:

(1)   "Postsecondary school" refers to an institute of education, including private or public and for-profit or non-profit, that provides students with a postsecondary education.

(2)   "Postsecondary education" refers to the formal education that follows elementary and secondary schooling.

Section 2:   Any person residing in the State of Olympus shall be eligible to enroll as a degree-seeking student in any postsecondary school offering two-year or four-year associate's or bachelor's degrees or in any postsecondary school offering graduate degrees.

Section 3:   Any person attending postsecondary school in Olympus shall be eligible for any public or private financial support including, but not limited to, scholarships, loans, grants, and work study.

Section 4:   Any person who graduated secondary school in Olympus shall be eligible to pay in-state tuition at any postsecondary public school in Olympus. Private postsecondary schools in Olympus shall decide for themselves if they will offer an in-state tuition rate. No public or private postsecondary public school in Olympus shall charge undocumented persons in-state tuition unless it charges legal residents, citizens and non-citizens alike, the same exact discounted rate of tuition.

IN THE SUPREME COURT
OF THE UNITED STATES

No. 2017–2018

William DeNolf, Petitioner

v.

The State of Olympus, Respondent

On writ of certiorari to the Supreme Court of the State of Olympus

---

ORDER OF THE COURT ON SUBMISSION

IT IS THEREFORE ORDERED that counsel appear
before the Supreme Court to present oral argument
on the following issues:

1.) Whether the Functional Brain Mapping Exam (FBME) conducted by the State of Olympus facially violates the right against self-incrimination protected by the Fifth Amendment, as applied to the states through the Due Process Clause of the Fourteenth Amendment?

2.) Whether the sentence of solitary confinement, as applied to Petitioner, violates the Cruel and Unusual Punishment Clause of the Eighth Amendment, as applied to the states through the Due Process Clause of the Fourteenth Amendment?

A violation of the Fourth Amendment is not a certified question and thus is not properly before this Court. Judges are not to ask about if the warrant was valid or why this is not an issue. While a direct appeal from the trial record, advocates may raise the issue of prison conditions. This is because the sentence imposed how Petitioner would serve his time in prison.

SUPREME COURT OF THE STATE OF OLYMPUS

No. 2017–2018

MR. WILLIAM DENOLF, PETITIONER

v.

THE STATE OF OLYMPUS, RESPONDENT

Before: Chief Justice PEREZ, and Justices BONNER, CRAIG, EATON, FAIRBANK, LEDFORD, AND STEFFENSEN.

Chief Justice PEREZ delivered the opinion of the Court, joined by Justices BONNER, EATON, AND STEFFENSEN. Justice FAIRBANK filed a dissenting opinion JOINED BY Justices CRAIG AND LEDFORD.

I.   Factual Background and Procedural History

Petitioner, William DeNolf, appeals the constitutionality of his conviction for murder and his subsequent sentence from an Olympus trial court.[1] All of his claims arise under the Federal Constitution of the United States. No claims were brought under the Olympus State Constitution or any Olympus law.

A.   The Functional Brain Mapping Exam ("FBME")

In an effort to crack down on crime in Olympus, scientists and crime scene investigators have teamed up to develop new diagnostic technology that will aid law enforcement officials during their investigations. The Functional Brain Mapping Exam ("FBME"), also known as forensic neuroimaging or brain finger-printing, is a brain mapping test that allows investigators to determine whether a suspect has memory of being at the scene of a crime. The exam applies a combination of neuroimaging techniques predicated on the mapping of biological quantities (neurons) onto spatial representations of the brain. In essence, certain areas of the brain will "light up" during an

---

[1]   The State of Olympus is the fifty-first state in the United States of America. Olympus does not have an intermediate trial court system. Under Olympus law Petitioner has a right of appeal to this court.

FBME exam if the subject has memories of being at a crime scene when he or she is shown pictures of it. The FBME uses an electroencephalograph to monitor activity of the brain. Electrodes are placed on the scalp and the temples. These electrodes are harmless and cause no pain to the subject. During the test, the subject is shown several images. The brain reacts to these images in certain predictable manners—meaning that the brain reacts in a noticeable manner when it views pictures of locations with which it is familiar. Thus, images, such as a loved one or a place that one has visited, will produce predictable activity in the brain that can be measured. This activity differs from the reaction to a photo of a person or place that is wholly unknown to the subject. Technicians are able to map or record the activity of the brain. High activity indicates the subject has vivid memory of a particular image, while low activity indicates the subject has little to no memory of a particular image. Investigators and law enforcement officials around the country are beginning to use the FBME as a way to retrieve information regarding criminal activity, including homicides.

According to all scientific studies, this brain mapping technique is very reliable. These studies are not included in the record. The parties before the Court have stipulated to the FBME's accuracy and scientific validity, as well as to the fact the test is generally accepted by the relevant medical and scientific communities. In fact, Petitioner did not question the scientific validity of the FBME at trial. Thus, this issue was not preserved for this appeal. FBMEs are performed by trained technicians, often physicians, who work with law enforcement agencies as well as private industries. Typically, they are not law enforcement officers themselves. In this regard, they are similar to the polygraph examiners who perform polygraph tests, but are not themselves law enforcement officers. In this case, the use of the FBME was at the direction of Olympus law enforcement officers. The parties have stipulated and the trial court agreed that the FBME was admissible under the controlling standards for reliability and accuracy. The parties and the court further agreed that the test procedure and its result were

within scientific standards and are accurate. Mr. DeNolf objected on
Fifth Amendment—self-incrimination grounds to the admissibility of
the evidence in question before us today.

B. The Sleep Suites Incident, the Questioning of Petitioner, and the Trial

Ms. Andrea Somerville was a twenty-eight-year-old woman who
worked by day as a biologist specializing in the study of retromingents,
and by night, as a prostitute in Olympus. Mr. William DeNolf is a fifty-
five-year-old real estate agent of sound mind who recently moved to
Olympus.[2] On March 17, 2014, Mr. DeNolf met Ms. Somerville late at
night in the parking lot at a motel called Sleep Suites in the city of
Knerr.

Jay Carney and Ashleigh Hammer are detectives for the Knerr Police
Department. They are members of a special state and local task force
that was established to investigate prostitution in Olympus. Detectives
Carney and Hammer were parked under a Sleep Suites lamp post in an
unmarked vehicle on the night that Mr. DeNolf and Ms. Somerville
arrived at Sleep Suites. Detective Hammer recognized Ms. Somerville
from past stakeouts and thought that the situation was suspicious. The
detectives debated for a while about whether to intercede on suspicion
that the woman was a prostitute and that Mr. DeNolf was her "john."
The detectives observed Ms. Somerville exit Mr. DeNolf's vehicle and
visit the reservations office where she rented a room from the clerk.
Meanwhile, DeNolf purchased two sodas from a vending machine. As
Mr. DeNolf and Ms. Somerville met up at Mr. DeNolf's car, Detective
Hammer observed that Ms. Somerville was handed a roll of money and
walked with Mr. DeNolf to the motel. Detective Carney approached
the two, identified himself as a City of Knerr Detective, and asked to
see their driver licenses. Both parties produced their driver licenses,

---

[2] According to briefs filed in this case, there is a history of major depression in his family
and he alleges that after the time he has spent in prison he has trouble sleeping and little appetite.
Major depression is the most severe form of depression. Expert witnesses for the State and Mr.
DeNolf concur that he has shown signs of major depression: however, both have testified that
such is common among individuals serving lengthy prison terms.

along with voter ID cards for Olympus. Mr. DeNolf and Ms. Sommerville said they had just met and were only talking. Detective Carney returned their IDs and left the two outside the motel. He and Detective Hammer were called to investigate a sex trafficking tip at a suspected brothel found in a neighborhood of Knerr known as La Grange. The locals have nicknamed the suspected brothel "The Home Across the Road." The local police call it "The House of the Rising Sun." The suspected brothel, which is owned by local gambler Frankie Lee, claims to be a restaurant and bar that goes by the formal name of "Paradise." Detectives Carney and Hammer did not return to Sleep Suites that night.

The following morning on March 18, 2014, Knerr Law Enforcement officials were called to the scene of a homicide. Two maids at Sleep Suites, Aleah Fisher and Abigail Kennefick, found Ms. Somerville dead inside room 417 at Sleep Suites—the same room she had rented the night before. Emergency responders quickly arrived at the scene of the crime, but were unable to revive Ms. Somerville. Mr. DeNolf was not present. The Knerr homicide detective who was assigned to the case, David Cazzarubyus, was aware of the deceased's suspected role in prostitution. Consequently, he contacted Detectives Carney and Hammer and informed them of Somerville's death and shared his suspicions that she had been tortured before she was murdered. The killer had written "whore" in the victim's blood on the walls of the room.

Detectives Carney and Hammer drove to Mr. DeNolf's home and asked if he would be willing to accompany them to the Knerr police department for questioning in connection with the murder of Ms. Somerville. Mr. DeNolf asked if he was under arrest and if he needed an attorney. Detective Hammer responded, "You are not under arrest—whether you want an attorney is up to you." Mr. DeNolf agreed to accompany the detectives. He did not call an attorney because in his words, "I am 100% innocent and I want to help you arrest the killer." The detectives transported Mr. DeNolf to the Knerr Police Department and took Mr. DeNolf into a room where investigators began interrogating him. Before doing so, they reminded him that he was not under arrest and was free to leave or stop talking if he wished. When asked if he had ever been inside any rooms at Sleep Suites, Mr. DeNolf answered "no." Mr. DeNolf was asked a few questions about being inside Sleep Suites, specifically room 417. He answered all their questions. Mr. DeNolf stated quite clearly that he had not been inside the motel, but that he had visited the exterior of the motel.

Mr. DeNolf admitted that he intended to pay Ms. Somerville for sex, but he consistently denied having killed or harmed her in any way. Mr. DeNolf stated that the transaction had not even occurred between himself and Ms. Somerville because he received a phone call from his wife telling him to "get home now!" Mr. DeNolf further said, "We didn't even have time to get into the motel room before my wife was yelling at me!" After answering these questions cooperatively, Mr. DeNolf informed the detectives that "I do not like the tone, or the direction of your questions." He also stated "I no longer want to speak with you and I will not say anything else to you guys." At this point, the detectives told Mr. DeNolf that they were done questioning him, but wanted to administer a test. The detectives requested a warrant for an FBME, which was granted by an Olympus trial judge Caitlin Wood. The parties stipulate that the warrant was valid.

After the warrant was issued, Mr. DeNolf was asked to accompany the detectives from the police department to an Imaging and Screening facility. Mr. DeNolf did not respond, but he did walk with the detectives to the facility located two buildings away from the police department. Mr. DeNolf was not handcuffed and he walked alongside the detectives. He had his wallet and identification. They walked past a bus stop and a few taxicabs that were parked outside the building. Once they reached the facility, Detectives Carney and Hammer left Mr. DeNolf alone with two FBME technicians. The technicians, Bobby Bronner and Chester Comerford, are both medical doctors who work by contract for the Knerr Police Department and were acting at the detectives' direction. They identified themselves to Mr. DeNolf as physicians. He asked, "Are you cops?" to which one answered, "No, but we work with the police in certain investigations such as this one today." Mr. DeNolf did not ask to leave or to speak to an attorney. Drs. Bronner and Comerford explained the FBME to Mr. DeNolf. They informed him that the FBME was "purely procedural, much like drawing blood or taking fingerprints." They also informed him that the test would not require any needles, unlike a blood test. Mr. DeNolf expressly said that he would not answer any questions or say anything more. Drs. Bronner and Comerford conducted the FBME test without asking Mr. DeNolf any further questions. The test took less than thirty minutes. The test does not involve any communication, verbal or otherwise, between the technicians and Mr. DeNolf. They simply show him a photograph and measure his brain response. He did not speak or make any faces or gestures nor did the technicians. There was no recording of the process.

Mr. DeNolf did not resist the FBME and was cooperative during it. During the FBME, the technicians used images from the scene of the crime, including from room 417 and from other locations in and around the motel, as well as images from non-crime scenes in and around other hotels.[3] In the image of room 417, Ms. Somerville's corpse had been removed from the area but there was still blood about the room. The results of the FBME demonstrated high activity when images from Sleep Suites were shown, indicating that Mr. DeNolf had memory of being at the hotel and being in room 417. The results

---

[3]   In total, Mr. DeNolf was shown fifty-six photographs. He was shown seven images from eight different hotels. From Sleep Suites, he was shown a photo of room 417 (the crime scene), a photo of room 110 and a photo of room 212 (not affiliated with the crime scene), as well as a photo of the motel reservations desk, a photo of the vending machine on the 4th floor, a photo of the front of the hotel, and a photo of the parking lot. He was shown similar photos of other hotel rooms, lobbies, front doors, parking lots, and vending machines from other hotels. These included images from several well-known hotel and motel chains (Days Inn, Holiday Inn, Drury Hotel and Suites, and Courtyard by Marriott), as well as several iconic hotels, such as the Pink Hotel in Waikiki, the hotel featured on the cover of the Eagles LP *Hotel California* and Trump International Hotel in Washington, D.C. Four of the rooms he was shown were crime scenes (they had blood about the room) and four were not. The photos from the hotels without crime scenes were randomly selected. The photos from the four hotels with crime scenes were not randomly selected—however the technicians were careful to randomly select images of hotel crime scenes from a pool that included twenty possible hotel crime scenes.

demonstrated low activity for all the other hotels that were shown. The test indicated that Mr. DeNolf only recognized one other hotel.[4] Based on these results, the police arrested Mr. DeNolf and he was arraigned for the murder of Ms. Somerville.

Mr. DeNolf filed a motion to suppress the results from the FBME. The trial judge, D.R. Fair, denied the motion. During trial, evidence was presented against Mr. DeNolf, including the results of the FBME and his statement to the police that he had not been inside Sleep Suites or in room 417. There were no witnesses other than Detectives Carney and Hammer who witnessed Mr. DeNolf at Sleep Suites, as the reservation clerk, "Big Dom" Noble, only interacted with the deceased. No DNA evidence was introduced at trial. The technicians who performed the FBME testified at Mr. DeNolf's trial. At trial, Judge Fair found that Mr. DeNolf showed no signs of mental deficiency (a point he did not contest). Neither at trial nor at sentencing did he present any mitigating factors that should be considered in assessing his guilt or penalty. Mr. DeNolf did not testify at his trial and instead invoked his Fifth Amendment right against self-incrimination.

A jury found Mr. DeNolf guilty of the murder of Ms. Somerville. After Mr. DeNolf was convicted, Judge Fair, pursuant to Olympus law, sentenced him to 30 years of solitary confinement within a Supermax prison known as Poseidon Penitentiary. This was not a mandatory penalty, and under the terms of the statute the judge could have sentenced Mr. DeNolf to death or to a longer or shorter term of years. The judge did not explain why he chose this exact period of years rather than a longer sentence, but he indicated that he sentenced Mr. DeNolf to solitary confinement because "he tortured his victim." In 20 states, inmates can be kept in solitary without definite release dates. While it is not unheard of for inmates to serve 15 to 30 years in solitary confinement, such a term is not the most common outcome. In fact, a few of these 20 states have no inmates serving without definite release

---

[4]   According to the test, the only hotel images that Mr. DeNolf recognized were the hotel from the cover of the Eagles LP *Hotel California* and images from the Sleep Suites.

dates." Mr. DeNolf entered prison on July 7, 2014. He has been in solitary confinement, without exception, since that date.

C. Olympus Law and Petitioner's Sentence

Olympus has a population of 10,000,000 people. .11% of the population (11,000 persons) are incarcerated. In Olympus, 385 (3.5%) of its 11,000 inmates are in jail for homicide and aggravated assault.[5] In Olympus, convicted murderers are subject to the death penalty, though it is a sentence that is rarely issued. Sentences such as life without parole or long terms such as fifty years without a possibility of parole, are much more common for those convicted of murder.

Under Olympus law, the sentencing authority possessed by judges includes the authority to sentence convicts to a variety of forms of what the state labels "restrictive housing."[6] Olympus is the only jurisdiction that grants judges this authority. Trial judges have the additional authority to determine how long an inmate will serve in restrictive housing and the level of that restrictive housing. Although Olympus does not grant parole to persons convicted of murder, a warden may elect to move a prisoner from solitary confinement back into the general prison population once the inmate has served half of the sentence. This can be important as studies find that inmates who are released directly from solitary confinement as opposed to from general population are more likely to reoffend and likely to do so quicker (12 vs 27 months) and that inmates who have served in solitary confinement are more likely to reoffend than those who have not. Olympus law provides six levels of restrictive housing, the most extreme of which is solitary confinement. This penalty tends to be reserved in Olympus for the most violent criminals.[7] Under Olympus

---

[5] These figures are comparable to figures released by the United States Federal Bureau of Prisons (BOP), which in 2015 found that 5,537 (3.1%) of all federal inmates were in jail for homicide, kidnapping, and aggravated assault.

[6] This authority is not being challenged on its face.

[7] The six forms of restrictive housing in Olympus are: (1) Protective custody, which protects an inmate from threats of violence and extortion from other inmates; (2) Segregation due to acute or serious mental health needs; (3) Segregation due to acute medical needs other than mental health needs; (4) Investigative segregation, which temporally segregates an inmate

law, inmates who "torture" their victims are eligible to be sentenced by a judge to solitary confinement at trial. Mr. DeNolf is one of 100 inmates in prison in Olympus who tortured a murder victim.[8] Inmates who torture their victims are not the only inmates sentenced to solitary conferment in Olympus.

In Olympus, solitary confinement is defined in the state code as "the physical and social isolation of individuals who are confined to their cells for 22 to 24 hours a day with no environmental or sensory stimuli and almost no human contact for a period of up to 30 consecutive days." Presently, 6% of the Olympus inmate population, or 660 inmates, are in some form of restrictive housing: 25 inmates in protective custody, 100 inmates in segregated housing due to mental health issues, 40 inmates in segregated housing due to non-mental health medical issues, 20 in investigative segregation, 75 in disciplinary segregation, and 400 in solitary confinement. The State can house 750 inmates in restrictive housing. Olympus does not subject juveniles to solitary confinement. The decision to sentence inmates to solitary confinement is based on their offenses for which they are serving a prison sentence. *See supra* footnote 5. 100 of these 400 inmates are in prison for murder or aggravated assault. The rest are in prison primarily for sexual offenses (150 inmates) or gang-related crimes (150 inmates). Some of these 400 inmates also suffer from mental illness.

D. Solitary Confinement in the United States

The use of solitary confinement in the United States dates to the early 1820s. According to the U.S. Bureau of Justice Statistics (BJS), the Federal Government and 40 states use some form of solitary confinement. Of the 1.5 million adults incarcerated in federal and state

---

while serious allegations of misconduct are investigated; (5) Disciplinary segregation, which punishes an inmate for a violation of a major disciplinary rule; and (6) Solitary confinement, which segregates inmates based on crimes they committed while they were a member of the non-prison general population.

[8]   It is not clear how many murderers who tortured their victims were not sentenced to solitary confinement by a judge or assigned to solitary confinement by prison officials. But majority of those who tortured their victims were sentenced to solitary confinement.

facilities,[9] about 80,000 to 100,000 are in some form of solitary confinement. With respect to the federal inmate population, the United States Bureau of Prisons (BOP) reported that as of January 2017, 5.75% (or 8,819) of inmates in custody are in segregated housing units (SHU). This is the federal equivalent of solitary confinement.[10] The BOP states that of these 8,819 inmates in SHU, 1,274 (14.45%) are in SHU for disciplinary reasons (disciplinary segregation). The BOP reports that 7,545 (85.6%) are in SHU for administrative reasons (administrative segregation), such as "they are under investigation for misconduct and/or criminal behavior." No equivalent data is available for the states that subject inmates to some form of solitary confinement. What is known is that 15 (30%) of the states automatically sentence gang-members to some form of restrictive housing. This is due to fears that gang members will pose a threat to other inmates as well as prison officials. As noted, however, Olympus subjects a similar percentage of its inmates to such confinement. Where federal and Olympus data differ is that Olympus subjects inmates to solitary confinement based on their crimes committed before they entered prison (400 of 660 or 60.6%). The Federal Government uses the term "restrictive housing" instead of the term "solitary confinement." However, the federal practice of restrictive housing is functionally the same as solitary confinement despite the terminological difference. Simply put, the United States practices solitary confinement; it just calls it restrictive housing.

---

[9] The BJS estimated in 2015 that on average nearly 2.2 million persons are incarcerated in the United States. This includes 154,389 federal inmates, 1,345,611 state inmates, 585,000 persons in local jails, 86,000 in juvenile facilities, 13,000 inmates in U.S. territories, 10,000 persons detained by Immigration and Customs Enforcement, 2,000 in inmates in Tribal facilities, and 1,600 persons held in military installations.

[10] The United Nations has observed "there is no universal definition of solitary confinement." Many nations, including the United States and many of its 51 states, do not use the term solitary confinement to describe its sentences. If there is one yardstick by which to distinguish what is solitary confinement from what is not, it is that the reduction in stimuli inflicted upon inmates is not only quantitative it is also qualitative. Put simply, it is not just the reduction in time outside one's cell, there is an overall diminished quality of life that occurs wherever the inmate may be.

The proliferation of restricted or segregated housing, which reflects the drive toward Supermax facilities, was driven in large part by: economics, trends in the 1980s and 1990s toward mandatory sentences, the rise of gang-activity in prisons, and the threat that gang-associated inmates posed to both officers and the general prison population.[11]

E. Conditions of Segregated Confinement at Poseidon Penitentiary

Poseidon Penitentiary is a Supermax prison located in central Olympus.[12] It is one of three Supermax prisons in Olympus. The other two are located in northern and southern Olympus. Each facility has the capacity to house a total of 500 prisoners—250 of whom are housed in single-inmate cells, which are designed to "separate dangerous prisoners from the rest of the general prison population." Currently, each of these Supermax prisons has about 30 open single-inmate segregated cell units. Olympus does not double-cell inmates who are serving solitary confinement. Not all prisoners at Poseidon Penitentiary are in solitary confinement.

Incarceration at the Poseidon Penitentiary is synonymous with extreme isolation. Within solitary confinement, almost every aspect of an inmate's life is controlled and monitored. The cells have solid metal doors with metal strips along the sides and bottoms, which prevent communication with other inmates. These doors block most light and vision and are operated by electronic command rather than by a guard using a key. The rooms and hallways all look similar and are comprised of concrete that is painted white. Each cell has a video surveillance

---

[11] Supermax facilities were designed to house dangerous inmates long-term with minimal interaction with other persons—for example, other inmates or court personal. A study by the group Judicial Watch and several newspaper accounts reported that of the 80,000 to 100,000 inmates in solitary confinement, 25,000 are presently in Supermax prisons. In addition, 50,000 to 60,000 more are in conditions approaching or consistent with solitary confinement in the nation's Secure Housing Units, Restricted Housing Units, and Special Management.

[12] A Supermax prison is comprised of "control units." In these units one typically finds the most dangerous offenders as well as offenders who may be segregated to protect them or because they are awaiting trial on additional charges unrelated to their original incarceration. Supermax prisons have high levels of security.

system that is constantly monitored by correctional officers. The cells have no windows. A light remains on in the cell at all times, though it may be turned off using a clap-sound operated light switch if the inmate so chooses. Restroom facilities, which can be flushed by the inmates, are available within the inmate's cell.

Basic conditions of hygiene are provided: all cells have air conditioning and heating options. There are no allegations of issues related to lack of water, air quality, or sanitation. Three meals a day are delivered to the inmate's cell where he or she eats alone instead of in a common eating area. The food is reported to be palatable. Inmates have limited access to books and mail, and they have a mattress of their own which must remain in their cell at all times. There is a recreation area that is located outside. It has a 20-foot wall around it and a plastic cover to protect inmates from the rain. The floor is a synthetic type of turf that absorbs the sunlight. There is room for inmates to run short sprints and to perform other exercises. There is a basketball and a soccer ball, but no other recreational equipment or facilities are available. The guards inflate the balls so they can be used.

Inmates must remain in their cells, which measure 7 feet by 14 feet, for 24 hours per day, for up to 30 consecutive days. Once every 30 consecutive days, the prisoner is allowed in a recreational cell for four hours where he or she can hear and talk to (but not see) other inmates. Some inmates yell at other inmates throughout the four-hour period and others try to intimidate guards during all their hours within the recreational cells. While inmates are deprived of almost any environmental or sensory stimuli and almost all human contact, their basic needs are met and they are provided comfortable accommodations that meet the Restrictive Housing Standards set forth by the American Correctional Association. The American Psychological Association estimates that half of all inmates in correctional facilities in the United States suffer from some form of mental illness. This rate increases for inmates housed in segregated units.

Inmates can request religious counseling, which is provided by two chaplains on the prison staff. There can be a delay of up to a week before inmates are able to meet with prison chaplains. It is unclear from the record whether Mr. DeNolf has ever requested such a meeting. Prison staffers do not interact verbally with the inmates and inmate behavior is observed by closed circuit televisions. Prisoners are not allowed to visit with outsiders, but they can correspond through mail once it has been reviewed and censored by prison staff. Prisoners are allowed to communicate uncensored with their lawyers, though few do after their appeals are finished.

The prison is staffed by guards 24 hours a day under the supervision of Warden Beta Diego. Prison guards must have at least a high school diploma and have passed a CPR class. Prison guards have the authority, if they choose, to report if an inmate is in need of medical or mental health attention. In fact, they perform medical/mental health triage to the extent that it occurs. However, prison guards have not received any training in mental health issues. When an inmate is reported to have mental health issues, or if an inmate requests mental health services, mental health services are provided by licensed professionals who have a minimum of a master's degree in social work. In fact, 90% of mental health professionals working at Poseidon Penitentiary received their degrees online from either Kedesh College or Olympus State University. These professionals are randomly chosen from a pool of mental health professionals to deal with inmates who are referred for evaluation. While none are full-time employees at the prison, there are always three mental health professionals on-call for residents in restricted housing. On average, there is one for every 200–220 inmates in restricted housing. Psychiatric outpatient treatment and medications are available on-site, but intensive psychiatric inpatient treatment is not available. Due to security concerns, inmates who need such care cannot be transported off-site to state mental health facilities. The mental health staff can participate in a voluntary system of peer review. Not all of the mental health professionals participate. This is the closest system of professional oversight of the mental health staff that exists at Poseidon Prison. Poseidon's record keeping on mental health referrals appears adequate.

Both the American Psychological Association and the BJS estimate that half of all inmates in the United States suffer from some form of mental illness. In addition, the BJS has reported that acute levels of mental illness are associated with persons who are subject to restrictive housing, such as solitary confinement (the term used by Olympus), segregated housing (a term used by many states), Security Housing (the term used by California), Special Housing (the term used in New York), Intensive Housing Units (the term used by Oregon), Isolation Confinement (the term used in Arkansas) and Administrative Housing (the term used by the United States Government). Not all who suffer from mental illness are in segregated housing.

Both sides have stipulated that mental health is a serious issue in American correctional facilities. In addition, both sides have stipulated that an estimated 75% of the prisoners who leave Poseidon Penitentiary have psychological disorders. No data has been gathered on the number of psychological disorders possessed by intimates before their incarceration in solitary confinement. In fact, prison staff does not perform any mental health screening of inmates before their sentencing or housing decisions.

F. Petitioner's Appeal

Mr. DeNolf alleges Fifth Amendment and Eighth Amendment violations of his constitutional rights as they are applied to the states through the Due Process Clause of the Fourteenth Amendment. We review the substantive merits of the constitutional arguments raised below. The parties to the case have stipulated to the aforementioned facts. We review all questions *de novo*. We AFFIRM the ruling of the trial court.

Chief Justice PEREZ delivered the majority opinion, joined by Justices BONNER, EATON, AND STEFFENSEN.

I.

Petitioner argues that the use of the FBME facially violates the Fifth Amendment's guarantee of the right against self-incrimination. We reject this argument and find no such violation to be represented by the facts before us today.

We hold that Mr. DeNolf's Fifth Amendment rights were not violated. Historically, the legal protection against compelled self-incrimination was directly related to the question of torture for extracting information and confessions. In modern times, this Court has focused on coercive methods that fall short of torture. The general presumption is that evidence that a defendant produces involuntarily is compelled. However, Mr. DeNolf did not resist the FBME conducted by law enforcement officials. Therefore, he was aware that he gave up his privilege against self-incrimination. In addition, the FBME is constitutional for several of the forthcoming reasons.

In *Schmerber v. California*, 384 U.S. 757 (1966), petitioner was convicted of driving an automobile while under the influence of alcohol. The United States Supreme Court held, over the petitioner's objection, that the analysis of petitioner's blood, which was taken by a physician in the hospital, was admissible because it did not violate the Fifth Amendment privilege against self-incrimination. *See id.* at 765 ("Since the blood test evidence, although an incriminating product of compulsion, was neither petitioner's testimony nor evidence relating to some communicative act or writing by the petitioner, it was not inadmissible on privilege grounds.").[13]

The blood test at issue in *Schmerber* was a reasonable one, which is generally accepted by medical and scientific experts as a highly effective means of determining the level of alcohol in a person's blood. The test in that case was performed in a reasonable manner in a hospital environment and in accord with accepted medical practices. These facts bear a strong resemblance to the case before us today. Mr. DeNolf's

---

[13] Although the police lacked a warrant in *Schmerber*, the Court rejected Schmerber's Fourth Amendment claims.

FBME was a reasonable and highly effective test performed by medical doctors in an appropriate environment and manner. Unlike the test in *Schmerber*, the FBME did not physically invade Mr. DeNolf's body. Contrary to Mr. DeNolf's claims, the FBME does not capture thoughts. Rather, like a blood test conducted to ascertain one's blood-alcohol level, the FBME simply reveals electrical impulses in the body—namely what one remembers. The facts that no fluid is withdrawn and no part of the body is penetrated make the FBME less likely to violate the Fifth Amendment than the blood test in *Schmerber*. There is nothing in the Constitution to protect electrical impulses of the body being passively read by a reliable machine.

The course of action taken by law enforcement was lawful. We affirm the lower court's finding.

II.

We hold that Mr. DeNolf's Eighth Amendment rights were not violated. The penalty here is not cruel and unusual for a number of reasons.

It is a slippery slope to determine how much solitary confinement is cruel and unusual for an individual. Cases involving such claims need to be decided on an independent, case-by-case basis that follows precedent. Typically, the state need only advance one legitimate penological justification to save a law or policy controlling prison conditions. The state has at least three legitimate penological justifications that support this penalty. It is important to note that the record finds that Mr. DeNolf is an adult who showed no signs of mental deficiency at trial and he presented no mitigating factors that would have prevented him from performing the cost-benefit analysis necessary for a punishment to satisfy the demands of the Eighth Amendment. See *Roper v. Simmons*, 543 U.S. 551 (2005). Thus, the state's interest in deterrence is rational, not vindictive. Further, the state has a valid interest in special deterrence, which is served by this penalty. Thus, it meets the standard set in *Ewing v. California*, 538 U.S. 11, 29–31 (2003) (plurality).

While not a case involving a challenge to solitary confinement, *Rhodes v. Chapman*, 452 U.S. 337 (1981), is illuminating. In that decision, the first to involve a challenge to prison conditions, the Court noted that while conditions can be unconstitutional, "[t]o the extent that such conditions are restrictive and even harsh, they are part of the penalty that criminal offenders pay for their offenses against society." *Id.* at 347. *Rhodes* establishes that prison conditions imposed by judges or by statute must be judged by "objective factors to the maximum possible effect." *Id.* at 346 (internal citations and quotations omitted). In a more recent prison conditions ruling, *Helling v. McKinney*, 509 U.S. 25, 28 (1993), the Court heard an Eighth Amendment claim that McKinney, an inmate in a Nevada prison, was put in serious health risk by second-hand smoke and as a result subject to a penalty forbidden by the Constitution. The Court, without ruling on the merits, held that McKinney could prevail in the future if he established that "he himself is being exposed to unreasonably high levels of [environmental tobacco smoke]." *Id.* at 35. The Court in *Helling* looked to clarify how inmates bringing suits alleging unsafe prison conditions must proceed:

> [W]ith respect to the objective factor, determining whether McKinney's conditions of confinement violate the Eighth Amendment requires more than a scientific and statistical inquiry into the seriousness of the potential harm and the likelihood that such injury to health will actually be caused by exposure to ETS. It also requires a court to assess whether society considers the risk that the prisoner complains of to be so grave that it violates contemporary standards of decency to expose *anyone* unwillingly to such a risk. In other words, the prisoner must show that the risk of which he complains is not one that today's society chooses to tolerate.

Id. at 36.

This was the approach followed in *Madrid v. Gomez*, 889 F. Supp 1146 (N.D. Cal. 1995).[14] In that case, the Northern District Court of California considered whether the direct conditions of solitary confinement as practiced at a specific prison violated the Eighth Amendment. *See id.* at 1260–79. *Madrid* stemmed from a class action suit brought by prisoners in California's Pelican Bay State Prison alleging a range of Eighth Amendment violations, including excessive force, inadequate physical and mental health care, and inhumane conditions in the prison's housing units. *Id.* at 1155–59. In that case, the district court held that there was unnecessary and wanton infliction of pain and use of excessive force, and prison officials did not provide inmates with constitutionally adequate medical and mental health care, among other conditions. *Id.* at 1279–80. The *Madrid* analysis, however, is starkly different from the case at bar. Given the conditions at the Poseidon Penitentiary, Mr. DeNolf's sentencing will not inflict pain nor involve the use of excessive force. The facts of the case present no evidence of the same sort of harsh conditions found to be unconstitutional in *Madrid*. The record reflects that Mr. DeNolf has an adequate amount of physical and mental health care within his solitary confinement facility, and there is no evidence in the record of inhumane conditions.

Madrid found that "[t]he Eighth Amendment simply does not guarantee that inmates will not suffer some psychological effects from incarceration or segregation." *Id.* at 1264. The same is true here. Like the court in *Madrid*, we find that the degree of psychological trauma inflicted on the average prisoner—in this case, Mr. DeNolf—by itself is not enough to violate the Eighth Amendment. Much like the *Madrid* court found, we recognize that for prisoners with pre-existing mental health conditions, as well as those with an abnormally high risk of suffering mental illness, being subjected to solitary confinement

---

[14]   The Ninth Circuit addressed this case on appeal in 1999, but that ruling focused solely on the issue of attorney's fees and did not reach the issue of whether the confinement was constitutional. *See Madrid v. Gomez*, 190 F.3d 990 (9th Cir. 1999). Therefore, that ruling is neither relevant to this case, nor part of this record.

conditions may be serious enough to constitute cruel and unusual punishment in violation of the Eighth Amendment. However, according to the facts of this case, Mr. DeNolf is of sound mind.

With regard to the dissent's belief that solitary confinement might jeopardize an individual's psychological state, we highlight Justice Stevens' concurrence in *Hudson v. McMillian*, 503 U.S. 1, 13 (1992) (Stevens, J., concurring). There, Justice Stevens argued that the Eighth Amendment forbids "unnecessary and wanton infliction of pain." The majority in *Hudson* found use of excessive force against a prisoner might constitute cruel and unusual punishment even though the prisoner does not suffer serious injury. *Id.* at 1. In Mr. DeNolf's case, there is no serious injury. In fact, Mr. DeNolf has not alleged any injuries. In their dissent to *McMillian*, Justices Thomas and Scalia found that the facts of the case emphasized that petitioner's injuries were "minor." *Id.* at 26 (Thomas, J., dissenting).

This case asks whether Mr. DeNolf has established that he has suffered a significant injury and that the conditions of confinement are "so grave" that they offend "contemporary standards of [human] decency." *Helling*, 509 U.S. at 36. We find that Mr. DeNolf has failed to carry this burden. The sentence in question is not cruel. We find that a use of force that causes only insignificant harm to a prisoner may be immoral, torturous, and despicable, but it is not cruel and unusual punishment. Furthermore, for an act of murder such as the one committed against Ms. Somerville, thirty years of "alone time" seems less severe than other possible punishments.

The use of solitary confinement, by any name, is both widespread and hardly new. Simply put, even if solitary confinement is found to be cruel, it is not unusual. To violate the Constitution, it must be both. To hold otherwise would be to rewrite our Constitution—an authority that we as judges lack."

Conviction and sentence of William DeNolf is AFFIRMED.

Justice FAIRBANK dissenting, joined by Justices CRAIG and LEDFORD.

I.

The first issue before the Court is whether or not the Constitution protects a person from the production of maps of cognition. The majority errs in its decision that Mr. DeNolf's constitutional rights were not violated because the Functional Brain Mapping Exam (FBME) did not force Mr. DeNolf to incriminate himself. The actions of the state are unconstitutional under the Fifth Amendment predominately because brain-based testing wrongly condemns the accused and tramples on the civil liberties of individuals.

The Fifth Amendment of the United States Constitution provides in pertinent part that "[n]o person . . . shall be compelled in any criminal case to be a witness against himself." U.S. CONST. amend. V. The notion that the state has the authority to, in essence, read the minds of its citizens is unconstitutional on its face, regardless of a warrant. The FBME enables the state to discover our thoughts. It is an appalling concept that appears to come straight from the most dystopian of science fiction. That our public officials would even consider using such a technology is shocking and their actual use of such power in this case constitutes a shocking attack upon our civil liberties. It is an abomination too terrible in its potential for misuse to even consider. Put simply, it is the stuff of which nightmares are made. The simple truth is that as society changes, the law as applied in practice has and must evolve alongside it. *Trop v. Dulles*, 356 U.S. 86, 101 (1958) (plurality) (recognizing that the Eighth Amendment draws its meaning from "the evolving standards of decency that mark the progress of a maturing society."). It is common knowledge that in the arena of civil rights and civil liberties, laws pertaining to segregation, reproductive rights, regulation of homosexual conduct, and marriage equality have all evolved as society has evolved. Times change, people change. The law must keep pace with it. The right against self-incrimination should be no exception.

Many policies which have been addressed by the Court reflect the basic concern of protecting the individual from unfair and inherently coercive government attempts to extort information involuntarily and inadmissibly. The privilege of self-incrimination was designed to halt the sort of physical invasions represented by the FBME. The majority in *Schmerber v. California*, 384 U.S. 757, 762 (1966), viewed the privilege against self-incrimination as a constitutional guarantee that the government will gain convictions "by its own independent labors, rather than by the cruel, simple expedient of compelling it from his [the suspect's] own mouth."

Mr. DeNolf's constitutional right was abridged. The Constitution protects against communication that is "testimonial, incriminating, and compelled." *United States v. Von Behren*, 822 F.3d 1139, 1144 (10th Cir. 2016) (internal citation and quotation marks omitted). This standard is satisfied in the immediate case. The majority's reliance on interrogation cases in which the accused either offered evidence that incriminated him on his own accord without being subject to questioning or allowed the accused to leave the police station and go home, is misplaced. *See, e.g., Rhode Island v. Innis*, 446 U.S. 291, 302–03 (1980) (upholding confession where officers exchanging "a few offhand remarks" could not have reasonably expected suspect to confess). These holdings are easily distinguishable from the case before us today.

The FBME may be a fairly unique test in how it operates and in what it reveals. Nevertheless, it is analogous to a polygraph test in many ways. Other courts have found that the use of polygraph results can violate the Fifth Amendment. *See Von Behren*, 822 F.3d at 1151. While the facts of the record and *Von Behren* may differ slightly, they are similar enough for *Von Behren* to be instructive. In that case, the Tenth Circuit held the polygraph test in question compelled Von Behren to testify against himself. *Id.*

Mr. DeNolf was required to submit to a process that produced images from his own brain, which were ultimately used against him. Given that fact, the most analogous case is *Pennsylvania v. Muniz*, 496 U.S. 582 (1990). In that case, the content of the answers was considered part of the accused's mind and off-limits to prosecutors and the police, who used them against defendants, without a warrant. *Id.* at 598–600. In the same way, the content of the brain impulses belongs to Mr. DeNolf and, again similarly, this content was used against DeNolf.

The Fifth Amendment privilege protects "the accused from having to reveal, directly or indirectly, his knowledge of facts relating him to the offense or from having to share his thoughts and beliefs with the Government." *Doe v. United States*, 487 U.S. 201, 213 (1988). In my view, *Doe* is the controlling case. There the Court held that, at a minimum, the privilege is triggered when a suspect is confronted with the "cruel trilemma" of truth, falsity, or silence. *Id.* at 212. When a suspect is forced to make a choice between truth, falsity, or silence, the suspect "disclose[s] the contents of his own mind," thereby implicating the privilege. *Id.* at 211. Much like an MRI, the FBME essentially rips the thoughts out of the accused and cannot be considered constitutional. Mr. DeNolf was ensnared by ambiguous circumstances, and therefore his Fifth Amendment rights have been violated. The same was true in *United States v. Hubbell*, 530 U.S. 27 (2000). In that case, the Court held that the cognition necessary to produce evidence sought by the state was of a testimonial nature. Where *Doe* stressed process, *Hubbell* stressed cognition. Under both approaches, a violation occurred. What is more, Justice Thomas, in his concurrence to *Hubbell*, offers an interpretation of what the term "witness" means in the text of the Fifth Amendment that is instructive to this case. *United States v. Hubbell*, 530 U.S. 27, 49 (2000) (Thomas, J. Concurring).

The Constitution evolves with the changes in science and new types of technology that may be created in the future. This new technology reads minds. No warrant can fix the constitutional violations caused by a mind reading device.

II.

The majority errs in ruling that Mr. DeNolf's sentence of 30 years of solitary confinement did not violate the Eighth Amendment. Our nation has a long history with the use of solitary confinement—one that dates back over 200 years. But that hardly disqualifies it from being cruel.

Solitary confinement is not only cruel—it is also unusual—and accordingly unconstitutional (except perhaps in the most unusual of circumstances).[15] It is time that the judiciary brings an end to this form of punishment.

The Eighth Amendment of the United States Constitution prohibits the federal government from "inflicting cruel and unusual punishments" onto individuals. U.S. CONST. amend. VIII. This prohibition applies to the states. *See, e.g., Ewing v. California,* 538 U.S. 11, 20 (2003). The Eighth Amendment forbids punishments that are at odds with "the evolving standards of decency that mark the progress of a mature society." *Trop v. Dulles,* 356 U.S. 86, 101 (1958). I know of no opinion issued by any court in the United States holding that the Eighth Amendment does not protect mental or psychological health and is instead limited solely to physical health.[16] The case for such a statement has arrived. I find that Olympus has inflicted cruel and unusual punishment onto Mr. DeNolf on the following reasoning.

The ruling of the District Court for the Northern District of California in *Madrid v. Gomez,* 889 F.Supp. 1146 (N.D. Cal. 1995) is instructive. In that case, the court wrote:

---

[15] I do not here address the issue of whether suspected terrorists, for example, or persons believed to be at risk from others, can or cannot be placed into some form of solitary confinement for the good of others or for their own good.

[16] In fact, the opposite is true. *See Rhodes v. Chapman,* 452 U.S. 337, 364 (1981) (Brennan, J., concurring) (noting that "[i]n determining when prison conditions pass beyond legitimate punishment and become cruel and unusual . . . . [C]ourt[s] must examine the effect upon inmates of the condition of the physical plant (lighting, heat, plumbing, ventilation, living space, noise levels, recreation space); sanitation (control of vermin and insects, food preparation, medical facilities, lavatories and showers, clean places for eating, sleeping, and working); safety (protection from violent, deranged, or diseased inmates, fire protection, emergency evacuation); inmate needs and services (clothing, nutrition, bedding, medical, dental, and mental health care, visitation time, exercise and recreation, educational and rehabilitative programming); and staffing (trained and adequate guards and other staff, avoidance of placing inmates in positions of authority over other inmates)."

> Regardless of whether there is an "exact syndrome" associated with incarceration in solitary confinement or security housing units, the Court is well satisfied that a severe reduction in environmental stimulation and social isolation can have serious psychiatric consequences for some people, and that these consequences are typically manifested in the symptoms identified above.

Id. at 1231–32. The following analysis is particularly important:

> Certain inmates who are not already mentally ill are also at high risk for incurring serious psychiatric problems, including becoming psychotic, if exposed to the SHU for any significant duration. As defendants' expert conceded, there are certain people who simply "can [no]t handle" a place like the Pelican Bay SHU. Persons at a higher risk of mentally deteriorating in the SHU are those who suffer from prior psychiatric problems, borderline personality disorder, chronic depression, chronic schizophrenia, brain damage or mental retardation, or an impulse-ridden personality. Consistent with the above, most of the inmates identified by Dr. Grassian as experiencing serious adverse consequences from the SHU were either already suffering from mental illness or fall within one of the above categories.

Id. at 1236 (internal citations omitted).

> In contrast, persons with "mature, healthy personality functioning and of at least average intelligence" are best able to tolerate SHU-like conditions. Significantly, the CDC's own Mental Health Services Branch recommended excluding from the Pelican Bay SHU "all inmates who have demonstrated evidence of serious mental illness or inmates who are assessed by mental health staff as likely to suffer a serious mental health problem if subjected to RES conditions."

Id. (internal citations omitted).

In order to determine whether a particular restriction constitutes "cruel and unusual punishment," the conditions of the confinement, as well as the length of confinement, should be considered. Studies, not included in this record, have shown that a high percentage of prisoners in the United States have reported suffering from heightened anxiety (91%), hyper-responsivity to external stimuli (86%), difficulty with concentration and memory (84%), confused thought process (84%), wide mood and emotional swings (71%), aggressive fantasies (61%), perceptual distortions (44%), and hallucinations (41%). Moreover, fully 34% of the sample experience all eight of these symptoms, and more than half (56%) experience at least five of them.

While Mr. DeNolf was found guilty of the murder of Ms. Somerville, I find that a near lifetime sentencing of solitary confinement is cruel and unusual. It is not that Mr. DeNolf will be eighty-five years old upon his release from Poseidon Penitentiary that is problematic—after all life in prison is frequently the sentence for murder—rather it is *how* he will spend the next thirty years that is a problem. This analysis more than meets the requirements set by the Court in *Helling v. McKinney*, 509 U.S. 25 (1993). I cannot understand how this sentence serves any valid penological purpose and as such it is vindictive and forbidden. *See Rhodes*, 452 U.S. at 364 (stating that "[w]hen 'the cumulative impact of the conditions of incarceration threatens the physical, mental, and emotional health and well-being of the inmates and/or creates a probability of recidivism and future incarceration,' the Court must conclude that the conditions violate the Constitution") (internal citation omitted); *Trop*, 356 U.S. at 102 (finding denationalization unconstitutional in part because it "subjects the individual to a fate of ever-increasing fear and distress").

Mr. DeNolf is deprived of human contact for thirty-day cycles within the Poseidon Petitionary; a need that is so basic it is essential to quality of life. Prisoners in solitary confinement suffer a loss that is both quantitative and qualitative in nature. The Court, in *Hudson v. McMillian*, 503 U.S. 1 (1992), found that the Eighth Amendment prohibits unnecessary psychological as well as physical pain. The harm to which

DeNolf is sentenced qualifies as such. In light of these facts, and our legal traditions, I judge this sentencing to be cruel under the Eighth Amendment.

Turning now to the issue of unusualness, solitary confinement is not new and is fairly widespread in terms of the number of states that utilize solitary confinement. That said, the number of inmates who are subjected to solitary confinement is a small percentage of the overall inmates in prison in the United States. The number enduring prolonged periods of solitary confinement is also low.

These facts reveal that solitary confinement, even though it occurs daily, is an unusual penalty. Moreover, there is a clear trend among the states toward reforming the nation's reliance on solitary confinement. This pattern began in 1998 when West Virginia banned the use of solitary confinement for juveniles for longer than ten days. Ten years later, New York banned its use for the mentally ill. In 2010, two states (Maine and Mississippi) reformed its use. In 2012, two states, Colorado and Massachusetts, took action to limit its application to juveniles and the mentally ill. In that same year, Alaska, Connecticut, Mississippi, and West Virginia took action to ban the use of solitary confinement for juveniles and the mentally ill. In 2013, five states (Illinois, Nevada, New York, Oklahoma, and Virginia) and the United States took actions that limited, if not discontinued, the use of solitary confinement. In 2014, at least ten states (Arizona, California, Colorado, Indiana, Michigan, Nebraska, New Mexico, New York, Ohio, and Wisconsin) adopted or formally proposed solitary confinement reforms meant to ease or reduce the practice.

The Supreme Court has held that "[i]t is not so much the number of these States that is significant, but the consistency of the direction of change." *Roper v. Simmons*, 543 U.S. 551, 556 (2005) (internal citations omitted). The history before us today indicates a trend away from the expansion of solitary confinement toward its easement, if not prohibition—a history that dates over fifteen years and has been consistent in its direction. Since 1998, twenty states[17] and the United States Government have adopted laws limiting or banning its use. In addition to those twenty states, there are seven additional states that prior to 1998 already did not subject inmates to solitary confinement. No state since 1998 has adopted laws adding or increasing its use. What is more, the United Nations has issued a report on torture and other cruel, inhumane, and degrading treatments or punishments that condemned the use of solitary confinement. That report found that while states around the world continue to use solitary confinement extensively, it is a penalty that is exceedingly rare among Western style democracies. Admittedly, of all Western style democracies, the United States was by far the nation that practiced solitary confinement the most. That said, as a percentage few prisoners are sentenced to solitary confinement and the direction of the trend is away from its adoption.

All of this evidence compels me to conclude that solitary confinement is an unusual penalty both in terms of real practice and adoption by the state. Perhaps there may be conditions under which it is constitutional, but this is not one of them. To my way of thinking, the public would be shocked that a prisoner would go straight into solitary confinement and that public would be shocked at what it entails. Simply put, solitary confinement is at odds with the modern standard of decency that exists in the United States. I find its use unconstitutional in Mr. DeNolf's case. Short of that, at a minimum, I would rule that its use must be curtailed and better regulated.

Because I judge these acts to violate the Fifth and Eighth Amendments, I respectfully dissent.

Cases Cited:

Schmerber v. CA, 384 U.S. 757 (1966) https://supreme.justia.com/cases/federal/us/384/757/case.html.

---

[17]   They are: Alaska, Arizona, California, Colorado, Connecticut, Illinois, Indiana, Maine, Massachusetts, Michigan, Mississippi, Nebraska, Nevada, New Mexico, New York, Ohio, Oklahoma, Virginia, Wisconsin, and West Virginia.

Rhode Island v. Innis, 446 U.S. 291 (1980) https://supreme.justia.com/cases/federal/us/446/291/.

Doe v. United States, 487 U.S. 201 (1988) https://supreme.justia.com/cases/federal/us/487/201/case.html.

Pennsylvania v Muniz, 496 U.S. 582 (1990) https://supreme.justia.com/cases/federal/us/496/582/.

United States v. Hubbell, 530 U.S. 27 (2000) http://caselaw.findlaw.com/us-supreme-court/530/27.html.

United States v. Von Behren, 822 F.3d 1139 (10th Cir. 2016) http://caselaw.findlaw.com/us-10th-circuit/1734539.html.

Rhodes v. Chapman, 452 U.S. 337 (1981) https://supreme.justia.com/cases/federal/us/452/337/.

Hudson v. McMillian, 503 U.S. 1 (1992) https://supreme.justia.com/cases/federal/us/503/1/case.html.

Helling v. McKinney, 509 U.S. 25 (1993) https://supreme.justia.com/cases/federal/us/509/25/case.html.

Madrid v. Gomez, 889 F. Supp. 1146 (N.D. Cal. 1995) http://law.justia.com/cases/federal/district-courts/FSupp/889/1146/1904317/.

Ewing v. California, 538 U.S. 11 (2003) https://supreme.justia.com/cases/federal/us/538/11/case.html.

Roper v. Simmons, 543 U.S. 551 (2005) https://supreme.justia.com/cases/federal/us/543/551/.

Contributors

NICHOLAS D. CONWAY (PhD, Texas A&M University; JD, Indiana University-Bloomington) is Assistant Professor of Political Science at San Francisco State University, where he serves as coach to the moot court team. He teaches and researches in the fields of public law and judicial politics. His research has appeared in *Social Science Quarterly* and the *Washington University Journal of Law and Policy*. He previously practiced law in the areas of civil rights and constitutional litigation, and served as an administrative law judge.

MCKINZIE CRAIG HALL earned a BA and MS in Political Science from the University of North Texas and a PhD in Political Science from Texas A&M University. She is an Assistant Professor at the University of Louisiana at Lafayette, where she founded the moot court program in 2015. Kinzie is the only current AMCA coach to qualify teams for the AMCA national tournament from three different institutions in five years. When she's not teaching courses on law and government or researching Supreme Court decision-making, she loves traveling with her husband Will and daughters Katie Belle and Ellie and streaming marathons of police procedural dramas with her Wheaten Terriers Beau and Sully.

KIMI LYNN KING (JD/PhD SUNY-Buffalo) is a Distinguished Teaching Professor at the University of North Texas whose teaching expertise focuses on American government and Constitutional law, while her research examines transitional justice, international war crimes tribunals, sexual violence, and victim witness-centered justice.

She has authored or co-authored two books (Cambridge University Press and University of Michigan Press), nine book chapters, and 17 articles in *Political Research Quarterly*, the *Journal of Conflict Resolution*, and *Social Science Quarterly* among others. She served as UNT's pre-law advisor, is the founding coach for UNT's nationally ranked Moot Court team, and she helped established the Women's Faculty Network which provides mentoring and advocacy for female faculty. She has won over 20 teaching or service awards including the American Political Science Association's Award for Innovative Teaching.

LEWIS RINGEL attended Trenton State College (now the College of New Jersey) and earned his PhD from the University of Maryland at College Park. He has been the Moot Court Director at California State University (CSULB) since 2006. Before coming to CSULB, He ran moot court simulations at the United States Naval Academy and Louisiana State University. Professor Ringel serves on the Executive Board of the American Collegiate Moot Association (AMCA). In that capacity he chairs the Case Committee and serves on the Rules and the Tournament Committees. To date, his teams have won six regional titles for oral advocacy and advanced to three national quarter-finals—reaching the semi-finals twice and the national finals once. In addition, his teams have won a national championship for written brief and been the runners-up for national written brief twice. Professor Ringel is the Winner of the 2018–19 John and Phyllis Jung Faculty Award. He is married with two children and has two dogs.

ANDREW B. SOMMERMAN is a practicing attorney in Dallas Texas. He has instructed law students and undergraduate students on Moot court at the Southern Methodist University, Texas A&M Law School, the South Texas college of Law Houston, the University of Texas at Arlington. He received his Juris Doctorate Degree from the South Texas College of Law where he was National Champion at numerous intercollegiate competitions. He has various publications on the subjects of moot court, damages, pleadings, expert witnesses, medical records and medical malpractice. He is Director and member of several legal associations.

PAUL I. WEIZER received a Master's degree in Public Administration and a PhD in Political Science from Temple University. Currently, he is a Professor of political science at Fitchburg State University in Massachusetts. He is the author of *The Supreme Court and Sexual Harassment* (Lexington Books: 2000), *Sexual Harassment: Cases, Case Studies, and Commentary* (Peter Lang Publishing: 2002) and *The Opinions of Justice Antonin Scalia: The Caustic Conservative* (Peter Lang Publishing: 2004) as well as numerous articles on sexual harassment and civil liberties. Dr. Weizer has served on the Executive Board of the American Collegiate Moot Association (AMCA) since its inception and is a past president of the organization. He founded the moot court program at Fitchburg State University in 2000 and has overseen one of the top programs in the nation, winning numerous awards and qualifying teams for every AMCA national moot court competition.

Index